RICHARD FLURY
The Life and Music
of a Swiss Romantic

RICHARD FLURY
The Life and Music of a Swiss Romantic

Chris Walton

TOCCATA PRESS

This book was first published by Toccata Press, 2017.

British Library Cataloguing in Publication Data
A catalogue record for this book is available from the British Library.

ISBN 978-0-907689-44-7

This publication has been made possible by donations
from the City of Solothurn
and the Rosmarie und Armin Däster-Schild-Stiftung, Grenchen.

STADTSOLOTHURN

Set in 11 on 12 point Minion Pro by KerryPress, St Albans

Contents

List of Illustrations

Richard Flury, portrait by Cuno Amiet in 1948

Introduction: A Man in a Hurry

The Swiss city of Solothurn, capital of the canton of the same name, sits on a gentle bend in the River Aare roughly halfway between Basel on the German-French border to the north, and the federal capital of Bern to the south. Looming over the city at its northern edge is the Weissenstein (literally 'white stone'), a ridge in the Jura mountain chain that cuts across this corner of Switzerland. It is not especially high, but is impressive in its uniformity, and on wintry days the clouds hover along its surface so that one could almost, for a moment, imagine that Table Mountain had been transposed from the Cape of Good Hope into pre-Alpine climes. Bordering the city to the south is the parish of Biberist, a former farming village. It was here, in 1896, that the composer Richard Flury was born, to the watchmaker-turned-restaurateur Adolf Flury and his wife Rosa. Biberist was back then already a *de facto* suburb of Solothurn, and although Richard retained a lifelong affection for the place of his birth, it was in Solothurn that he went to school and made his career as conductor, teacher and composer, benefiting on the one hand from all that a small town in the provinces can offer a gifted man, while often also chafing under the small-town yoke.

In many ways, Flury's career was to conform to a pattern already well established among Swiss-German composers since the mid-nineteenth century. Starting with Wagner's composer friends Johann Carl Eschmann (1826–82) and Wilhelm Baumgartner (1820–67), and moving through the generation of Fritz Brun (1878–1959), Volkmar Andreae (1879–1962) and Othmar Schoeck (1886–1957) to the Schoenberg pupil Erich Schmid (1907–2000), they all followed the same pattern: initial education in Switzerland followed by further studies in Germany or Austria, then a return home to work as a conductor of choirs or orchestras and/or as a teacher at a conservatoire or cantonal high school. Richard Flury took composition lessons with Hans Huber at the Basel Conservatoire and with Joseph Marx in Vienna before coming back to conduct the Solothurn Orchestra and teach the violin at his former school. Like his above-mentioned compatriots, he too remained thereafter in Switzerland, bar holidays or performances abroad, until he died.

To be sure, they all had excellent financial and political reasons for staying put. Even when it was still a largely agrarian nation in the nineteenth century, Switzerland was more than once an island of peace amidst a sea of European revolution, war and unrest. The attraction of the place (and its currency) was particularly acute in the 1920s and '30s (in his memoirs, *Lebenserinnerungen*, published in 1950, Flury recalled being only one of many Swiss visitors populating the boxes at the Vienna Opera in 1921, all of them – like him – profiting from the strong franc that was the envy of the Austrians[1]). Although Flury's life followed a set pattern, it also exudes a certain fascination because of the well-known figures who entered it; and that is also how Flury himself seems to have seen it. His memoirs are full of tales of his encounters with the famous, all told with a light touch and a charming sense of self-deprecation. There are the stories of how he conducted Pablo Casals in Solothurn, for example, and of the time he introduced the sweet-toothed Richard Strauss to Solothurn's high art of cake-baking. And those eager for sensation can even find a hint of it in Flury's fascination for a certain young actress at the local theatre who in the 1940s inspired him to write two dozen songs before she embarked for Hollywood, where she starred alongside Yul Brynner and Gary Cooper and graced the cover of *Time Magazine* as one of the beauties of the age.

Yet a life intertwining with other, more famous lives, although undoubtedly enriching to the figure thus intertwined, is of limited interest to posterity. Nor does Flury seem to have possessed any truly damning character traits that might afford the biographer or his readers a dash of spice. Even when one listens between the metaphorical lines of the recollections of family and friends, there seems to have been little untoward about him, with everyone insistent both that he was a decent, sympathetic man, and that their insistence was genuine ('A lovely person. His [second] wife too. Lovely person. Both lovely people. A lovely man. Lovely people', one interviewee told me[2]). It does indeed seem that everyone liked him (with the notable exception, reputedly, of his first wife). And since Flury's career confined him both to the provinces and to norms long established by others, he might seem a composer whose interest to posterity is in the end at best peripheral.

However, there is only one thing that really matters here, and it is what makes a discussion of the life of Richard Flury worthwhile: he wrote good music. Some of it is very good indeed. A few of his orchestral works – such as the *Altisberg Suite* – ought to be in the repertoire of the big Swiss orchestras and would not disappoint if heard on the international concert-stage. The Third Violin Concerto is another such case. It was premiered and recorded for the radio by the star violinist Georg Kulenkampff and would repay being rediscovered by violinists today. There are also many delights among his piano works and chamber music. Financial constraints might prevent his operas from gaining a proper foothold in the theatre, but that is a shame. The early *Eine florentinische Tragödie* is a fine work that foreshadows the

[1] Richard Flury, *Lebenserinnerungen*, Habegger AG, Derendingen, 1950, p. 89.
[2] Conversation with the musician in question (name withheld) in Biberist, 28 August 2012.

late *parlando* style of Strauss and would be straightforward to stage (it could even hold its own despite competition from the Zemlinsky opera of the same name). But at only 45 minutes in length it would require a partner for a double bill, which always complicates budgets in an opera house. The other operas would be trickier to get performed on account of their larger casts, though *Die helle Nacht* looks highly promising in score and ought at least to be recorded. And the overture to the opera *Casanova e l'Albertolli* deserves to have a life of its own for it is as catchy and as spirited as, say, Reznicek's overture to *Donna Diana*.

In stylistic terms, Flury saw himself as a lifelong committed Romantic, a fact to which he alludes repeatedly in his writings, even going so far as to use the word 'Bekenntnis', with its resonances of religious avowal, in the title of a lecture he gave in 1953 detailing his aesthetic stance.[3] But even a cursory perusal of the scores confirms that Flury was not simply subservient to conservative norms, and his more adventurous works of the 1920s and early 1930s are also arguably his best (such as his piano pieces of the time, the First String Quartet and the early operas, where he sometimes even goes beyond the bounds of tonality). All the same, his later years also offer sporadic riches from a time when he was most firmly wedded to a Romantic aesthetic, one then regarded as *passé* almost everywhere else (though our own postmodern age has mercifully ceased to castigate composers for returning to tonality after having once ventured away from it).

The very fact that Flury's later years were prolific is a significant bucking of the Swiss trend. For although he may have followed the pattern of his compatriots by venturing abroad to study and then returning home to conduct and teach, a major difference lies in the fact that many of those others later abandoned composing altogether. In the nineteenth century, Wilhelm Baumgartner best fits this pattern, but more striking are the twentieth-century cases: Marcel Sulzberger (1876–1941), Volkmar Andreae, Erich Schmid and Adolf Brunner (1901–92) all fell (almost) silent as they grew older. The trend seems to have infected even those who arrived in Switzerland from abroad. Czesław Marek (1891–1985) and Paul Kletzki (1900–73) were two of the finest composers Poland ever produced, both of them compelled by world wars to flee to Switzerland (in Marek's case the First, in Kletzki's the Second). But both stopped composing before they were 50. Why so many men should stop doing what they did best is not a question to be answered here; I must let it stand as a strange but undeniable fact of Swiss music history.

Richard Flury seems to have had no such problem. Although his *œuvre* is not vast, it does cover almost every possible genre, from the biggest to the smallest, both instrumental and vocal. When one considers that he earned his living by teaching the violin at a high school and that he spent

[3] Flury, 'Mein Bekenntnis zur musikalischen Romantik. Vortrag gehalten in der Jugendgemeinde für Musik in Solothurn 20. Januar 1953'. Special supplement (undated) to the *Solothurner Zeitung*.

much of his spare time conducting, then his fecundity becomes even more remarkable. He was by all accounts a workaholic. In his reminiscences of his stay in Vienna in 1921, he recalls cramming so many concerts and operas into his few weeks that he all but collapsed from exhaustion.[4] A similar determination to use his time to the full seems to have predominated in later life. More than one former student has testified to me how most teachers at the Kantonsschule would use breaks between lessons to smoke and socialise; Flury, on the other hand, would take manuscript paper out of his desk drawer and work until his next violin pupil arrived, oblivious to any noise coming from the other classrooms (some claim he composed, others say he was orchestrating, but all agree that he used his spare time to work on his compositions). Nor have I come across any example of Flury having turned down a commission. Even when his prodigious capacity for work was inadequate to the task, he still did not say no. Thus when he had the chance to write a comic opera for Lugano in 1937 he agreed, though Eduard Favre had to be drafted in to orchestrate the work because of Flury's other commitments. Flury even on occasion embarked on large-scale works without the certainty of a commission or performance, as in the case of a 'mystery play' scheduled for open-air performance in Solothurn in 1945 but cancelled for reasons of cost shortly after the score was finished, with no financial recompense to the composer.

One of Flury's former students offered a note of criticism that seems important, not only because of the general rarity of adverse comment in my interviews with his associates but also because the student in question was a composer himself and thus accustomed to wrestling with notes on paper. Flury, he said, lacked thoroughness; he had a distracted, nervous air about him and was in too much of a hurry to put a finished work behind him and move on to the next. It would have been wiser, he said, if Flury had spent more time going back to revise what he had written in the light of the experience of its performance.[5]

There is some truth in this criticism. When he conducted his First Symphony in the early 1920s, Flury made numerous changes, but left both score and parts in such disarray that immense efforts were needed to decipher his intentions when it came to be recorded nearly 90 years later. He also on occasion left works unfinished. Thus his Second Violin Concerto of 1940, a present for his young second wife, was tactlessly left unorchestrated, whereas he made sure to finish the score for his next, the Third Violin Concerto of 1943–44, because he was able to win Kulenkampff for its premiere. It was left to Richard Flury's son, the composer and violinist Urs Joseph Flury, to orchestrate and record the Second Concerto after his father's death. But all the same, if Flury had not been a man averse to going

[4] *Lebenserinnerungen*, *op. cit.*, p. 89.

[5] Conversation with Alban Roetschi, Solothurn, 11 January 2013.

over ground already trodden, and if it had not been for his nervous energy and the steady flow of his inspiration driving him on to the next project, and then the next and the next, he would hardly have produced such a comprehensive output. His enthusiasm for his craft can also on occasion reveal his approach to other aspects of life. For example, as he himself recounts in his memoirs,[6] his second opera, *Die helle Nacht*, begun in 1932, had no chance of success in Germany because the (deceased) poet on whose work the libretto was based, Paul Zifferer, was of Jewish descent. But when the opportunity arose in 1943 to collaborate on a new work with Peter Lotar, a Jewish Czech refugee from the Nazis who was in exile in Solothurn (the 'mystery play' referred to above), Flury did not hesitate. Others in the Swiss artistic fraternity were more careful in their wartime associations, keeping an eye on the possible consequences to their music and their royalties in Germany, should they work with those the Nazis deemed undesirable. As shall be seen in the course of this narrative, Flury had no such qualms.

Richard Flury: an avowed Romantic, immensely enthusiastic, but unwilling to retrace his steps; a man, it seems, in a hurry. This book retraces his steps for him.

Acknowledgements

I would like to thank all those individuals and institutions who have helped me in my research for this book, first and foremost Urs Joseph Flury, who has offered more encouragement than a biographer could hope for, and who without demur gave complete access to all the materials I needed, with no conditions attached. The Richard Flury Foundation has similarly been highly supportive, in particular its board members Verena Bider, Hans Dudle, Heinz Lehmann, Ueli Steiner and, most of all, Ulrich Lips. I also wish to thank the following individuals for their assistance (in alphabetical order): Mr and Mrs Paul von Arb, Maria Böhlen, Elisabeth Bürki-Flury, Niklaus Bütikofer, Simone Chiquet, Stefan Dell'Olivo, Marie-Louise De Ycaza, Hildegard Dieke, Charles Dobler, Madeleine Elmer, Markus Erni, Therese Flury, Dani Gloor, Susanne Grulich, Renate Gygax, Thomas Leibnitz, Attila Lengyel, Ulrich Lips, Werner Lüchinger, Jost Meier, Rosette Mengi-Schaad, Verena Monnier, Meike Olbrich, Peter Palmer, Carlo Piccardi, Max Reber, Mr and Mrs Alban Roetschi, Christine Ryser, Angelika Salge, Robert Scholl-Sulzer, Hermann Wichers, Martina Wohlthat, Mr and Mrs Gottfried Wyss, Fabio Zali and Nora Zimmermann.

I should like to express my particular thanks to the Zentralbibliothek Solothurn, whose personnel have shown immense patience and goodwill over the course of my many visits (in particular Verena Bider, Hans Braun, Allard Eekman, Cecile Eggenschwiler, Sabrina Hofmann, Ian Holt and Franziska Jäggi). I am also grateful to the following companies and institutions: the Bibliothèque cantonale

[6] *Lebenserinnerungen, op. cit.*, p. 204.

et universitaire de Lausanne, the cantonal and city authorities of Solothurn, the Deutsches Literaturarchiv Marbach, the Eidgenössisches Departement des Innern EDI, the Schweizerisches Bundesarchiv BAR, the Musikakademie Basel, the Bibliothek Musikwissenschaft der Universität Bern, the Musikhochschule Basel, the Österreichische Nationalbibliothek, the Universitätsbibliothek Basel, the Staatsarchiv Basel-Stadt, Universität Bern – Universitätsarchiv and the Zentralbibliothek Zürich.

For permission to reproduce the illustrations seen here, I am grateful to the Zentralbibliothek Solothurn (the city of Solothurn, public domain, p. 18; Solothurn Art Museum and Concert Hall, shelfmark ZBS P 06101, p. 20; Kantonsschule Solothurn, shelfmark ZBS P 06050, p. 32; Hotel Krone, public domain, p. 36; Mühledorf, shelfmark ZBS P 01147, p. 187); to the Zentralbibliothek Zürich (Hauptgasse Solothurn, Sammlung Photochrom, http://dx.doi.org/10.3931/e-rara-45371 / Public Domain Mark, p. 19); to the Bibliothek Musikwissenschaft der Universität Bern (Ernst Kurth, p. 54); and to Photoramacolor AG (Mühledorf, p. 187). The photo of Maria Schell (p. 184) is from a private collection. For permission to use the cover portrait by Amiet I am grateful to the Flury family heirs. All other illustrations are reproduced with kind permission of Urs Joseph Flury.

In certain instances in this book, the names have been withheld of interviewees when the topics we discussed might cause them embarrassment if named. But I naturally have detailed records of these conversations.

Paul Mann kindly set all the music examples. The copyright to the music rests with Urs Joseph Flury, to whom I am grateful for permission to reproduce them here. Proofreading help from Bruce Goatly and Máire Taylor is gratefully acknowledged. Special gratitude goes to Martin Anderson of Toccata Press, for his initial and undimmed enthusiasm for a book on a composer as yet little known in the English-speaking world, and for his untiring aid in bringing the manuscript into its current form.

Where the text below refers to 'Flury's archives', it means the Zentralbibliothek Solothurn in the case of his music archives; all other such archival materials (letters, reviews, photos, etc.) are held by Urs Joseph Flury unless otherwise stated.

Chris Walton
Solothurn and Törbel
September 2016

1
First Musical Endeavours

Solothurn is not large: the city itself has some 16,000 inhabitants, though its various adjoining satellite towns, such as Biberist, mean that far more come and go each day. The origins of the city lie in the Stone Age, but its Roman incarnation, Vicus Salodurum, is its effective starting point. Remnants of the Roman walls remain visible here and there in the old part of town, having been incorporated into whatever buildings sprang up in their place (always with a polite little plaque to inform passers-by of their venerable age). It was two Roman legionnaires from Thebes, Urs and Viktor, who provided the city with its joint patron saints, having supposedly chosen to be beheaded here in c. 300AD rather than abandon their new Christian faith (Richard Flury would commemorate them in a play with music in the early 1940s).

The late Middle Ages saw the city buildings expand, adding walls, towers and ever more churches. Solothurn joined the Swiss Confederacy in 1481, and in 1530 it became the seat of the French Ambassadors to Switzerland. During the religious turmoil of these years it avoided conversion to the new Protestant faith. This fidelity to Rome, coupled with the gentrification appropriate to its status as a diplomatic hub, resulted in the erection of the more glamorous of its early modern edifices, including numerous villas catering to the upper crust. Solothurn today markets itself proudly as 'Switzerland's most beautiful Baroque city', and with good reason. A Jesuit Church stands on the main street, its façade so well inset into the row of shop fronts that it is almost easy to overlook. But once inside, one finds a riot of white stucco to rival almost any southern German cathedral. And only a few yards away, at the end of the Hauptgasse, there is the imposing early Classical cathedral of St Urs, seat of the Bishop of Basel, designed by Gaetano Pisoni and completed in 1773. It dominates the skyline of the city and is situated at the top of a series of magnificent steps graced by elaborate fountains on either side, all constructed, like the cathedral itself, from the gleaming white limestone quarried from the cliffs below the Weissenstein. The effect is overwhelming but somewhat incongruous, as if some grandiose eighteenth-century Roman edifice had been transplanted into a town too small to cope with it.

In the nineteenth century, the sometime swamplands to the west of the city towards Biel were drained, and massive canals built to control the flow of water in the Aare. In spring and summer today, pleasure cruisers glide

The city of Solothurn in the second half of the nineteenth century, seen from the farmland of Biberist, with the Jura mountain chain in the background. Richard Flury lived close to this spot in his later years, and often went walking in the woods near here.

back and forth along the river between Solothurn and the Lake of Biel, though low-lying bridges keep all larger vessels upstream, ensuring that the venerable city centre remains undisturbed by nautical intrusions save for the occasional hoot of a distant ship-horn. The watch industry also arrived in the late 1800s, and though in more recent times most of its craftsmen have disappeared except at the luxury end of the market, a newcomer can still discern the residual finickiness of the archetypal watchmaker in so many aspects of Solothurn, from the punctuality of its buses to the breathtakingly precise chocolate, cream and meringue creations in the windows of the local *confiseries*.

Not long after the outlying region was reclaimed from the marshes, the Solothurn authorities embarked on a major cultural facelift of the city itself. A ring road was constructed outside the old city walls, and parks were laid out where once the city moat had been. In the resultant narrow green belt, a magnificent concert hall was built at the turn of the twentieth century – a kind of mini-Musikvereinssaal, though without the gilt – and next to it a museum that today boasts a collection of late-nineteenth- and early-twentieth-century art worthy of comparison with almost any other. Here, Van Gogh nestles alongside Klimt and Matisse and a whole host of Hodlers and Amiets. (Not long ago, Philip Hensher of *The Independent* wrote how

The Hauptgasse – 'main street' – in Solothurn, c. 1902. The Cathedral of St Urs is at the end of the street, the Jesuit Church on the right.

he had once taken the wrong train from Bern to Geneva and ended up visiting Solothurn instead; astonished at the artistic riches on display, he wrote 'Am I the only person in the world who didn't know about the museum at Solothurn?'[1])

Of no less significance to the cultural history of Solothurn, though somewhat more modest than its art collection, is the City Theatre. The Jesuits ran the main school in Solothurn throughout the Baroque, and as was the case with their brethren in Lucerne and elsewhere, music and theatre were for many decades an integral part of their educational offerings. It was the Jesuits who in the mid-1700s built a bespoke theatre near the banks of the Aare, adjacent to their church and its school. Whereas arch-Protestant cities such as Zurich forbade plays and operas as the devil's work until well into the nineteenth century, the Jesuit centres of Lucerne and Solothurn had long before been enjoying operas and plays on a regular basis. Some of the scores and parts used in Solothurn in the late eighteenth century have survived to this day in the local library.

The Solothurn theatre was taken over by the secular authorities in the early nineteenth century and subjected to assorted renovations over the decades. But squatting between other buildings at the front and back, and

[1] Philip Hensher, 'Rake's still making perfect progress', *The Independent*, 13 August 2010.

The Solothurn Art Museum (right) and Concert Hall (left), c. 1915, just outside the old city wall. The former fortifications have here been replaced by a park.

hemmed in by the river and the school on its sides, its various renovations did not offer any possibility of expansion, and so the city theatre remained far smaller than any of the buildings that sprang up elsewhere in the nineteenth century to cater for the fondness for drama of the emergent Swiss bourgeoisie. It was only in 1927 that a professional company began running the theatre. The pit could never cope with more than 30 musicians (nor can it today), but that did not stop the staples of the operatic repertoire from being given on a regular basis without regard to size or suitability, as was the general custom at all the smallest theatres on the Continent (a fact about which Richard Strauss was wont to despair). When Richard Flury's own first opera, *Eine florentinische Tragödie*, was given its world premiere in the Solothurn Theatre in 1929, the composer had to unscrew the first two rows of seats in the stalls so that his late-Romantic orchestra could squeeze in.[2]

Flury's birthplace of Biberist grew up around the banks of the River Emme just before it flows into the Aare (the Emme is the same river that features in the name of the Emmental cheese we all know). Not even the most patriotic of locals could claim any particular beauty for Biberist itself. Its few delights are listed swiftly: two pretty churches (one for each denomination, Catholic and Protestant); a delightful villa on the edge of town that boasts an art collection donated in 1968 by Fritz Moos, Richard Flury's brother-in-law; then there are the woods of the Bucheggberg that rise up gently to the west and were one of Flury's favourite hiking haunts ('even as a child I loved

[2] *Lebenserinnerungen*, *op. cit.*, p. 203.

the little hills and dales of the Bucheggberg, which, untouched by railways and factories, left their mark on my soul as an ideal landscape', he wrote[3]). Until the mid-nineteenth century, Biberist was only a farming village on the main road to Bern, but then everything changed with the erection of a paper factory. The river Emme is surprisingly broad and shallow here, and it had long proven ideal for powering mills of all sorts, one of them a powder mill that had blown up in the early 1800s. When industrialisation reached the region in the early years after the founding of the Swiss Federal State in 1848, the potential of Biberist was spotted and promptly exploited. A canal was built parallel to the right bank of the river so as best to harness the power of the water, and a paper factory built on top of it. The mills of Biberist were hardly dark and satanic, but still left a permanent mark on the place. Paper production began in 1862, and the factory was long the main employer all about until it finally closed in 2011. This factory was also the reason that little Biberist remains today the proud owner of two different railway stations: to the west is the station on the branch line that was opened in 1916 and today takes one to the Solothurn main station in two minutes in one direction, and to Bern in half an hour in the other; and on the eastern banks of the Emme is the appropriately named 'Biberist East' station, on the line from Solothurn to Burgdorf that opened in the 1880s. The tracks here run alongside the factory they used to serve and that today sits as a near-empty shell. A 'masterplan' has been promised for the site by the local authorities, with agro-industrial landscaping, sport fields and massive public artworks to be realised by the year 2033.[4] We shall see.

With so many factory workers to feed, several restaurants were soon established nearby. One of these was the Emmenbrücke Restaurant, named because it stood on the corner of a bridge ('Brücke') over the river Emme, a minute or so on foot from both the paper factory and the 'Biberist East' station. The restaurant was set up by one Josef Gamohn, a former stonemason, and his wife Elisabeth, and they lived in the floors above it. The Gamohns were originally from the Vorarlberg in the west of Austria. Before the First World War, the borders of continental Europe existed in reality only on maps, not as physical barriers, and so it was quite natural for a mason such as Josef to wander across the land and take up work in Switzerland, as he did in the 1860s. According to family history, he found a job helping to build the schoolhouse in Biberist, then afterwards worked at the paper factory, and settled down when he got married.

Josef and Elisabeth in time passed on their restaurant and its living quarters to their daughter Rosa and her husband, the watchmaker Adolf Flury. It was in this house that Rosa and Adolf raised their children, of whom Richard, born on 26 March 1896, was the third of four. Rosa had been born

[3] *Ibid.*, p. 225.

[4] *Cf.* www.papieri-biberist.ch/#vision, accessed September 2015.

and bred in Switzerland, but retained a link with her father's homeland. Just as expatriate Britons often revere the House of Windsor from far-off foreign fields, so too did Rosa Gamohn retain an affection for Kaiser Franz Joseph I and things Austrian, demonstrating it often in the way she knew best, by cooking Tyrolean dumplings.[5] She also kept in touch with her cousins back across the border, and family ties remained close enough for mutual visits every now and then – a tradition that her son Richard upheld into adulthood.

As their former overlords in mediaeval times, the Austrians were long a natural bogeyman for the Swiss and became the butt of their jokes, as the Irish are to the English or the Belgians to the French (an Austrian accent overheard in Zurich as late as the 1980s and '90s would prompt visible disdain among the Swiss natives within earshot). But for Richard Flury, Austria was home both to family and to the rich musical traditions he would always hold dear. He later chose a Viennese expatriate to teach him counterpoint, and two years after that he went to Vienna itself to complete his music studies. He composed several Viennese waltzes that are more than worthy of the name and offer ample proof of his melodic gifts. But artistic admiration and familial connections seem never to have prompted Richard or his near family to any sense of political kinship. A letter exists from Richard to his brother Adolf, written from Laufen on 27 May 1943 when Richard was on military service; he is forwarding a letter received from a cousin in Austria, Hans Gamohn, he says, whose son has just been killed in the war. Richard remarks: 'But as far as I'm aware, Hans G. was himself always a supporter of this "blessed" annexation[6] that is bringing beautiful, poor Austria so much ill'.

Richard's paternal family, the Flurys, originally came from the region around Genoa in Italy (so he claimed), but fled to Switzerland on account of revolutionary activities.[7] There might be more fiction than fact in this suggestion. But what can be stated with certainty is that the name is particularly common in the Solothurn area (also in its variant of Fluri), and that Richard Flury's family had lived there since at least the eighteenth century. His grandfather, Urs Josef Flury, was a stone-carver by trade and even owned his own quarry. But he gave this profession up to go and run the Café Spitz in Solothurn, which was more lucrative. In later years he regaled his grandsons with tales from his time in the Solothurn army during the 'Sonderbundskrieg', the brief Swiss civil war of 1848 that resulted in a rapid defeat for the independent-minded, conservative cantons and made possible the emergence of a more liberal, federal state. Urs Josef Flury and his wife Anna had seven daughters, but only one son survived into adulthood: Adolf, Richard's father, who trained for four years

[5] *Lebenserinnerungen*, *op. cit.*, p. 12.

[6] The *Anschluss*, Hitler's annexation of Austria in March 1938.

[7] *Lebenserinnerungen*, *op. cit.*, p. 11.

The Emmenbrücke Restaurant in Biberist c. 1900, with Rosa and Adolf Flury

as a watchmaker, and later kept a workshop above the restaurant that he and his wife took over from her parents in Biberist. They earned extra money by renting out four small apartments in a nearby house to local workers and their families.

Adolf's real passion seems to have been music. He played the trumpet in the army, ran a little band, practised for an hour a day and also played in the amateur orchestra in Solothurn. Adolf even helped to found a small-scale orchestra in Biberist (to ensure adequate numbers, all four of Adolf's children, including Richard, were drafted in to play). He must have been a remarkable man; he was fascinated by modern technologies, was the principal photographer in Biberist (it is thanks to him that there are so many family pictures from the time), and he even took part in local politics as an active member of the Liberal Party.

Information on Richard Flury's family life and childhood is largely dependent on his own memoirs, but since neither the (brief) typescript reminiscences of his elder brother, Adolf, nor the family's oral history offer anything contradictory, one can probably assume that the picture Flury paints for posterity is accurate. The wealth of detail he offers also suggests keen powers of observation and recall; and since he had his memoirs published and distributed freely among family members and friends, it seems unlikely he would have intentionally indulged in excessive fiction.

Adolf Flury Sen., trumpeter, second from left, c. 1900

Young violinist: Richard Flury, at age seven or so, with his sister Erika, outside the restaurant 'Zur Emmenbrücke'

Richard Flury recalled his parents' marriage as having been a 'harmony of souls',[8] his mother a 'saint'.[9] But no marital harmony is without its discordant notes, and since Flury was writing at a time when his own experience of marriage had proven problematical, it would have been natural for him to have idealised his parents' union in an act of compensation. But all the sources nevertheless suggest that Richard and his three siblings enjoyed a happy childhood and a solid family life – Adolf, born in 1891 and clearly the dominant personality in the family; Rosa, born in 1892; and Erika, born in 1898 and thus Richard's junior by two years. It was Erika to whom he felt closest in his youth, though he admits that his desire to exercise his elder rights often came into conflict with her superior physical strength and intelligence, prompting him to take revenge on her dolls instead.[10] Flury praises her equanimity of spirit (perhaps implying that this was a gift not equally bestowed on her siblings), and to judge from surviving photos she was also the beauty of the family. She played second violin in the Biberist orchestra alongside her brothers and sister, and later took her commercial diploma in Solothurn before marrying a wealthy engineer, Fritz Moos, who became a colonel in the army. Regrettably for Richard – though family loyalty precluded open complaint – Fritz had little interest in music,

[8] *Ibid.*, p. 10.
[9] *Ibid.*, p. 13.
[10] *Ibid.*, pp. 18–19.

lavishing his wealth instead on the visual arts and becoming a major patron on the Swiss scene. As mentioned, he left his substantial art collection to the local authority, with enough money to ensure that it was kept accessible to the general public through the offices of the 'Moos-Flury Foundation' which exists to this day.

Flury's other sister, Rosa, played the piano in the Biberist orchestra, presumably to fill out the harmonies in what must have been at times a lopsided ensemble. She was sent off to a finishing school in Auvernier some forty miles away on the shores of Lake Neuchâtel, and afterwards returned to help out her mother in the household. Richard later recalled his admiration for her being able to recite Schiller's play *Wilhelm Tell* from memory in its entirety. She married an engineer by the name of Walter Jud, and they took on the family house and restaurant after her parents' death. Running a restaurant naturally situates one at the centre of local society, and Walter was one of the co-founders of the Biberist carnival celebrations in 1945.[11]

Where Richard tended to be mild-mannered, dreamy and keen to compromise (thus the opinion in word and print of almost everyone who knew him), Adolf was by all accounts goal-oriented, practically minded and hot-tempered, occasionally choleric – even his own reminiscences begin with an admission of his 'restless, impetuous temperament that even today [1950] often cannot be constrained by reason'.[12] But Adolf was also very clever. Richard recalled how he feared his brother's keen intelligence as a child, for he would always struggle to grasp whatever Adolf tried to explain to him. Adolf seems early on to have adopted a paternal, didactic role towards his younger brother. He would play a major part in getting Richard admitted into grammar school, into the local student fraternity 'Dornachia' and also into the 'Sankt Lukasbruderschaft' ('Fraternity of St Lukas', a local society which had survived in Solothurn since the sixteenth century and which remains in existence to this day). Indeed, Adolf generally seems to have supervised Richard's entrance into adult society – even more so than their father. Richard later recalled that 'he gave me advice at important times of my life, which to my detriment I did not always follow';[13] he is here perhaps thinking of one specific life-changing matter to which I shall return at its proper place in this narrative.[14] Adolf was a keen amateur cellist and proficient on horn, trombone and double-bass, and later also dabbled in conducting and singing (he was apparently good enough to sing solo tenor in local choral and operatic performances). After a year studying engineering at the Eidgenössische Technische Hochschule in Zurich (the 'Swiss Federal Institute of Technology', today known as 'ETH Zurich'), Adolf returned home to tell his father that he was abandoning his studies

[11] *Cf.* www.schnaegg.ch/history/dieerstenjahre/dokumentevon1945.php, accessed October 2015.

[12] Adolf Flury, [Reminiscences], typescript, p. 2.

[13] *Lebenserinnerungen*, *op. cit.*, p. 14.

[14] *Cf.* p. 91, below.

The Flury family, c. 1914:
Richard, Adolf Sen., Erika, Rosa Jun., Rosa Sen., Adolf Jun.

in favour of music. He was met with a strict refusal; the family's financial limitations would not allow it. Being the loyal eldest son, named after his father, Adolf obeyed and continued with the path he had chosen first. He later had a highly successful career with his own engineering company, first in Biberist, then in Bern, which brought him money and status. He also rose in the ranks of the Swiss Army, serving as a first lieutenant during the Second World War (unlike Richard, who had an aversion to things military and never quite fitted in). Adolf's two daughters were equally determined and successful in their turn – they both later became architects, at a time when it was still an unusual profession for a woman in male-dominated Swiss society.

Adolf seems always to have acknowledged that his brother possessed musical gifts far beyond his own, though his self-confidence, his financial success and Richard's own acknowledgement of Adolf's superior intellect seem to have helped prevent any overt envy on Adolf's part that his younger sibling had been allowed the career choice he had been denied. And in any case, after their father's death Adolf remained for many years a figure of quasi-paternal authority for Richard. When Richard had the opportunity to buy a Blüthner grand piano in 1928, for example, it was to Adolf that he turned for assistance. Adolf promptly gave him 1,500 francs for it – though as a loan, to be repaid monthly with interest over several years, all signed and sealed in an official contract.[15] Their correspondence makes it evident that similar arrangements were made for Richard to be able to pay a visit to Vienna soon after, and to attend a conducting course given by Felix Weingartner in Basel.[16] To be sure, Adolf was probably not (yet) wealthy enough to give such sums as a gift, but one suspects that these contracts had a didactic intent: Richard was never overly gifted in financial matters, and Adolf probably reckoned that lending the money with interest allowed him to offer dual assistance to his younger brother – by helping him get the instrument he wanted, but also by teaching him the lesson for life that everything comes at a cost (in this case, at 40 francs a month plus two per cent interest). Altogether, the Flurys could be said to be remarkably representative of German Swiss society from the late nineteenth century onwards, characterised as it still is by a rigorous meritocracy that values hard work and individualism. Over the space of only three generations, a family of intermittently migrant stonemasons was transformed into a dynasty of well-to-do engineers, architects, artists and art patrons.

Richard Flury's first musical endeavours apparently comprised attempts to pick out tunes at the family piano that stood in the restaurant dining room. But it was the violin that fascinated him from early on. The members of his father's orchestra were generally unworried about practising between their weekly rehearsals and so would often store their instruments in the Flurys' large living room. Richard later recalled how he would creep in, take out a violin from its case and try it out. His secrecy was in vain, for he usually forgot to wash his hands in advance, leaving sticky traces of jam, honey and butter on the body and fingerboard. When repeated admonishments from his father failed to have any effect, he was given his own tiny violin the next Christmas.[17] His first violin-teacher was Richard Spiegel, a local primary-school teacher, the co-organiser of the Biberist Orchestra along with Adolf Flury, and its regular conductor. Spiegel and Adolf were close friends, and they had travelled together on occasion as far away as the Munich Oktoberfest. When it came to the violin, Spiegel was more of an enthusiast than an expert, though Flury later maintained that he had been a 'brilliant' pedagogue and had been crucial in instilling a love of music in him early on. Spiegel was able to draw, and to improvise verses, and was also gifted in maths and the sciences – but he later lost his job because a love of the bottle apparently provided ammunition to prominent locals who disliked him. Spiegel died in 1917, not long after being sacked, but his nephew Cäsar (1918–98), a highly gifted painter, would later also play a role in Richard Flury's biography.

[15] Contract dated 13 March 1928 in Richard Flury's archives. As stated in the Acknowledgements (on p. 16, above), Flury's music archives are in the Zentralbibliothek Solothurn, while his other archives are held by his son Urs Joseph Flury.

[16] Assorted letters from Flury to Adolf, in Flury's archives.

[17] *Lebenserinnerungen*, *op. cit.*, pp. 38–39.

Richard Flury in costume for a performance of the 'Kindersinfonie' in the Solothurn Concert Hall, c. 1907

An injury to his left index finger caused by a broken bottle meant that Flury had to abandon the violin for three years. Piano lessons were tried instead – he was sent to the teacher of his elder siblings, Klemens Allemann, who was also a primary-school teacher and the conductor of the local Catholic church choir. Flury showed little interest and stopped when Allemann declared his embarrassment at taking money for lessons that brought no progress. But when Allemann was appointed Flury's classroom teacher in the third and fourth years of primary school in Biberist, Flury enjoyed the singing lessons he gave; soon he was also able to take up the violin again, this time with a young teacher in nearby Solothurn, Maria Schaad, who was a graduate of the Zurich Conservatoire. He took the train to Solothurn for his lessons – profiting from the proximity of the family home to the station by delaying his departure until he heard the station bell signalling that the train had left the previous station, Gerlafingen. By his own admission, on his journey home he would so often forget to take his violin with him when alighting from the train that the staff at the terminus station, Burgdorf, soon knew its provenance and simply sent it on the next train back to Biberist.[18]

When he reached the sixth year of primary school, Richard's father decided it was time to send him to a more advanced teacher – much to the boy's horror, for he had grown accustomed to Miss Schaad. So he was enrolled instead with Gustav Langenhagen, who was also the director of the venerable Solothurn city band, the 'Stadtmusik Solothurn', which had been in existence since 1845 (and which still thrives). But Flury soon grew to like Langenhagen, who had broad experience on several wind instruments as well as the violin – he was the 'perfect embodiment of the sturdy, old German regimental Kapellmeister', Flury wrote many years later.[19]

[18] *Ibid.* p. 42.

[19] *Ibid.* p. 43.

2
High-School Music

In Flury's time, as is still the case today, Swiss high schools were run as a selective system, with the 'Gymnasium' the school for the highest stream, equivalent to a grammar school in Britain. Its prime purpose is to prepare its students for university entrance. In Switzerland, the grammar school is a 'Kantonsschule', a high school run by the canton, not the local municipal authority. These schools are based in the larger centres of population, which in Canton Solothurn means the city of Olten – back then a largely proletarian place on account of its importance as a crossing point for the main Swiss railway lines – and the more patrician city of Solothurn itself.

Solothurn has a long tradition of public education. The canons at its various monasteries began teaching the local youth several centuries ago. In the sixteenth century, two pupils of the famous music-theorist Heinrich Glarean settled in Solothurn and played a major role in running its schools: Johannes von Aal (c. 1500–51) and his nephew, Hanns Wagner (1520–90).[1] Both von Aal and Wagner composed music and wrote plays,[2] and the latter's drama about Urs, Solothurn's patron saint, would be one of the sources for the mystery play with music that Richard Flury composed in the early 1940s.[3] This early, deep-seated connection between the city's intellectuals, its schools, music and theatre remained significant over the ensuing centuries. The Jesuits took over the running of the city schools in the mid-seventeenth century, and then passed on that task to the local authorities two hundred years later. The Kantonsschule Solothurn was founded in 1833 on the premises of the former Jesuit School, then moved in 1882 into the former palace of the French ambassadors to Switzerland, the Ambassadorenhof.[4] By the end of the nineteenth century, this cantonal school essentially featured three in one: the grammar school proper, then

[1] *Cf.*, for example, Johann Mösch, 'Der Einfluss des Humanisten Glarean auf Solothurn', *Jahrbuch für solothurnische Geschichte*, Vol. 11 (1938), pp. 69–87, and Peter Frey and Justin Arber (eds.), *1833–1983. 150 Jahre Kantonsschule Solothurn*, Kantonsschule Solothurn, Solothurn, 1983, p. 14.

[2] *Cf.* Mösch, *loc. cit.*, and Rolf Max Kully, 'Aal, Johannes', and 'Wagner, Hanns', in *Historisches Lexikon der Schweiz*, www.hls-dhs-dss.ch/textes/d/D11462.php and www.hls-dhs-dss.ch/textes/d/D12374.php respectively, accessed October 2015.

[3] *Cf.* Rolf Max Kully, 'Hanns Wagner und das Solothurner "Festspiel" vom Jahre 1581', *Jahrbuch für solothurnische Geschichte*, Vol. 55 (1982), pp. 109–28, and Peter Lotar's diary entry for 20 May 1943, held by the Schweizerisches Literaturarchiv in Bern.

[4] *Cf.* Stefan Blank and Markus Hochstrasser, *Die Kunstdenkmäler des Kantons Solothurn*, Vol. II, *Die Stadt Solothurn II. Profanbauten*, Gesellschaft für Schweizerischer Kunstgeschichte, Bern, 2008, pp. 219–23.

The Kantonsschule in Solothurn (centre right), c. 1915. It lies directly opposite the Art Museum.

a grammar school with a technical focus (whose students would often progress to study at ETH Zurich), and the 'Lehrerseminar' or pedagogical school, for those intent on a career as a teacher.

Since entrance into it was on academic merit alone, the Kantonsschule was an ideal place for the upwardly mobile. Richard's elder brother Adolf was a high flyer in matters mathematical and scientific and gained entrance to its portals with ease. He later reminisced fondly about the 'free, progressive spirit' of the school.[5] Richard was hungry for knowledge and so also aspired to move up to the Kantonsschule upon completing his sixth year of primary school. But his marks in mathematics were so dreadful that he failed to make the grade, landing instead in the bottom 25 per cent of his class of 48 children.

Richard's mother suggested that he move to her family's native Feldkirch across the border in Austria, where he might be allowed to attend grammar school, but this prospect did not appeal to her husband – presumably for lack of funds. The alternative was for Richard to complete his last two years of statutory education at his primary school in Biberist, along with the rest of the mathematically challenged, and thereafter to take a job as a worker at the local paper-factory. It was now that brother Adolf intervened. He was in his second-last year at the Kantonsschule and took it upon himself to march into the principal's office to insist that his brother be allowed into the school on at least a provisional basis. Its democratic traditions notwithstanding, Switzerland was long a preserve of patriarchal hegemony, and so for a boy

[5] Adolf Flury, *loc. cit.*, p. 3.

in his mid-teens to take such a step, seemingly against the natural order of things, is a testament to Adolf's strength of character. Luckily, Richard's inadequacy in maths was made up for by very good marks in most other subjects; accordingly, they let him in, and within six weeks the provisional nature of his status had been made permanent. He also applied himself sufficiently to pass the necessary maths exams for the remainder of his school education.

Flury seems to have enjoyed his years in the Kantonsschule far more than one might suppose, given the problems he faced in getting there and the hard work required to stay in it. A letter he wrote to his father some four years after leaving school (in fact, the last letter he wrote before his father's death) suggests that not all went smoothly: 'With regard to my nervousness, many former school friends have said that I've become much calmer compared to when I was at the grammar school'.[6] But one should not read too much into this statement. Flury did retain a certain nervous sensibility throughout his adult life – friends mention minor physical tics, such as absent-mindedly writing in the air with the little finger of his left hand while deep in thought. But puberty can in any case bring out all manner of quirks and habits that often disappear again naturally, once the hormones have settled. And although he admits that he did not make too many close friends in his class, the fact that Richard gladly attended school alumni gatherings over the ensuing decades would seem to suggest that in truth he fitted in quite well, and that his generally happy reminiscences of his schooldays were not too pink-tinged in retrospect.

Teaching at a Swiss cantonal grammar school has long required and accorded an academic status similar to that of university lecturers, and most of Flury's teachers possessed a doctorate (at least one would later be appointed to a university professorship). No documents about Richard Flury's schoolboy years have survived in the official Solothurn archives,[7] but thanks to his fastidiousness in documenting his life and work, several of his old school books lie in his private archives. There are copious notebooks filled with information on logic, ancient history and the like. As one would expect, Flury's enjoyment of individual subjects depended considerably on the character of his teachers, about whom he writes in his memoirs. He praises his maths master – who was also the school rector – for the clarity of his explanations; drawing lessons were popular (not least because the boys were allowed to eat the fresh fruit bought by their teacher for their still-life classes); Latin, Greek and Italian were also among his favourite subjects; his French teacher introduced them to modern literature (though his explanations tended to the highfalutin), whereas their German teacher stuck to the classics and also directed the school productions of

[6] Letter from Richard Flury to his father, dated 22 January 1920, Geneva, held in Flury's archives.
[7] E-mail to the author from Ursula Naef of the Kantonsschule Solothurn, dated 28 January 2015.

Flury (third from left, back row) as a member of the Dornachia fraternity, 1915

Schiller, Goethe and the like. Botany and gymnastics did not appeal much to Flury. And although history lessons with Ferdinand von Arx were enjoyable – he was a leading local historian and author of a history of Switzerland for schools – the lessons with their other history professor, Eugen Tatarinoff, were as dry as dust, despite the man's exotic pedigree (he was the son of a colonel in the Russian army). Odd though it may sound today, Flury's curriculum even included subjects such as crystallography and astronomy – the latter being made possible by the construction of a planetary observatory for the school in 1908, financed partly by the state and partly by private sponsors.[8] Their teacher for religion did not believe in evolution, though it is perhaps a sign of the progressive nature of the school that Richard Flury wrote of having argued passionately with him about Darwin without inviting censure (and culminating in his teacher's declaration, he recalled, that 'if you personally insist on being descended from apes, then I shan't argue against it'[9]). Class music and singing lessons were with Edmund Wyss (1867–1929), a Solothurn native who had studied at the Leipzig Conservatoire. He made a name for himself with the music for a festival play in 1899 about the Swiss victory at the Battle of Dornach in 1499 in which the Swiss Confederacy defeated the Swabian League from

[8] Frey and Arber, *op. cit.*, p. 71.

[9] *Lebenserinnerungen, op. cit.*, pp. 61–62.

the north (twenty years later, Richard Flury would himself orchestrate the 'Festmarsch' from Wyss' play). According to Flury, Wyss even incorporated the eurhythmics of Émile Jaques-Dalcroze in his teaching. In objective terms, Flury's school-years were certainly successful, as his school-leaving certificate, dated 1 April 1916, records uniformly excellent marks. The Swiss school system grades its papers from 6 (the best mark) to 1 (the worst), and in German, philosophy, history and drawing Flury was awarded a 6; in everything else – from Latin, Greek and French to all the sciences – he was given a 5.

Flury also partook of the more convivial aspects of life at the Kantonsschule, primarily through the offices of the 'Dornachia', one of three student fraternities ('Verbindungen') that existed at the school at the time, and which was named after the site of the aforementioned battle.[10] In Germany such fraternities are usually found at universities, but in Switzerland and Austria they are also commonly found in grammar schools. Each fraternity has its own colours, which feature in the uniforms its members wear. The practices and vocabulary of the Dornachia are similar to those of its parallel fraternities at the German universities, though it is not a 'duelling fraternity' such as one still finds north of the Rhine. Its members met (and still meet) every week in its private rooms underneath the Roter Turm Hotel in Solothurn. Their activities included sports, hearing lectures by other members or alumni, and drinking beer – the last of these was compulsory, though Flury disliked the bitter taste and so drank only the statutory minimum amount. His memoirs wax lyrical about their Saturday-evening gatherings, and how groups from the fraternity would wander about the streets on summer nights, he with his violin, his friends with guitar, mandolin or clarinet, serenading themselves and others. Richard's admission to the Dornachia was again a favour he owed his brother, for Adolf presided over the Verbindung during Richard's first year at the Kantonsschule.

Gustav Langenhagen remained Flury's violin-teacher for his first year at the Kantonsschule, but he then left the city, at which Flury switched to the instrumental teacher at his school, Hans Heutschi – a wise move, since Flury had become aware that Heutschi disliked any of his school students taking tuition with outside teachers. Heutschi was a bachelor and lived opposite the grand Baroque cathedral in a room in the Hotel Krone, which for some two centuries had been the stopping-off point for anyone of note passing through, from Casanova to James Boswell.[11] Flury's description of Heutschi – 'He was [...] very nervous in his gestures and it was not difficult to guess that he was a sensitive musician possessed of delicate nerves'[12] – suggests that

[10] *Cf.* www.dornachia.ch/, accessed October 2015.

[11] *Cf.*, for example, Frederick A. Pottle (ed.), *Boswell on the Grand Tour: Germany and Switzerland, 1764*, McGraw-Hill, New York, 1953, pp. 208–11.

[12] *Lebenserinnerungen*, *op. cit.*, p. 44.

The Hotel Krone in Solothurn, with the Cathedral of St Urs on the left. Since its most recent renovations, the Hotel looks today very much as in this nineteenth-century aquatint.

the man struck a sympathetic chord in Flury, for it sounds remarkably like descriptions given of Flury himself by assorted contemporaries. Heutschi conducted the school orchestra, in which the students of the Kantonsschule were joined by musicians drafted in from other schools. Flury was among the violins, and it was here, he recalled, that he first became acquainted with symphonies by Haydn, Gluck's overture to *Iphigenie in Aulis* and Mozart's overtures to *Idomeneo* and *Die Entführung aus dem Serail*. Nor was this the only orchestra in which Flury was active. His father and Richard Spiegel had meanwhile restarted the Biberist Orchestra, after it had petered out during Richard Flury's childhood. Richard was now appointed concert-master, though he had just entered his teens. The Biberist Orchestra never had more than 25 members and its repertoire was very much geared to amateurs (both in the ensemble and in the audience), eschewing the symphonic and concentrating instead on lighter overtures by composers such as Auber, Boieldieu and Rossini (though with a dash of Mozart thrown in too).[13] Spiegel conducted, though apparently with more enthusiasm than talent, smoking his pipe while he did so. The musicians themselves all had either a litre or half-litre jug of beer next to their stands (except for Richard, who was restricted to raspberry juice on account of his age).[14]

[13] *Ibid.*, p. 53.
[14] *Ibid.*, p. 51.

It was also in his first years at the Kantonsschule, the composer later wrote, that he saw his first operas. It would be another one-and-a-half decades before Solothurn got its own professional opera ensemble, but a small troupe of instrumentalists and singers came up from Bern every year to put on guest performances of light fare in the city theatre – Flury mentions seeing operas or operettas by Friedrich von Flotow, Albert Lortzing, Jacques Offenbach, Johann Strauss (presumably the Younger), Franz von Suppé and even Mozart. The conductor played at a piano in the pit (no doubt to fill in missing orchestral parts) and Flury, his brother Adolf and others were drafted in to turn the pages for him.[15]

Exactly when Flury began to compose is not known, but his earliest surviving efforts are all dated around 1911. They are uniformly awful – he was no prodigy – although given his amateur, provincial background, that is not overly surprising. There is a trio for three violins or two violins and viola from 1911, in which it is obvious that Flury has no idea how to write in the viola clef, and in which he demonstrates no real knowledge of harmony, melody, rhythm or notation. A duo for two violins from the same year is no better. His ambition already far outstripped his abilities – he was soon writing 'concert overtures' for orchestra. The first of these, also from 1911, is in C major, and in fact almost never leaves that key, as Flury also wryly admits in his memoirs.[16] The Biberist Orchestra had the misfortune to try it out, and it seems to have been the first of his works to receive a (more or less public) performance, about a month after its completion. The card-catalogue that Flury later compiled of his *œuvre* lists it as having been performed in the Hotel Bahnhof in Biberist on 6 January 1912, with the Biberist Orchestra conducted by Richard Spiegel.

A second Concert Overture, from 1912, is in F major, which key is similarly retained throughout. Then there is a Concert Waltz for orchestra written in November 1912, which is again in C major (and again never really leaves it). But an overture for orchestra written in 1912–13 shows a considerable improvement (relatively speaking). There is a definite sense of forward momentum, and the string-writing is more idiomatic. But Flury still has problems moving out of his home key, and his modulations tend to have the grating feeling of a car changing gears without the driver having depressed the clutch. An overture entitled *Tarquinius* from 1913 is more promising. The wind parts have now gained a certain degree of independence, though the prevalence of root-position harmonies looks at times like very bad mock-Berlioz. The style of the overture is actually rather more akin to Rossini, and it is cast in three short movements – though one has the impression that the brevity was necessary so that Flury didn't have to develop his material. There are two more 'concert waltzes', written while

[15] *Ibid.*, p. 46.

[16] *Ibid.*, p. 52.

The Biberist Orchestra in Mühledorf, c. 1912. Adolf Flury Sen. is at the back, far left; Richard is in front of him with his violin; Richard Spiegel is fourth from left in the back row; Adolf Flury Jun. is seated in front of him, with Rosa Flury to the right of him.

he was still at the Kantonsschule. They are also ambitious – the second, completed on 12 September 1914, is a full 60 pages of orchestral score – but one also suspects that the format of the waltz-sequence, mimicking the practice of the (Johann) Strauss family, is again a means for Flury to circumvent having to develop his themes.

There is also a small amount of piano and chamber music extant from Flury's years at the Kantonsschule. Five waltzes for piano from December 1912 have a slightly better sense of harmonic direction than his orchestral music of the time, though there is still a tendency for the bass to get stuck in root position. The fifth of them, by contrast, has a few inventive touches, and sounds at times like a cross between the 'folksy' Grieg and an alphorn melody. The marches for piano from this period are similarly replete with melodic and harmonic clichés from the popular literature (Johann Strauss and others), though the phrase-lengths aren't always properly judged, leaving the harmony hanging too long on the dominant and making of the piece less of a march than a limp (as in his *Gruss an Biberist. Marsch* of 1912). There is a bundle of pieces for violin and piano from 1912–14, one of which Flury mentions in his memoirs.[17] It is entitled *Erotikon*, and he recalls how his teacher urged him in vain to change the title. He apparently performed it before his peers to such applause that he had to play it again. It begins passionately on the G string, incorporates lots of tricky double-stops, features an accompanied cadenza and then proceeds

[17] *Ibid.*, p. 48.

into a passage where semiquavers cross the strings in a manner requiring vigorous wrist movements of near-Freudian import. Ever more bizarre harmonic progressions finally give way to a return of the opening melody. It has the look of a piece intended to impress someone – obviously a member of the opposite sex, as the title suggests, though Flury remains otherwise silent about it. If one had to settle on a candidate, it would probably be Gertrud Getzner, the daughter of family friends in Maria-Grün, just outside Feldkirch, whom he mentions as the object of his adoration during the summer holidays he spent with his mother's family.[18] She died during the First World War while working as a nurse in a hospital in Munich; Flury would later dedicate his first and only piano sonata to her memory.

Flury later claimed[19] that it was Gustav Langenhagen who had first given him advice on matters of instrumentation when he embarked on the composition of his orchestral overtures, although the chronology he gives elsewhere seems to contradict this assertion. He also recalled Heutschi having asked him to write an overture for the school orchestra, though his teacher died suddenly of a stroke before Flury was able to deliver.[20] These early works give little impression of the composer having had any tuition in harmony and counterpoint – Flury does mention having had a few harmony lessons with Julius Tschirner, Langenhagen's successor as conductor of the city band,[21] but one can only surmise that these hours were either very few or that Tschirner was an awful teacher. The progress Flury made in composition at this time seems to have been more the result of sheer willpower on his part. This dogged determination would stand him in good stead on many an occasion in the years to come. Playing as much music as he did also meant he learnt by osmosis – besides the orchestras of Biberist and the Kantonsschule, he played string quartets with school friends, and the smallness of Solothurn meant that he also had ample opportunities to play chamber music with adults. These included the pianist and composer Casimir Meister (1869–1941), who taught at the Kantonsschule and conducted the local choral societies during these years. Flury was particularly impressed by his piano technique, though he remarked also that Meister was too modest to play much in public.[22] Meister's own teachers had included Josef Rheinberger in Munich and Charles-Marie Widor in Paris, and so it is perhaps a shame that he did not offer Flury regular instruction in composition.[23] But at least Hans Heutschi's successor, Heinrich Wydler, began to give Flury proper lessons in 'Harmonielehre' to

[18] *Ibid.*, pp. 68–72.

[19] *Ibid.*, p. 43.

[20] *Ibid.*, pp. 45–46.

[21] *Ibid.*, p. 47.

[22] *Ibid.*, p. 48.

[23] For more information on Meister, *cf.* Hans-Rudolf Dürrenmatt's catalogue of his archives: *Casimir Meister, 1869–1941. Verzeichnis der handschriftlichen und gedruckten Werke in der Zentralbibliothek Solothurn*, Zentralbibliothek, Solothurn, 2009.

Flury around the age of twenty

prepare him for his subsequent studies at the conservatoire. Flury wrote warmly of Wydler in later years, also of his gifts as a violin-teacher: 'Of all my teachers before attending the conservatoire, I owe Professor Heinrich Wydler the most', though he noted, too, that Wydler came too late to correct all his bad habits as a violinist.[24] It would seem that towards the end of his years at the Kantonsschule, Flury realised that he had much lost ground to cover. So it must be judged all the more remarkable that he would master late-Romantic harmony and the art of orchestration in little more than five years after leaving school.

[24] *Lebenserinnerungen*, *op. cit.*, p. 48.

3
War and Muses

Before he could start his music studies proper, Flury had to fulfil his duties as a male Swiss citizen. His statutory military service began the day after he completed his final school exams, meaning that he was not even able to attend the general school-leaving festivities. The Swiss army, created after the establishment of the federal state in 1848, is a militia force in which recruits spend several months of basic training before returning to civilian life. They are then called up for refresher courses on a regular basis, and in times of European war the army is mobilised to defend the neutrality of the country and to ensure that its borders are respected. Right from the start, the army was based on Prussian principles, and during the First World War its commander-in-chief was General Ulrich Wille, the son of a Prussian exile and husband to a member of the von Bismarck family.

Although Flury's memoirs include many tales of his time in the military, he rarely mentions the First World War itself – and even then, it is music that he recalls first. On the evening of 1 August 1914 – the day that Germany and Russia went to war – he and his friends in the Dornachia fraternity had played a serenade to a Swiss soldier standing guard at the Wengibrücke, one of the bridges that cross the River Aare in the centre of town (exactly why the Swiss army should have been guarding the Aare – with a single soldier – is something of a mystery, but that is how Flury remembers it). Switzerland remained neutral during the War, but the civilian population suffered nonetheless from the inflation, rationing and overall economic malaise that war brings in its wake. Perhaps Flury did not want to dwell on the less pleasant aspects of these years in his memoirs – though it is more likely that he was not too adversely affected. Little Solothurn was spared the demonstrations and civil disturbances that were prompted by inflation and food shortages in the major Swiss cities as the War dragged on, and given the self-centredness common to almost everyone in their late teens and early twenties, it should not be surprising that Flury's prime concerns seem to have been getting on with his career in music, getting access to the opposite sex, and getting through his bouts of military service with as little incident as possible.

Flury's initial military training took place in the summer of 1916 in Liestal, to the south of Basel. It was unproblematic, even enjoyable. He had no problem with the physical exertions of night-long slogs through the Swiss countryside, but he wasn't good at synchronised marching, as his head – he claimed[1] – was too full of syncopations. And a tendency to confuse left and right proved awkward when trying to follow the bayonet instructions given by their Major, a former member of the French Foreign Legion. But Flury proved good at shooting – which he attributed to having a steady bowing arm from his violin practice – and he tells us that this skill was the reason he was recommended to do a seven-week-long, non-commissioned officer's training course in Porrentruy in north-west Switzerland.[2] Porrentruy lies some 25 miles west of Basel as the crow flies, on the French side of Switzerland's language boundary. It is a geographical oddity in that it is a kind of peninsula that juts out into French territory. Although the Western Front was relatively calm on its southern fringes, Flury and his companions were nevertheless on occasion able to watch dogfights between German and Allied planes overhead.

Flury had an ambivalent attitude to the army. While acknowledging its defensive tasks as a necessity and acquiescing in his concomitant duties as a citizen, he was never able to sympathise with those who took undue pleasure in the rigours of military life. (During his active service in the Second World War, for example, he gave expression to these feelings in letters home that in other countries would have been censored or withheld and used as proof of sedition at a court martial.) In any case, Flury was soon found unsuited to assuming command over other soldiers and, after reaching the rank of corporal, he was not sent on to train as an officer (his elder brother Adolf, by contrast, was by this time already a lieutenant). But at least the fact of his having become a non-commissioned officer gave him the right to live in a rented room away from the barracks of the rank-and-file. And he was in due course appointed 'Trompeter-Wachtmeister', literally 'trumpeter-sergeant', and put in charge of the company band. Directing brass bands would henceforth be his principal military activity during his intermittent army career, prompting him to compose numerous marches for these ensembles himself (his archives contain two such marches written in Vendlincourt on the French border, just outside Porrentruy, in September 1917, both of them competent but impersonal; the archives also contain another march, undated, as well as several composed during his active service in the early years of the Second World War).

Flury's early military service alternated with his studies. He applied for admission to the Basel Conservatoire in mid-1916, although he does not reveal precisely why he chose this particular institution. His French was probably not yet good enough for him to have considered Geneva as a serious possibility (despite that '5' in his school certificate), but the conservatoires of Bern and Zurich would have been excellent alternative options for the two main subjects he wanted to study (violin and theory – the latter

[1] *Lebenserinnerungen*, *op. cit.*, p. 92.

[2] *Ibid.*, pp. 94–95.

Sergeant Flury's regimental band (Flury in the back row, third from left)

presumably with a view to gaining the necessary basics for a future career as a composer). Zurich's music life was dominated by Volkmar Andreae, the director of the Zurich Conservatoire, conductor of the Tonhalle Orchestra and a successful composer in his own right; in Bern, the leading musical personality was Fritz Brun – another composer-conductor, like Andreae. Flury admired the work of both men, and had either of them been willing or able to give him composition lessons, he would surely have profited from it. But given the current state of his compositional technique he was not in any position to pick and choose his teachers. Perhaps more importantly, the director in Basel, Hans Huber, was a well-known pedagogue, an excellent composer in the Brahmsian tradition, and a native of the canton of Solothurn who had gone to school there himself.[3] Edmund Wyss, Flury's teacher in Solothurn, had also studied with Huber some thirty years before. It seems that Flury wrote directly to Huber when applying for admission to the Conservatoire. Huber's friendly reply of 26 August 1916 – written in his own hand, not dictated – has survived in Flury's archives (Flury later recalled that Huber 'never left a letter unanswered'[4]). Huber asks whether Flury wishes to take violin or theory as his main subject, and says that if he chooses the former, then he can take theory and piano as secondary

[3] *Cf.* Edgar Refardt, *Hans Huber, Leben und Werk eines Schweizer Musikers*, Atlantis Verlag, Zurich, 1944, especially its biography on pp. 13–73.

[4] *Lebenserinnerungen*, *op. cit.*, p. 79.

'Trumpeter-sergeant' Flury on active service, Vendlincourt, October 1917

subjects and take part in assorted ensembles, string quartets and the like (though at a total fee of 400 francs, he adds). Huber goes on to say that the entrance exam will take place at 9 in the morning on 2 October, with term itself beginning on 5 October. A brief note from Huber has also survived, written on 9 September, in which he mentions in passing a 'Prof. W.' – and so presumably Edmund Wyss had indeed put in a good word for his student.

The violin-teacher in Basel was Fritz Hirt, the leader of the Basel Symphony Orchestra. He was the only teacher present at Flury's entrance exam (though Richard's elder brother Adolf came along to give moral support). Flury played a study in double-stopping by Kreutzer and had to recognise different intervals that were played to him. He was accepted, although he recalled that Hirt said his general musicianship was more advanced than his violin-playing. That doesn't seem to have surprised Flury, whose continued self-doubts on the instrument were hardly alleviated in the performance classes in the months to come. In his own words, '14-year-old girls played virtuosic pieces in a flawless manner that put my own technique in the shade, cramped and encumbered by inhibitions as it was'.[5]

[5] *Ibid.*, p. 77.

The ongoing war might actually have acted to Flury's advantage in getting a place to study. Basel had been popular with students from north of the Rhine, but the outbreak of hostilities had made it almost impossible for them to continue their studies on the Swiss side of the border. Student numbers accordingly dropped from 519 students in 1913–14 to only 309 a year later[6] (which will have meant a corresponding drop in income from fees). But if the economic situation meant a better chance for Flury to get accepted as a student, it seems in any case that his teachers – Huber in particular – saw that he indeed possessed talent. Flury and Huber remained in contact by correspondence long after Huber's retirement, and Huber later advised him on other teachers he might approach. The tone of the older man's letters and cards to Flury always remained warm and encouraging.

Flury took theory as his principal subject at the Conservatoire, with violin as a secondary subject. He seems to have found his teachers sympathetic: Hirt for the violin, Eduard Ehrsam for the piano, and Fritz Ziegler for harmony (though Flury's meagre pianistic ability meant he found figured-bass exercises particularly difficult at the beginning). Karl Nef's music-history lectures, by contrast, he found boring. Flury also writes that Huber did not give any composition lessons during his first year, but that he joined Huber's class the next year. In fact, what Flury fails to mention in his memoirs is that his 'two years in Basel'[7] were really only two semesters, namely the winter semesters of 1916–17 and 1917–18; furthermore, as a note from Huber's wife to Flury reveals (dated 19 September 1917),[8] Huber was on leave for the first half of his second semester. So it would seem that Flury didn't have much tuition from the man at all. The matriculation books of the Conservatoire also confirm that he paid for only one semester in each year (his fees in his first year were thus 200 francs, exactly half of the sum mentioned by Huber).[9] Nevertheless, of all his teachers in Basel it was Huber who made the biggest impression. Flury's reminiscences are here worth quoting, as they are the first time he recalls any kind of systematic instruction in composition:

> Huber knew that you can't learn composing, and so adjusted how he treated his students accordingly. He used several Beethoven sonatas to explain in broad terms the structure of classical forms, and after only the second class did he send us off with the task of writing a sonata ourselves, either for piano or orchestra. He taught us how to compose like you teach animals to swim, namely by throwing us into the water without further ado and observing how

[6] Hans Ehinger, 'Geschichtlicher Überblick' in Musik-Akademie der Stadt Basel, *Gedenkschrift zum fünfzigjährigen Bestehen der Abteilung Konservatorium 1905–1955*, Verlag der Musik-Akademie, Basel, 1955, pp. 5–46 (here 14–15).

[7] *Lebenserinnerungen*, *op. cit.*, p. 81.

[8] Held today in Flury's archives.

[9] I am grateful to Martina Wohlthat for providing access to the matriculation books of the Basel Conservatoire.

> we managed to save ourselves. He didn't gripe long about our attempts at composition. He would read through them swiftly, which was enough for him to form his opinion. What was usable was allowed to remain. What was weak was either struck out or dispatched to the waste-paper basket.[10]

Students at the Conservatoire were allowed free entrance into the rehearsals of the Basel Symphony Orchestra under Hermann Suter. Flury went to these rehearsals, and although it is not known how many he attended, his determination to improve himself means he probably made full use of the opportunities he was given. His orchestral experience had hitherto been largely confined to the amateur scene, which in itself can be highly instructive (just as driving a small Fiat with a dodgy engine will teach one more about how a car works than one might learn from sitting at the wheel of a new Rolls-Royce). Many composer-conductors in the generations before Flury had learnt their craft during 'galley years' spent working in a provincial, semi-professional environment – most notably Richard Wagner. But being able to hear a professional orchestra play and rehearse under a good conductor will have opened Flury's ears and eyes to what is really possible with a first-rate ensemble. He was unable to attend many actual concerts or opera performances in Basel for the simple reason that he didn't have the money. But he did occasionally go to the theatre, and a Basel performance of August Strindberg's *Dance of Death* with Alexander Moissi, in a guest performance by Max Reinhardt's ensemble from Berlin, was an event he remembered all his life.[11]

Flury also made the most of his months in Basel by enrolling at the same time in the Philosophical Faculty of the University (again only for the winter semesters of 1916–17 and 1917–18, but not for the summer semester in between). He attended Nef's lectures on Beethoven (for Nef was on the staff of both institutions of higher education in the city), although he found these as dull as the man's classes at the Conservatoire. He did, however, enjoy the lectures in philosophy, ethics and psychology given by Karl Joel and those in art-history by Friedrich Rintelen (Flury's official study booklet lists the latter course as 'Italian painters from Titian to Rubens [*sic*]'). Flury never took any exams at the University, and so there is no further information about his activities there.[12]

During his first semester in Basel, Flury rented a room at Steinenvorstadt 69, and in his last semester at Austrasse 107, in both cases within walking distance of Conservatoire and University. He apparently ate mostly at a teetotal restaurant on the Totengässlein near the University, but like many

[10] *Lebenserinnerungen*, *op. cit.*, pp. 78–79.

[11] *Ibid.*, p. 81.

[12] I am grateful to Hermann Wichers of the Staatsarchiv Basel-Stadt for information on Flury's matriculation dates. Flury's study booklet, in which the courses he attended are entered by hand and signed by his professors, is in his private archives.

students before and after, he found the local cuisine not a patch on that of his mother, later becoming convinced that he had suffered from malnutrition as a result – though perhaps wartime economics were at least in part to blame. And since his parents ran a restaurant and will have had direct access to local farm produce throughout the war, his mother probably made sure her offspring remained well fed when back in Biberist.

In between his two semesters in Basel, Flury was given an opportunity to put into practice what he had learnt as a 'trumpeter sergeant' and from observing Hermann Suter on the podium in Basel, for in early 1917 he was appointed the director of the Stadtmusik Solothurn (the city band[13]) on an interim basis. The war had apparently made it difficult to get suitable candidates to run the band, and so Flury was drafted in. He stayed for only a few months and was unconvinced of his efficacy, not least because of his own meagre proficiency as a trumpeter: he had taken up the bass trumpet in the army, but had by his own admission[14] not been unduly conscientious in probing its mysteries. His archives hold a letter signed by the president and secretary of the Stadtmusik on 17 January 1918, after the end of his year as its director, in which they confirm him to have been a 'duteous, knowledgeable and hardworking musician. We were very satisfied with his very fine accomplishments'.[15] And although one can never be wholly certain of the honesty of such general pronouncements, Flury must have done a good job because he was asked to jump in again to conduct the Stadtmusik five years later. All the same, the fact that he isn't mentioned in the brief history of the Stadtmusik published by the band on its website suggests that his impact was of only incidental significance.[16]

Flury remained luckless in his love-life, and by his own account was so tongue-tied that he resorted to writing a love-letter in Latin to a blonde girl he fancied at the Conservatoire but who, it seems, had not noticed him. It would be a while yet before Flury's luck would change. But he began composing songs in his late teens, dedicating them to the assorted girls by whom he later claimed to have been inspired.[17] Flury wrote of having had a chaste relationship with a girl for four years until the end of his time at the Kantonsschule – presumably the 'Fridy Lüthi' who was the dedicatee of songs such as 'Yearning' ('Sehnsucht', to a poem by R. Baumbach, September 1915), 'When I look into your eyes' ('Wenn ich in deine Augen seh', Heine, 5 January 1916) and another 'Yearning' (by Goethe this time, 25 January 1916). The titles are on the whole more expressive than the music. The first 'Sehnsucht', for example, begins with a promising two-bar motif in the bass, but abandons it for blandness as soon as the song proper

[13] *Cf.* p. 30, above.

[14] *Lebenserinnerungen*, *op. cit.*, p. 108.

[15] The letter is in Flury's archives.

[16] *Cf.* www.stadtmusiksolothurn.ch/fileadmin/Dateien/geschichte.pdf, accessed October 2015.

[17] *Lebenserinnerungen*, *op. cit.*, p. 142.

starts. Flury can't even make his note stems go the right way yet. There are then three songs from mid-1917 dedicated to one Paula von Arx: 'Dead love' (Böhm), 'To Helmine von Chezy' (Chamisso) and 'Melancholy' (Julius Arent). The first two of these are characterised by odd stops and starts and show little sense of how anything should hang together. 'Melancholy' is full of competent sequences, albeit of little overall consequence; but it is pretty, more assured than what had gone before it, and a sign at last that Flury's harmony lessons in Basel had exerted a positive impact. It would later be his earliest work to find its way into print.

A sudden spate of songs was unleashed in 1918, many of them to texts by Heine, and some of them dedicated to one Grety Siegrist, a 'blue-eyed, golden-blonde' girl from Thun.[18] There is 'I greet you' ('Sei mir gegrüsst', 27 January 1918), with an impossibly high vocal line that was later corrected (a middle section is marked 'complainingly' - 'klagend' - presumably for autobiographical reasons). Then there is 'From my tears' ('Aus meinen Tränen', 10 April 1918) and 'In the lovely month of May' ('Im wunderschönen Monat Mai', written on the same day). There are several further Heine settings from this time not expressly dedicated to Grety, though she was presumably their addressee too. Their titles alone seem to suggest that Flury is communicating to someone in particular: 'The blue eyes of spring' ('Die blauen Frühlingsaugen', 18 April 1918), 'Your face so loving and mild' ('Dein Angesicht so lieb und mild', 14 June 1918) and 'When I look into your eyes' ('Wenn ich in deine Augen seh', 19 June 1918, marked 'mournfully!' - not the same setting as that of 1916 mentioned above). The best of these is 'In the lovely month of May' (Ex. 1), which is proof enough that Huber's tuition - however brief - had really left its mark. To be sure, at times the song seems almost demonstrative in the way it avoids reminiscence of Schumann - it was bold of Flury to set so many texts already made famous by the earlier composer. Its diction is somewhat foursquare, the phrasing too (as is the case in all the other above songs), and its harmonies are largely untroubled by dissonance; the ironic questioning of Schumann's fragmentary cadences gives way here to unequivocal rapture. At first glance, one feels this song ought to sound rather dull and formulaic. And yet there is a *Schwung* to the piano part and a sense of trajectory to the vocal line and to the accompanying harmonies that make it stand out in stark contrast to what had gone before. Even the handwriting of the autograph looks more assured. The youthful naivety of this song could so easily have become irritatingly post-pubertal, but instead it manages to err on the side of charming. This is the first work by Flury that gives an intimation that its author might be a real composer after all, and so there is reason to be grateful to Grety Siegrist, whoever she was.

[18] *Ibid.*, p. 142.

Ex. 1

Voice
Piano
Im wun - der - schön-en Mo - nat Mai, Als al - le Kno - spen spran - gen, Da
L.H.
5
ist in mei-nem Her - zen Die Lie - be auf - ge - gan - gen. Im
9
wun - der - schön - en Mo - nat Mai, Als
11
al - le Vö gel san - - - - gen, Da

13
hab' ich ihr ge - stan - - - - den Mein
6
15
Langsam
Seh - nen und Ver - lan - gen. Im
L.H.
20
wun - der - schön - en Mo - nat Mai, Da hab' ich ihr ge-stan - den Mein
3
24
Seh - - nen, mein Seh - - nen, mein Seh - nen und Ver - lan - gen.

4
Counterpoint in Bern

However much Flury learnt in Basel, it seems that it only made him more aware of how much he still had to learn. At some point in 1917 or early 1918, he found out that 'Ernst Kurth, the most important musicologist of our time, had begun teaching in Bern',[1] at which he decided that this was the man who could teach him what he still needed to know in matters of harmony and counterpoint. Kurth (1886–1946), an Austrian, had taken a doctorate in musicology under Guido Adler (studying with him at the same time as Anton Webern, as it happens), had become acquainted with Gustav Mahler, and had then worked as a répétiteur in Leipzig, Bamberg and elsewhere. In fact, he was appointed to a lectureship in music at Bern University in 1912, not 1917. But Flury's mistaken chronology is instructive, for it was in 1917 that Kurth published his seminal *Fundamentals of Linear Counterpoint*,[2] and it was most probably Flury's discovery of this book that prompted him to want Kurth as a teacher. Thus in April 1918 Flury moved to Bern, where he matriculated at the university on the 22nd of the month.[3] As in Basel, he also enrolled at the nearby Conservatoire, taking violin lessons with Alphonse Brun, one of the best-known Swiss violinists of the day,[4] and piano lessons with Ernst Denhof. Brun's fastidiousness seems to have merely reinforced Flury's self-doubts and driven him into depression; but the lessons with Kurth always served to raise his spirits again. It was Kurth, he claimed, who gave him the confidence to pursue his chosen career as a composer:

> Twice a week I had private tuition with him in harmony and counterpoint. In recognising theoretical problems in music, Kurth was a genius, and I do not believe that I could have found a more suitable teacher to explain the concepts in this field.[5]

[1] *Lebenserinnerungen*, *op. cit.*, p. 82.

[2] Ernst Kurth, *Grundlagen des linearen Kontrapunkts: Einführung in Stil und Technik von Bach's melodischer Polyphonie*, Max Drechsel, Bern, 1917.

[3] I am grateful to Niklaus Bütikofer of the Bern University Archives for information on Flury's dates of matriculation and exmatriculation at the University.

[4] Alphonse Brun (1889–1963), violinist and later director of the Bern Conservatoire; no relation to Fritz Brun.

[5] *Lebenserinnerungen*, *op. cit.*, p. 82.

Flury spent three semesters in Bern altogether. His memoirs[6] record his having attended lectures in philosophy given by Paul Häberlin and Richard Herbertz, and in art history by Arthur Weese, though his study booklet lists only one course by Herbertz and none by either of the others (did he perhaps attend unofficially so as not to have to pay the course fees? Yet these were not high – Herbertz's course is listed in Flury's study booklet as having cost him 15 francs). Flury also attended Kurth's own lectures on assorted aspects of musicology and enjoyed them immensely, finding them a marked contrast to the dullness of Karl Nef in Basel. They were also wide-ranging. The summer semester of 1918 lists three lecture-courses by Kurth: in chorales and the harmonisation of folksong; the development of harmony in Mozart, Beethoven and Schubert; and Anton Bruckner's symphonies. Flury later remarked that it was Kurth to whom he owed his introduction to the music of Bruckner.

Military service intervened again in the summer of 1918, although this time it took on a less oppressive form than hitherto. In order to improve his band-leading skills he was sent on a three-week course for 'trumpeter sergeants' in Zurich (which included a visit from Volkmar Andreae, who was a colonel in the Swiss army), but thereafter Flury spent two summer months on military-band duty in Locarno by the banks of the Lago Maggiore, conducting a band of some sixty musicians in regular concerts on the Piazza Grande, eating excellent food, drinking the local wine and falling in and out of love with assorted local girls. Flury's letters to Ernst Kurth have not survived except for birthday greetings sent on Kurth's 60th birthday in 1946. But Kurth's letters were kept by Flury – or at least most of them. The earliest that survives dates from that summer of 1918, thanking Flury for a letter – presumably from Locarno – written on 27 July, and telling him that he will return to Bern on 1 September, after which date Flury may contact him to arrange their next meeting. Kurth writes:

> I am pleased that you feel inwardly more secure in music. I have also noticed it, though I have to emphasise that the end of the road is still a long way off; in particular, you have to develop a more deep-seated sense of calm. You ought to change your whole inner attitude to making music in order to allow the powers within you – which are undoubtedly highly promising – to develop freely. But I think that we can discuss these things with more clarity and more freely face to face. Until then, approach your military service calmly as a spiritual relaxation and convalescence. Then it will also further your professional development, which will thrive all the quicker and be the more uninhibited for it.[7]

[6] *Ibid.*, p. 82.

[7] Letter from Ernst Kurth to Richard Flury, Oberdiessbach, 7 August 1918, in Nora Schmid and Lea Hinden, [Inventar Nachlass Ernst Kurth] *Anhang II, Volltextbriefe zum Inventar Nachlass Ernst Kurth.* Institut für Musikwissenschaft, Bern, 2007, pp. 308–9.

Ernst Kurth

Kurth is here presumably alluding to the nervous side of Flury's disposition, already mentioned, to which numerous other sources also refer.

The relationship between Kurth and Flury cannot be reconstructed without the latter's side of the correspondence, but Flury clearly admired Kurth immensely. He also seems to have felt he could unburden himself to Kurth, who although only ten years his senior was more worldly by far, both in professional terms and (presumably) sexually (Kurth had married in 1917). The gap in experience between two men of 22 and 32 can be vast, as was the case here. Flury also seems to have sought out father-figures as his teachers; Huber had already acquired something of a paternal role, but this consideration applied even more to Kurth, and the same pattern would emerge when Flury later studied with Joseph Marx in Vienna. A close emotional bond with his teachers was clearly important. Perhaps Flury felt better able to open his heart to an outsider who both understood his craft and knew him well enough personally to be a sympathetic receptacle for emotional baggage, but was not so close as to be tempted to offer unwanted opinions (if he wanted uncomfortable truths, Flury knew he could always rely on his brother, Adolf).

Flury's lessons with Kurth coincided with a switch in his emotional affections, for his sometime infatuation with Grety Siegrist seems to have been superseded by another Grety late in 1918: one Grety Kunz, 'a talented pianist' with whom Flury played chamber music, and who accompanied him in three violin sonatas he wrote in 1918.[8] The first, in G major, was composed in Biberist in April (the first movement), June (the second) and July 1918 (the Scherzo and Finale); the second, in A major, was written in Schaffhausen between 19 and 24 September and was dedicated to Grety; and the third, in E flat major, between 5 and 15 November in Biberist (it bears no dedication, but was presumably also intended for Grety). There are promising moments in all three, but they suffer from a desire to be both expansive and ecstatic, and their composer does not yet possess the mastery of form to keep either tendency in check. The violin part is overly showy, with lots of double and triple stops, arpeggios scrubbing frantically across all the strings, and passages repeated an octave higher in order to show off the soloist's ability to soar up the E string. The second sonata (the one expressly dedicated to Grety) contains comments – in a different hand – such as 'stubbornly', 'mockingly', 'warmly comforting', as if trying to express emotions that the music simply cannot yet. Its second movement is entitled 'à la Marche funèbre'. The third sonata is the best of the three, being overall more effective despite possessing similar faults. Its Scherzo stands out: it eschews the prolixity of the rest, is short, clean in its textures, and uses a little more counterpoint than the other movements. Its Trio is of similar quality, and is written in contrasting metres (triple time for the violin and $\frac{4}{4}$ for the piano, though its syncopations do not sound as pronounced as they look on paper).

Flury sent the second and third of these sonatas to Hans Huber at some point in late 1918 or early 1919 – quite when cannot be established, since his letter has not survived, and Huber's long reply is undated. But Huber invested much time in looking at the sonatas, even quoting the odd bar in his letter in order to suggest possibilities for improvement. He, too, preferred the third sonata, liking the Scherzo best: 'The Scherzo in A flat major is probably the best piece because it is fresh and natural and rhythmically interesting in its invention'.[9] Of these three sonatas, only the second one was ever performed. Richard played the slow movement, accompanied by his brother, Adolf, in a concert in the Reformed Church of Biberist on 3 May 1919, and the whole sonata at the same venue (also accompanied by Adolf) in a concert of the Gerlafingen Men's Chorus on 21 June 1919 (Adolf also sang five of Richard's songs in the same concert).

Grety Kunz was also the dedicatee of a Suite for Piano written just before Christmas 1918 (one of its movements, entitled 'Trost' – 'Comfort' – was apparently written in the 'Caffè Flora, Solothurn' on 20 December). Its movements are far less ambitious than those of the violin sonatas, and the Suite is all the better and the prettier for it. But it seems that at some point

[8] *Lebenserinnerungen*, *op. cit.*, p. 141. Flury's memoirs do not give her name, but his description of the sonatas and the dedication to Grety on the manuscripts leave no doubt as to her identity.

[9] Undated letter from Huber to Flury in the latter's archives, presumably early 1919.

thereafter, Grety broke off relations with Flury (not that any 'relations' had actually taken place, he assures the reader of his memoirs[10]), for her family wanted to marry her off to the son of a wealthy factory-owner. Her engagement was announced only ten days after his own rejection, Flury recalled (adding that Grety soon broke off that engagement too, without returning to seek his own affections afterwards).[11] It is perhaps this event that hovers in the background of the next letter in the meagre surviving correspondence between Kurth and Flury. Again, Flury's own letter is lost, but Kurth's reply confirms his having already slipped into a paternal role. It is dated 13 April 1919, and was thus written at the start of Flury's last semester with him:

> Thank you very much for your detailed letter [...]. I am happy to talk with you about the things whose lack of clarity distresses you, or about the external experiences [that] sour your life, and I hope I will be able to offer you reassurance if this is what you seek. The great disappointment to which you allude is something you should regard as one of life's warnings not to expect others to join you wholeheartedly on your way: everyone who works on and in himself has to suffer this, suddenly realising that he cannot expect anyone else to understand him better.
>
> [It is[12]] true that young people ruin their character early on in a small town just as in the big city [...] and that young artists especially can project everything onto a woman that they only wish to see and feel in their own ideals. This is the reason for this everyday song of disappointment, this terrible contrast between what one wants to have seen and the truth one sees as soon as the phantom melts away. [...] And don't forget that the naivety that all true artists possess can easily become a curse. The fact that such an occurrence has churned up your other struggles and your disquiet is something I understand very well [...]. You can well bear a setback in your artistic development, and in this matter you can reassure your father, or at least not let yourself be worried by him. I believe that you are on the path to becoming something truly splendid and am always happy to help you. Come to Bern soon to talk more about this.[13]

This is the last text from the three semesters that Flury spent with Kurth – hardly surprisingly, because a student and his teacher meeting every week do not need to write each other letters. There is therefore no more detail about the 'struggles' to which Kurth refers. But even if Grety Kunz was not the specific origin of Flury's existential *angst*, these will have been the 'struggles' one might expect of a man of Flury's age and time – unrequited love(s), his father's worries about a son's career prospects in a difficult profession, and

[10] *Lebenserinnerungen*, *op. cit.*, p. 141.

[11] *Ibid.*, p. 141.

[12] Half a line is illegible here because of a fold that has worn away the paper.

[13] Letter from Kurth to Flury, Bern, 13 April 1919, in Schmid and Hinden, *op. cit.*, p. 309.

Flury's own self-doubts, compounded no doubt by the rest of the above. It is to Kurth's credit that he was willing to invest so much time and energy in guiding his student through personal crises, besides helping him to catch up with what he needed to know in matters of compositional technique. And along with the usual problems of post-adolescence, there were surely also other reasons why Flury's present situation was chafing at him. Previous generations of Swiss composers had spent their formative years across the border, studying in Leipzig, Cologne, Berlin or the other major centres of the *Land der Musik*. In his letter commenting on the violin sonatas, Huber had already suggested that Flury consider studying with Friedrich Klose in Munich. But Germany and Austria were in the midst of economic, social and political chaos. So even if Flury had been able to scrape together enough money to travel abroad, he would have found little there except hunger, insurrection and the impact of the Europe-wide influenza epidemic of 1918–19. This so-called Spanish Flu had claimed several thousand lives in sheltered Switzerland alone in the past months, and the number of its victims elsewhere on the Continent was now into the millions.[14] Flury was a small-town Swiss boy with feelings of inadequacy towards those who seemed to have had it far better, far earlier; but the current state of things in Europe meant that he had no real chance to break out of his small-town situation either. It will have been all the more important to Flury to have close personal contact with a teacher such as Kurth, who had enjoyed direct contact with the great Austro-German musical traditions he so admired.

Flury certainly soaked up all he could from Kurth. His study booklet at Bern University records his having attended four more lecture-courses by Kurth in his second semester (winter 1918–19), this time in musical form of the Classical era, Beethoven's life and works, exercises in musical styles and the history of opera. There were four more university courses in the summer semester of 1919 (Flury's last in Bern), in polyphonic forms, the development of the *Lied* from Schubert to Hugo Wolf, Bach's harmony and the principal writings of Richard Wagner. Flury's archives contain a wealth of notebooks that must date from this time, as their subject headings are similar to the titles of Kurth's lecture series. Although the lack of more detailed sources means one cannot be sure how expansive Flury's musicological knowledge was before he went to Kurth, it is clear that he had now developed a passion for it. The topics in his notes cover a broad spectrum of music and music history, from Cherubini and Spontini to Verdi, Wagner and Schopenhauer. A paragraph about E. T. A. Hoffmann even mentions that his *Undine* had appeared in a modern edition by Hans Pfitzner (published a little over a decade earlier). Flury's notebooks on harmony and counterpoint are even more extensive and methodical, and their long quotations from Kurth show that he was actively working through his published book on counterpoint.

[14] The final death-toll of the epidemic is usually put at between 20 and 50 million, although some estimates are as high as 100 million.

Whatever the worries and self-doubts that plagued Flury at this time, Kurth took practical steps to put him on the right track in the one area where he could truly make an impact: his compositional technique. Flury's archives contain a few harmony exercises from his time with Huber and almost nothing from his first semester with Kurth except for some chorale harmonisations *à la* Bach – the kind that every student of music learns to write. But from late April 1919 onwards, as the exercises in his archives prove, Flury underwent a rigorous course in counterpoint with Kurth. It is fascinating to read through the manuscript book in which they are written, because there is a new exercise every few days – sometimes more than one a day – and one can follow his progress step by step (luckily for his biographers, Flury was methodical in dating almost everything he wrote). Flury will have shown Kurth his violin sonatas, and Kurth (like Huber) will have recognised his tendency to prolixity and his inability to keep control of harmony and form. So he starts by getting Flury to write Baroque suite movements for solo violin (preludes, courantes, bourrées and the like). Had Flury been a pianist, Kurth would perhaps have given him other tasks, but instead he set him off on familiar territory. There are over a dozen of these movements, the last of them dated 13 May 1919. Then on 24 May, Flury begins writing two-part keyboard inventions. They limp along now and then, their chromaticism occasionally getting out of hand, but they show more and more coherence and signs of rhythmic life. There are nine of these pieces, written up to 17 June. They overlap at the end with more complicated exercises. On 13 June, for example, Flury writes a two-part canon in which the theme appears in the inversion halfway through. It isn't particularly good music, but he is beginning to show more control over his material. On 26 June 1919 he writes his first three-part fugue, and over the next month there follow three-part canons using chorale themes, and freely imitative inventions in three parts.

The composer who emerges still has a long way to go, but he is a very different man from the one who wrote the three gushing violin sonatas only months before. Flury could have gone away and wallowed after his romantic rejection and Huber's telling him he couldn't write counterpoint. Instead, his dogged persistence won through. Huber had told Flury of his violin sonatas that he had to 'use a lot more counterpoint. It is all so homophonous'.[15] So counterpoint is what he went off to learn. One must also recognise Flury's astuteness in choosing his teacher. Kurth was barely over thirty himself, he had only just published his first large-scale book, and the university where he lectured did not even have a proper music department. But Flury must have sensed something in Kurth's book that seemed to point the way forward for him – and indeed his works of the coming years would prove that all those counterpoint exercises had borne

[15] Letter from Huber, undated, in Flury's archives.

proper fruit. And Kurth believed in Flury, too. In a letter of 1926, Kurth told him that he was 'one of my best and dearest students'.[16] Over the years he frequently expressed high praise for Flury's works – and the fact that his compliments were also on occasion paired with critical comment confirms that Kurth truly engaged with the music. His high praise was no superficial exchange of pleasantries, but sincerely meant.

[16] Letter from Kurth to Flury, Spiez, 9 June 1926, in Schmid and Hinden, *op. cit.*, p. 312.

5
Geneva

The records of Bern University list Flury as having officially ceased his studies there on 27 September 1919; in his study booklet that year, Kurth himself wrote '20 Sept' in the column marked 'date of deregistration'. Flury's classes with Kurth had actually finished before the summer, so he must have made an extracurricular visit to get his teacher's signature. In fact, he might even have done so on his way to western Switzerland, for he registered for that winter semester as a student at both the University and the Conservatoire of Geneva. To attend several different institutions of higher education without actually getting a degree from any of them was not unusual in the nineteenth and early twentieth centuries when, in the German-speaking world at least, university and conservatoire education was something of a *smörgåsbord*. One didn't necessarily require a certificate at the end of it to have any hope of entrance into the world of work, as is the norm today. And in fact, Flury had just acquired a job – two of them, indeed. The Stadtorchester Solothurn – the 'City Orchestra', which despite its municipal designation was composed of amateurs – had been created in 1917 by merging two older such institutions. In 1919 the Orchestra found itself bereft of a conductor, and its president, Arthur Baumgartner, had approached Flury with a view to his taking on the position: it seems he had heard good things about Flury's interim stint as conductor of the city band. Not long afterwards, in August 1919, Flury was also appointed to the post of violin-teacher at the Solothurn City Music School, when the incumbent, Theodor Niemann, went into retirement. Flury still had a few months before he had to take up the job, and his post with the Stadtorchester was also subject to a probation period. He therefore decided to make the most of what must have seemed like his last chance to hone the musical skills he required, and set off for a semester in Geneva.

Flury's study booklet for Geneva lists his having attended lectures in the winter semester of 1919–20 in the history of philosophy by Charles Werner (later the Rector of the University) and in 'the science of art' by the archaeologist and photographer Waldemar Deonna. But the real reason for going to Geneva was to study composition and instrumentation with Joseph Lauber. It was Huber who had recommended him as 'the right man' in a letter of 'September'[1] (presumably of that year, 1919). 'But you'll have to work hard', he had warned.

Lauber was born in 1864 near Lucerne (thus making him the same age as Richard Strauss). He had studied in Zurich, Munich and Paris, his teachers including Josef Rheinberger and Jules Massenet. After teaching briefly at his alma mater, the Conservatoire of Zurich, he had moved to Geneva, where he worked variously as a staff conductor at the Grand Théâtre and as a teacher of piano and composition. His best-known pupil was Frank Martin, who towards the end of his life remembered his studies with Lauber with affection and admiration: 'In teaching me harmony, he always taught me to lead the parts properly, always melodically, and I am extremely grateful to him for that'.[2] Lauber's own music is a peculiar mixture of the Germanic and the French, managing to combine with remarkable success the Austro-German late-Romantic harmonies he would have learnt in Munich with the sound-colours of the Impressionists he subsequently heard in Paris. The subtlety of his orchestration will surely also have derived in part from his conducting experiences with a top-class orchestra in Geneva. In his memoirs, Flury wrote:

> Josef [*sic*] Lauber's knowledge seemed unlimited and the facility with which he was able to improve my exercises by deleting or adding a bar, adding a rest or changing a few notes or a chord could only be admired. [...] He knew the tonal effects and technical possibilities of every instrument, in all its detail.[3]

He would gladly have studied longer with Lauber, Flury continued, had duty not called him back to Solothurn. And as with his other teachers, Flury never lost touch with Lauber. There is little correspondence between them in Flury's archives, and none in Lauber's, but the few letters from Lauber (from long after Flury's studies had ended) display much affection on the part of the older man for both his former pupil and his compositions. Flury mentions having on occasion taken new scores to Lauber in his holiday home in Les Plans sur Bex, some fifteen miles to the south-east of Montreux. They also seem to have been united in a mistrust of the all-too-modern tendencies that emerged in the inter-War years – 'competent in its form, clear in its structure and instrumentation, fresh and without precipitating into any unclean, modern, artificial problems!', Lauber wrote over twenty years later of Flury's one-movement *Waldsymphonie* ('Forest Symphony').[4]

Flury's few months in Geneva were as important for the violin-teacher he engaged there: Paul Miche. Ten years older than Flury, Miche was a

[1] When punching holes in the letter for inclusion in his correspondence file, Flury happened to punch them so as to obscure the number before the name of the month. No year is given.

[2] Frank Martin and Jean-Claude Piguet, *Entretiens sur la musique*, Éditions de la Baconnière, Neuchâtel, 1967, p. 15.

[3] *Op. cit.*, pp. 84–85.

[4] Letter from Lauber to Flury, 8 August [1942?] in Flury's archives.

Joseph Lauber, signed for Flury: 'To my very distinguished former pupil'

professor at the Geneva Conservatoire, where he had himself been awarded a *premier prix* only a few years before. Flury knew of him because he had attended recitals Miche had occasionally given in Solothurn. Although Miche was born on the French side of the linguistic divide in Switzerland, his birthplace, Courtelary, was only twenty miles from Solothurn along the arc of the Jura mountain ridge, close to the village of Corgémont, where Flury's paternal grandfather had once worked as a stonemason. Flury does not specifically mention the proximity of their geographical origins, though when he waxes lyrical about Miche's own compositions having possessed the 'dreamy poetry and melancholy [...] of the autumnal colours of the Jurassian landscapes', he clearly feels a close affinity to him. He and Miche got on wonderfully, wrote Flury, and Miche's teaching managed to free him of what he felt had long held him back as a violinist:

> all my schoolboyish inhibitions disappeared as if by a miracle [....] the self-confidence that he instilled in me awoke a joy in music-making that I had not known since boyhood. I practised several hours a day and profited from the freedom and unimpeded individualism that makes the French manner contrary to the authoritarian standpoint of the German schoolmaster.[5]

[5] *Op. cit.*, p. 84.

In a letter to his father from Geneva, dated 22 January 1920, Flury writes that Lauber is convinced he will succeed as a composer, and adds: 'I thank you today with all my heart for your many sacrifices during my long studies and for your having agreed to my chosen profession'. The envelope bears the much later remark: 'Last letter to my father'; his father died five days later, from the results of an otherwise banal accident. He had been travelling in a local train and got out at his station as he always did, but without realising that work on the lines had meant the train had not yet properly arrived at the platform. He had opened the door and jumped out unthinkingly, and injured himself when he plunged into the little ravine that ran alongside the tracks. A telegram has survived in Flury's archives that his brother Adolf sent to Geneva on the day of their father's death; it reads 'come straight home. Adolf'.

Flury returned to Geneva after the funeral. A month after his father died, on 27 February 1920, Adolf wrote to tell him that the Music School needed to know how soon he might return to Solothurn to start his teaching job. So the requirements of family and career meant that his student life in Geneva had to end. But Flury had continued to be prolific as a composer, despite those several hours a day he spent practising. He had written another overture for orchestra in the summer of 1919 (his 'No. 4'), he had begun and then abandoned a string quartet, and had at the same time started a Mass for solo voices, chorus and orchestra or organ, which he completed in short score in August 1919. The overture is formulaic and full of dull sequences, its harmonic trajectory still limp, with the occasional burst from a solo trombone accompanied by cascading violins that altogether looks a little like Wagner's Wotan on a caffeine overdose; occasional arpeggiated figures in contrary motion in the strings seem to confirm that Flury had indeed become acquainted with Bruckner by now.[6] The aborted string quartet is more idiomatically written for its instruments, and the spacings of the inner parts are not cramped as they are in his orchestral works of the time. The Mass would seem to defy any serious attempt at performance – though he scored its Kyrie for chorus and orchestra and indeed had it performed at the annual festival of the Swiss Musicians' Association (the *Tonkünstlerfest*) four years later: diminished fifths for the bass voices and a soprano part that is both high and extremely chromatic suggest that Flury had never had much real contact with singers. At least his orchestration has improved (thanks to Lauber?). Nevertheless, there are two other works from late 1919 that show a real advance in his compositional skills.

Under Lauber's supervision, Flury wrote a three-movement piano sonata, the dates on its movements spanning 23 October 1919 to 25 February 1920. It is formally still a student work – the first movement is in sonata form, the second in a tripartite *Lied* form, the third a rondo – and the thematic

[6] Thanks to Kurth: *cf.* p. 53, above.

material is not particularly distinctive, with echoes of Grieg in the opening and of Wagner's Nibelung motif in the second subject of the first movement. But the structure is clear, the textures have been thinned out, and although the climax of the second movement is a little salonesque, Flury is starting to get a grip on chromatic harmony. This piano sonata – his only essay in the genre – was later published as his Op. 7. It thoroughly deserves an airing, and was in later years on one occasion played by no less a musician than Walter Gieseking. Flury dedicated it to the memory of Gertrud Getzner, one of his earliest childhood loves,[7] who had died working as a nurse during the First World War.

Flury's last work under the auspices of Lauber was a *Pastorale for Orchestra* that represents a much bigger leap. There are still stodgy moments, and now and then he unsubtly copies Richard Strauss' penchant for underpinning a climax with a held second-inversion chord. But his orchestration has become more idiomatic. He has learnt to score properly for woodwind, the trumpet now and then shares the melody nicely with the violins, and there are climactic swooshes on the harp. The harmony remains tonal, with a firm bass line, but there is otherwise a slippery, delightfully near-Delian quality to it. In objective terms, this *Pastorale* cannot compare with the orchestral works Flury would write only a few years later, but without the lessons learnt here, those works would perhaps never have become possible.

So Flury returned to Solothurn to take up his post as violin teacher and as the conductor of the local amateur orchestra. His salary as a part-time teacher was CHF 260 'per hour per year' for children of secondary school age, and CHF 220 for those still at primary school – in other words, if he taught ten secondary school pupils, his annual wage would be CHF 2,600 before taxes. He applied to be paid the same amount for every pupil, regardless of school age, but this bid was turned down in a letter of 28 May 1920 from the city council. While his salary was not a lot of money, neither was it ungenerous for a single man at the start of his career. The Swiss Federal Office of Statistics notes[8] that the average annual rent for a two-room apartment in Solothurn in 1920 was about CHF 420. Foodstuffs had increased drastically in price over the previous few years, and inflation in Switzerland reached a peak in 1920, with the average price of bread per kilo having nearly doubled since before the First World War. But prices soon declined again, at the same time that they exploded in the post-War hyper-inflation in Germany and Austria. Flury's employment meant he could live the life of a bachelor relatively comfortably, if with little financial wriggle-room. The economic collapse beyond the Swiss border, however, opened up

[7] *Cf.* p. 39, above.

[8] 'Eidgenössische Wohnungs-Enquete vom 1. Dezember 1920: Preise für Mietwohnungen ohne Nutzung nach Zimmerzahl in 17-20 Städten' on the website 'Historical statistics of Switzerland online', run by the Forschungsstelle für Sozial- und Wirtschaftsgeschichte of the University of Zurich, www.fsw.uzh.ch/hstat/nls_rev/ls_files.php?chapter_var=./h, accessed September 2016.

possibilities for anyone earning Swiss francs, and it was probably this fact that soon gave Flury the idea of making one last study trip to round off his compositional technique.

6
Flury the 'Marxist'

Not many documents have survived from Flury's first eighteen months in the world of work. But that is hardly surprising: given that his studies hitherto display a man possessed of both deep commitment and a fastidiousness in his approach to work, he will no doubt have spent a lot of time preparing for his lessons and learning scores to conduct. His compositional output certainly dropped. After returning to Biberist from Geneva he wrote a 'festive march' for the 25th anniversary of the 'Ruppigoner', the alumni association of his former school fraternity, the Dornachia. It is a return to the foursquare, popular vein of his much earlier works, though it is more assured in every way. The slithery harmonies of the *Pastorale* have disappeared – they wouldn't be much suited to marching – and although the piece probably goes down best after a night's drinking with one's schoolfellows, it is competent in form, content and orchestration. Roughly the same can be said of another occasional orchestral work, written a little over two months later (the score is dated 4 July 1920): a *Spanischer Tanz*, the result of an infatuation with a Spanish girl, Flury claimed.[1] It is salon music, and the outer sections – replete with castanets and tambourines – are really a little too banal; the middle section, by contrast, is much more interesting, with cross-rhythms and suspensions in the clarinets. The latter sound almost as if they're going to burst forth into a klezmer piece, but then the opening music returns and spoils the effect. There is little else to show for the next year except a few songs. Four from 1920 and 1921 were later published with four more from 1922 under the title of *8 Love Songs*, Op. 9, though they are really only individual songs grouped together for publication and are rather outshone by the colour title-page designed by Flury's friend, the Solothurn artist Max Kessler.

The other main opus from 1920 is *6 Little Songs*, Op. 8, to poems in Swiss-German dialect by the poet Josef Reinhart. These songs were to be Flury's first contribution to the annual *Tonkünstlerfest* of the Association of Swiss Musicians, into which he had meanwhile been accepted. Three of them were duly performed on 15 May 1921 at the festival, held that year in Lugano, with Hélène Stoss accompanied by Lily Mermino; they also performed Flury's 'Der Liebende' from his *8 Love Songs*. Flury's music was sandwiched in the middle of a programme that began with Frank Martin's

[1] *Lebenserinnerungen, op. cit.*, p. 124.

Max Kessler's title page for Flury's 8 Love Songs, *Op. 9*

Piano Quintet in D minor and ended with Hans Huber's Second Piano Quintet, in G major. The works at these festivals were (and are) selected by a jury whose task is a delicate balancing act to ensure that different genres and different styles can be heard, new voices given their chance and old voices not denied theirs, either. That task would become more complicated in the ensuing decades when the avant-garde and the late-Romantics and Neo-Classicists clashed with one another, but for the moment the tone at such gatherings was generally conservative, so that Flury still fitted in well. In this instance, though, his songs tend to lapse into the tweeness typical of many dialect songs in Switzerland in the late nineteenth and early twentieth centuries. The exception among the four performed in Lugano is 'Nemol', which is considerably superior to the other songs with which it shares its opus number.

Two months after his national debut, Flury made his international one, so to speak. In spite of the privations of the First World War and the years thereafter, Switzerland's tourist havens did their best to retain the ambience of the *fin de siècle*, and in Interlaken the Kursaal was still running the summer series of orchestral concerts that had been popular in the years before the outbreak of hostilities. These concerts were directed by Eduard Favre (1872–1946), who was originally from Fribourg near Bern, had studied the violin under Eugène Ysaÿe in Belgium, had played the viola in the Schörg Quartet and had then been prominent in the Dalcroze institutions, first in the garden town of Hellerau near Dresden and then in Vienna. Favre spent some twenty years conducting the Kurorchester (the 'spa orchestra') in the summer in Interlaken, which was where Flury first saw him in action shortly after the First World War. The Kurorchester comprised some fifty musicians, and what to an outsider from the Anglo-Saxon world might seem the kind of dubious, *ad hoc* ensemble that could once have graced a Victorian pier was in fact a far more professional institution – hardly surprising, in that the guests in resorts such as Interlaken included aristocracy and intelligentsia from across the Continent. Before the First World War, even the likes of Richard Strauss took the trouble to conduct a Kurorchester when the fee was right, and after the War he was to be seen among their audiences too when vacationing at his favourite spas (even, on at least one occasion, in Interlaken itself[2]). The Kurorchester in Interlaken was by all accounts of a far higher standard than anything in Solothurn, and so Flury summoned up the courage to send Favre his latest three orchestral pieces – the *Spanischer Tanz*, the *Ruppigoner Festmarsch* and the *Pastorale*. Favre wrote back shortly afterwards to say he'd already performed them in an afternoon concert (which in itself suggests that Flury had been so bold as to include parts with the scores he sent). The pieces had gone very well, and would be performed again at the evening concert of 10 July 1921. Flury didn't have the money for a train ticket, but since he couldn't possibly miss it, he decided to cycle there instead – some 40 miles as the crow flies, though since there are valleys and hills to traverse, it is a good deal farther by road. He set off early, reached the Kursaal by the afternoon – by his own admission reeking of bicycle oil and sweat – and went to greet Favre, only to be informed that the composer was expected to conduct his own works that evening. Waiving all sartorial objections aside, Favre told Flury to go to his apartment, get his household help to lend him an evening suit, and come back in time for the performance. Flury did as instructed, but as he was much thinner than Favre, the trousers threatened to descend all evening. And since the baggy trousers merely compounded his embarrassment at his odour, he was too ashamed to walk past the porter at the door on his return to the Kursaal. So he crept round the back and climbed over a fence

[2] *Lebenserinnerungen*, *op. cit.*, p. 137.

Flury around 1922

to get through a side door to the hall in time to conduct his pieces. By his own account the performance went swimmingly – a Kurorchester was a well-oiled machine, accustomed to playing a huge repertoire, and so there was little that could have gone wrong – and he was called back to the stage many times. Afterwards, he went back to Favre's apartment to change into his own clothes, then cycled through the night back to Biberist.

Besides his success in Interlaken, Flury also received words of encouragement from Hans Huber, to whom he had apparently sent copies of his newest works. Huber might even have heard his songs at the *Tonkünstlerfest*, for since retirement he was spending most of his time in nearby Locarno in Italian Switzerland. Huber's letter is undated, so one cannot know exactly when he wrote it. But he mentions the Piano Sonata as well as the recent songs, and in fact prefers the latter, he writes. He also finds the last movement of the Sonata the best of its three. In general he assures Flury of the 'great progress' he has made as a composer over the past two years. Huber had suggested a while back that Flury might consider going to study with Friedrich Klose in Munich, and it seems it was again Huber who suggested studying abroad to Flury, this time in Vienna, and he wrote letters of recommendation to this effect. Flury applied for leave from both orchestra and school in Solothurn and was granted both; his brother, Adolf, took over the orchestra for the next half year, while Flury's predecessor at the school, Theodor Niemann, left retirement one last time to deputise for him.

Flury always felt drawn to Austria, perhaps because he was part-Austrian himself, but mostly because it was for him, quite simply, the land of music. In purely personal terms he could hardly have chosen a better time to go to Vienna, because it was in the autumn of 1921 that the hyper-inflation began. The local economy nosedived, but for foreigners with hard currency – Swiss francs or dollars in this instance – everything became absurdly cheap. Flury later recalled being able to buy a full meal in a Viennese restaurant, including trout, a main course of meat and then a dessert with cream, for 60 centimes – less than the price of a loaf of bread back in Switzerland.

Flury found a room at Währingerstrasse 80, just around the corner from the Volksoper, only a mile from the Ringstrasse, and to his delight his landlady, Marie Hellmer-Werner, had known Hugo Wolf in her youth. She possessed several of his manuscripts and vividly remembered hearing him play and sing through his opera *Der Corregidor* to his friends. Her son-in-law Hans Zimmert was the leader of the orchestra in the Johann Strauss-Theater on the Favoritenstrasse (long since defunct[3]), where operettas by Emmerich Kálmán, Franz Lehár, Robert Stolz and others had their first performances, and during these months Zimmert and Flury often played through the latter's compositions. Flury's memoirs relate how he had

[3] The Johann Strauss-Theater was torn down in 1960.

Poster for the first performances of Flury's music in Interlaken, 5 July 1921

initially held hopes of studying with Richard Strauss. But Strauss never took on pupils, and he was in any case on a concert-tour of North America in the winter of 1921–22 (the best place to earn hard currency, of course). This setback did not dim Flury's ambitions, as he now tried to get lessons with another star on the international scene, the conductor-composer Felix Weingartner (1863–1942), who had succeeded Mahler as the director of the Vienna Court Opera from 1907 to 1910 and at the time of Flury's visit was still the chief conductor of the Vienna Philharmonic Orchestra. But Weingartner turned him down too, recommending him instead to Joseph Marx.

Marx was born in Graz in 1882, took his doctorate in music theory there in 1909, and thereafter established himself as a teacher and composer. His songs were much performed in these years, and confirmed him as a composer in the tradition of Hugo Wolf. In 1914 Marx moved to Vienna upon accepting a professorship in composition and music theory at the Academy of Music and Performing Arts in Vienna, where he taught alongside Franz Schreker.[4] Flury's first letter to him is dated 23 September 1921. He writes that he is in Vienna for three months to attend concerts, that he is contacting him on Weingartner's recommendation, and that he would like 'to work on an orchestral piece and several small things under your direction' in that time. He encloses several compositions (there is no record of which). Marx accepted him for private lessons twice a week. In his memoirs, Flury writes that they analysed works by Brahms, Debussy, Reger and 'new works by Russian composers'[5] (again, it is not known which). He also wrote piano pieces for Marx to correct and comment on. There are four of these in Flury's archives; two *Intermezzi* dated 25 October and 4 November, and two Preludes dated 5 November and 28 November. They are all short – each is around the two-minute mark. But there is a world's difference in quality between these pieces and everything in Flury's *œuvre* that preceded them. There is a turn of phrase here and there that suggests those 'newer Russian works' were in fact Stravinsky's, and if one strains hard, one can detect echoes of Debussy, Reger and others. But there is little point in trying, because these pieces are so full of invention that one soon listens to them on their own terms. The first Prelude (Ex. 2) is confined to the white notes – perhaps Marx felt it a practical way of keeping Flury's occasionally wayward chromaticism in check. It begins with a reminiscence of Chopin's Mazurka, Op. 17, No. 4, in the left hand, but then veers off on its own trajectory. Flury was justly proud of it. At its climax, he wrote 'All the notes of the scale' in the score when all seven sound at once. Whether thanks to Marx's tuition, or because getting out of Switzerland and sampling the musical life of a vast, imperial city had set his mind free, Flury ended his

[4] *Cf.* Erik Werba, *Joseph Marx*, Verlag der Österreichischen Musikzeitschrift, Vienna, 1964, pp. 9–11.

[5] *Lebenserinnerungen*, *op. cit.*, p. 87.

three months in Vienna a very different, far more mature composer than he had been when he had arrived.

Ex. 2

Flury certainly made full use of his time in the metropolis, and of the fact that everything was cheap for him. He wrote in his memoirs that he attended over a hundred concerts or theatre performances over the course of his three months,[6] and a list he apparently made at the time has survived, showing his attendances by date. He went to cello recitals, symphony concerts, quartet evenings, matinées with the Vienna Philharmonic, to operas at the Volksoper and State Opera, including Korngold's *Violanta*, Meyerbeer's *Robert le diable*, Offenbach's *Les Contes d'Hoffmann*, Pfitzner's *Palestrina*, Strauss' *Elektra* and *Der Rosenkavalier*, Verdi's *Il trovatore*, Wagner's *Das Rheingold*, Weber's *Der Freischütz*, and plays at the Burgtheater and elsewhere, including Gerhart Hauptmann's *Und Pippa tanzt* and Molière's *Le Malade imaginaire* – and much, much more. No wonder he claims he sometimes fell asleep at the theatre. It is astonishing that he had any time or energy left for his composition exercises with Marx.

Flury was long acquainted with the bigger towns of Switzerland and had sampled what Zurich and Geneva had to offer – in his papers, for example, there is a list of the concerts given by the Orchestre de la Suisse Romande for 1919–20, and in light of his thirst for knowledge and experience, he will have attended whatever concerts were affordable when he was living in Geneva. But even today, the sheer extent of cultural life in Vienna is overwhelming in comparison with any Swiss city. And the vastness of its parks, the stylishness of its boulevards, the size of its buildings – its museums, theatres and palaces – all this, despite the deprivations of a war economy, must have seemed staggering to Flury. The Viennese have long been notorious for their snootiness, as if somehow convinced that their city is still the capital of the biggest European empire. But Flury seems to have felt a part of it all. He would always love Vienna. He would always dream of being able to live there, he would always dream of going back, and in later years he visited whenever he could. And if his love of things Viennese instead found expression at a distance in the several Viennese waltzes that he later wrote, then at least one can be grateful for it, for they are some of his most charming pieces.

Marx was the last, and perhaps the most important, of the father figures Flury acquired during his studies. The fact that Flury's father had died some twenty months before might have played a role here. His next letter to Marx dates from 2 November 1921 – only a month or so after starting lessons with him. That date is All Souls' Day, and the day before, All Saints', is a national holiday in Austria, and traditionally a time when the dead are remembered. Perhaps the bank holiday meant that there was a break in Flury's lessons (in 1921 it fell on a Tuesday). But regardless of the reason, Flury now poured his heart out to Marx in a long, rambling, clumsily adolescent, poetic letter in which he covered almost everything that worried him: his mother, his

[6] *Ibid.*, p. 89.

Flury in 1923, lithograph by the Austrian artist Hans Zötsch (1886–1957)

work and even the opposite sex. Any teacher receiving such a letter would be taken aback, as it is oddly intimate coming from a new student whom Marx barely knew. But Marx seems to have taken it in his stride, for their lessons continued unabated. It also seems to have freed up something in Flury, for he wrote the best two of those little piano pieces within three days of sending the letter. Flury had at this time also fallen in love with Mimi, the niece of his landlady, though the latter's vehement opposition to a liaison[7] helped put paid to any notion of sampling more than Vienna's cultural delights in his brief stay in the city.

Violin lessons also featured in these jam-packed three months. Flury had hoped to study with the legendary Arnold Rosé, but he was about to go on tour, so on Rosé's recommendation Flury went instead to Samuel Bondi.[8] Flury probably knew of him already, because Bondi had published a book of finger exercises for octaves on the violin in Leipzig in 1913 that had been successful enough to be published in French and English as well.[9] Flury seems not to have been impressed because Bondi tried to sell him a violin and a bow – and this is the only time in his memoirs when Flury comes across as less than generous, for he also admits that the parlous state of the Austrian economy made Bondi's behaviour comprehensible. Flury mentions with some distaste how Swiss nationals in Vienna were regarded as 'potential objects of exploitation' by the Viennese,[10] and yet at the same time he admits that Swiss-German dialect was almost all you could hear in the expensive boxes at the State Opera,[11] since the Swiss bourgeoisie was flocking to the city to make the most of the favourable exchange rate. As someone who had until then lived all his life with little money, suddenly being able to afford everything and being treated as a rich man by all around him must have been as disconcerting as it will have been enjoyable. He notes with some relief that Marx made no attempt to swindle him, but charged him the same fee that he asked from all his local students. As for Bondi, Flury can't have taken too much of a dislike to him, as he dedicated a *Menuet viennois* to him that he wrote for violin and piano as a diversion from his more 'serious' pieces for Marx. It's Flury in Neo-Classical, Fritz Kreisler vein – and it is so charming that it would also have been worthy of Kreisler himself.

Flury returned to Biberist at the turn of the year, and wrote to Marx on 2 January 1922 to thank him for everything. It was the beginning of a correspondence that would last until Marx's death in 1964.

[7] According to Flury's memoirs, *ibid.*, p. 90.

[8] Letter from Rosé to Flury in the latter's archives, 20 September 1921.

[9] Flury calls him 'Sigmund' everywhere, but the name under which he published and is featured in the reference books is always 'Samuel'. Since Flury mentions his octave exercises, it has to be the same person.

[10] *Lebenserinnerungen*, *op. cit.*, p. 88.

[11] *Ibid*, p. 89.

7
Back to the Grind

For Flury, returning home meant putting his studies behind him and starting work. He also moved to Solothurn, where he could walk to work instead of taking the train from Biberist. He stayed with his aunt on the Lorenzenstrasse, in a building that today – appropriately – houses the Solothurn Music School. From there it was a ten-minute walk to the Restaurant Kreuz by the banks of the Aare, in the hall of which the Solothurn Orchestra held its rehearsals[1] (later the rehearsal venue was moved to the Restaurant Schwanen just across the river). With the exception of his periods of military service, Flury would spend the rest of his career much as he began it now: teaching the violin in Solothurn, and conducting the local orchestra. Both activities would always be somewhat incidental to his chosen vocation as a composer, but they naturally fed off one another. He undoubtedly chafed under the burden of teaching scales and exercises to the local youth, as also under the amateur status of his orchestra – his letters to Marx over the next decades return time and again to his 'regret' at not having a permanent professional ensemble under his direction. But the skill of his orchestration suggests a man keenly aware of the practicalities of the different instruments, and working with talented amateurs can make one far better aware of what balances and what doesn't. A professional orchestra tends to self-regulation, resorting easily to 'automatic pilot', whereas an amateur orchestra requires a more active engagement with the nitty-gritty of a score. And Flury was soon ploughing through swathes of the repertoire. His next letter to Marx, from 9 February 1922, mentions that his orchestra is currently rehearsing Schubert's 'Unfinished', and Haydn's 'La reine' and 'Oxford' Symphonies (Nos. 85 and 92). Of yet more interest, however, is the following passage in the letter:

> I've begun a 1st symphony, and have already sketched 300 bars of the first movement. I've firmly decided to write it to the end, even if it's bad, so that this long-longed-for monstrosity is finally in the world, whether as an encouraging example to me or as a deterrent for future work.

Flury spent over a year on this new symphony. His description of it as his '1st' implies an ambition to write more, and the fact that it was in D minor was in itself a statement of grand intent, given the significance

[1] *Lebenserinnerungen*, *op. cit.*, p. 158.

The Schwanen Restaurant in Solothurn,
where Flury's orchestra rehearsed for many years

of specific keys in the Austro-German Romantic imagination: D minor is the key of Beethoven's Ninth and his 'Tempest' Piano Sonata (No. 17) and of Bruckner's Ninth (and incidentally, when Richard Strauss wrote his first symphony at the age of sixteen, he also chose D minor). But Flury's symphony had to be put aside in the meantime because he was awarded a major municipal commission: to write a 'Festspiel' – a 'festival pageant' with music – for the 'Stadtschützen' in Solothurn. These 'city shooters' had formed a society at some point back in the fifteenth century, at a time when crossbows had not yet been replaced by guns. From 1472 onwards, their shooting range, the 'Schützenmatt', lay just outside the city walls (which part of town still bears that name today). In 1922 they moved their shooting range to Zuchwil, a tiny neighbouring town on the opposite bank of the river Aare, and decided to hold a festival pageant to celebrate their long history (although the pageant was officially announced as celebrating the 400th anniversary of the society, the choice of number seems to have been somewhat arbitrary, given that the society was in fact much older).[2] It was Flury's first-ever large-scale commission, and proof of his acceptance on the Solothurn cultural scene. The text was to be written by his old German teacher Walther von Arx (who had been responsible for directing the last big pageant in the town, back in 1899, for which Flury's revered music-teacher Edmund Wyss had composed the music). Von Arx first wrote the parts of the text that were to be set to music, and sent them to Flury in early 1922. But then he took ill and had to be replaced. The Festival committee chose in his stead Cäsar von Arx – no relation – who was only a year older than Flury, but who was already working as a director and author in Leipzig. This second von Arx now had to draft the actual drama around the numbers that the first von Arx and Flury had already prepared. The pageant was performed with much success in early August 1922, coinciding with the Solothurn shooting festival. Flury was responsible for the music direction of rehearsals and performances. Flury's musical climax was the final chorus, and he was horrified when Cäsar von Arx wanted to drop it in favour of a long speech.[3] After a protracted debate with the organisation committee, a compromise was found by placing the final chorus at the opening of the work instead – Flury's personal introduction to the vagaries of the theatrical world. The poster for the event, which was also used as the cover for the printed music, was a splendid painting of a Baroque marksman against a backdrop of old Solothurn and the River Aare. The overall event was a financial success, too (no doubt aided by the erection of a beer tent that catered for all-night drinkers), and as an extra reward Flury was presented with several gold napoleons by the chairman of the committee. All the same, Flury later recorded that he lapsed into depression after the performance

[2] *Cf.* the website of the Society, www.stadtschuetzen-solothurn.ch/, accessed February 2016.

[3] *Lebenserinnerungen, op. cit.*, p. 114.

Emil Scheller's cover picture for Flury's Festspiel *in 1922*

Flury marching with the city band across the Aare in the procession to the Zuchwil shooting range for the 1922 festival. The cathedral of St Urs can be seen in the background.

run: 'In place of the greatest sense of excitement there came a vacuum that gave way to anxious questions about the goals and justification of my future artistic endeavours'.[4]

The style of Flury's music for the pageant was of the accessible, patriotic-bombastic nature typical of the *Festspiel* genre. It is fluent and tuneful, but is unlikely to be resurrected, given that the costs involved would today outweigh its somewhat meagre artistic merit. He would later complain about the stylistic restrictions that such commissions for the masses imposed, but such limits have their uses (one thinks perhaps of Benjamin Britten's music for W. H. Auden's films *Coal Face* and *Night Mail*, written with limited resources for the General Post Office Film Unit). Like most composers of his generation and background, Flury probably already harboured operatic ambitions, not least because a successful opera was the best way to achieve financial independence as a composer. The format of a festival pageant presented him with an ideal entry into music drama. With its number format, it offered a relatively fixed, anxiety-free form while demanding a larger-scale dramatic trajectory. Cäsar von Arx soon afterwards moved back to Switzerland on a permanent basis. He first worked at the Schauspielhaus in Zurich (i.e., the Zurich theatre for spoken drama), but turned freelance in 1925 and embarked on a highly successful career as a dramatist. His 1922 *Festspiel* was the first of several such pageants he was to write. Von Arx and Flury stayed in contact – the only extant letter from von Arx to Flury,

[4] *Ibid.*, p. 114.

dated 26 March 1936, makes it evident that they were on first-name, 'Du' terms, though Flury's efforts to collaborate again with him were rejected for 'lack of time' (or perhaps their argument over the final chorus of 1922 still rankled a little with von Arx).

Flury's experience of preparing his *Festspiel* also brought other work in its wake. The city band, the Stadtmusik, was once again between music directors, and so Flury was asked to step in and conduct the concerts it was due to give in the large festival tent that summer. In late 1922 Flury was also elected the conductor of the Zurich Academic Orchestra, comprising students from ETH Zurich and the University of Zurich. He remained resident in Solothurn – he could not afford to give up his teaching and his local orchestra – and therefore commuted twice a week by train to his rehearsals in Zurich. There was only one big concert every year. The standard of the student members varied considerably, for none of them was a student of music (the university music department was not founded until 1927); any missing wind instruments were drafted in from the Tonhalle Orchestra for their concerts. Flury stayed in the job for four years. Apart from enabling him to obtain further experience as a conductor, his time with the Academic Orchestra will have helped to make him better known among Zurich musicians. He was also occasionally able to engage good soloists – such as his former teacher Paul Miche, who played under his direction at a charity concert in the Zurich Tonhalle on 9 February 1923.[5] By Flury's own admission, his time with the orchestra also gave him increased respect for double-bass players – though simply because he had a sympathetic, gifted example who also happened to be the son of the physicist Albert Einstein (who had won his Nobel Prize just the year before). Hans Albert Einstein had followed in his father's footsteps by attending ETH Zurich.[6]

It would be another five years or so before Flury wrote his first opera, but it is not impossible that his experience of drama in music in mid-1922 also spilled over into his First Symphony. Since Beethoven, the symphony has been the most inherently 'dramatic' of all the instrumental genres. In his Symphony, Flury was not bound by exterior stylistic considerations, and it is qualitatively far better than anything he had hitherto composed. It is also far bigger.

On 15 December 1922, Flury wrote to Marx to tell him about his recent election as conductor of the Zurich Academic Orchestra, and added: 'I'm still labouring with my troublesome 1st Symphony'. Ten weeks later, on 28 February 1923, he writes 'My 1st Symphony is being born with labour pains and is still a troublesome child'. He adds that he would like to send Marx six new songs in manuscript. He does not mention which ones; there are several from 1922 and 1923 and it was 1923 that saw the publication

[5] Newspaper clipping in Flury's archives.

[6] *Lebenserinnerungen, op. cit.*, p. 150.

of his *8 Love Songs*, Op. 9. But he does complain that writing love-songs does not seem to have the desired effect on the opposite sex: 'The success of such erotic outpourings ['Ergüsse'] is in every respect negative' (the Freudian vocabulary speaks volumes – in other contexts, 'Ergüsse' can mean 'ejaculations' in the specifically sexual sense of the word). The identity of the member or members of the opposite sex who were the desired vessels of Flury's outpourings are not known. But they were certainly on his mind for much of the year, and he must have alluded to them when he sent a copy of his *8 Love Songs* to one of the poets set therein, namely Isabelle Kaiser (1866–1925). His letter has not survived, but her reply has, and it is tactful and sympathetic, despite Flury's obvious tendency to unburden his heart to anyone whether solicited or not. She wrote from her home in Beckenried in Canton Nidwalden by Lake Lucerne on 7 June 1923, apologising for the 'months' that had elapsed since Flury had sent his songs, and thanking him for them:

> To be sure, the young girls to whom they are dedicated because their loveliness and unconscious poetry inspired you cannot in their May comprehend this mature art [...] and what one cannot understand, one cannot love! [...] Your day will come too! Just keep working steadfastly ... and don't let yourself be discouraged by any dismay or silence![7]

One can well imagine Kaiser – a famous writer in her day – offering similar words to all the other young artists who must have written to her on a regular basis, seeking encouragement. But there is otherwise little that is stereotypical about the letter, and for a man still as uncertain about himself as Flury, it must have been a considerable comfort, especially since he was about to present to the world his biggest composition to date: his First Symphony.

[7] Letter in Flury's archives.

8
The First Symphony

The picture of Flury as a nervous young man lonely for love and eager for professional approval is tempered by the tales of regular conviviality that he presents in his memoirs. During the 1920s, he and a group of like-minded fellow artists came together on a regular basis in one or other of the pubs of Solothurn, collectively calling themselves the 'Künstlerstübli' – literally the 'artists' room'. This 'room' was metaphorical, moving from place to place, depending on wherever they arranged to meet, talk, drink and argue. Sometimes it would be the back room of the Misteli Restaurant, at others the Café Schwarz. The 'artists' in attendance also varied. They included the painters Franz Bözinger, Max Kessler, Robert Rudolf, Paul Demme, Max Brunner and Emil Scheller, the writers Bernhard Moser and Robert Roetschi, the sculptor Walter Peter and many others. Reminiscing about 1923 and the period when he was finishing his First Symphony, Flury tells how he and friends from the Künstlerstübli would sit together every day, exchanging memories of the great cities of Europe they had visited, from Naples to Paris, Vienna, Florence and Rome, and discussing artistic projects current and future. Flury later expressed regret that he had no idea back then exactly how much time he frittered away in his twenties.[1] But apart from the fact that one's twenties are ideal for time-frittering, as anyone looking back on them will confess, Flury can't have frittered as much as he suspects when one considers the amount of music that he managed to write. And he himself admits that he kept a daily record on the wall calendar of the Café Schwarz as to how many bars of his First Symphony he had scored since the previous day.[2]

Once the score was complete, Flury sent it to Eduard Favre, who promptly accepted it for performance with his Kurorchester in Interlaken that coming summer. Flury had the parts copied by a local amateur copyist and sent them to Favre. The only rehearsal – an hour in length, not much longer than the symphony itself – took place three days before the world premiere of 27 June 1923, which Flury was to conduct himself. It was a disaster, because he had not bothered to check the accuracy of the parts in advance; among the copyist's worst mistakes was a tendency to count wrong numbers of rests in the wind parts. Flury writes in his memoirs that he only just managed to

[1] *Lebenserinnerungen*, *op. cit.*, p. 126.

[2] *Ibid.*, pp. 127–28.

run through the first three movements, and so the last was omitted, and he took the tempi at a generally moderate pace. In fact, the manuscript of the symphony gives '17 November 1923' as the date of completion of the last movement, and so perhaps Flury's memory played tricks on him as to why this movement was omitted. All the same, Flury recalled the performance of his symphonic torso as being an outstanding success. No objective report of the event has survived, since the concerts of a Kurorchester were not usually attended by the critics. But on 11 September 1923, a performance of the first movement took place, this time in Bern with the Bern City Orchestra under the direction of the composer. The director of the Orchestra, Albert Nef, had written to Flury on 19 August, offering him a slot of up to twenty minutes in a 'people's symphony concert', an institution common among the orchestras of the German-speaking world in the early twentieth century that provided cheap concerts for the general public, often with more accessible repertoire and with fewer rehearsals than the main subscription concerts. And this concert was indeed reviewed: by Gustav Renker, a Vienna-born Swiss who edited the daily paper *Berner Tagblatt* throughout the 1920s. Renker was a decade older than Flury, had worked as a staff conductor in Vienna, Graz and Nuremberg and had taken his doctorate in musicology in Vienna in 1913. He had worked as a ski instructor in the Austrian Army in the First World War and subsequently became one of the best-selling authors in the German-speaking world (Leni Riefenstahl's 1932 Alpine film *Das blaue Licht* was based on one of his books). He was, then, far from being an impressionable local light, and although his opinions were coloured by a generally anti-modern stance, his comments on Flury's First Symphony are worth quoting at some length:

> He is an unknown but can do much – indeed, very much. We should take note of this name: Richard Flury. An occasional work by the young composer once arrived on our desk, the music for a shooting festival. One couldn't take this too seriously, as it had been written for a close, probably very undemanding circle of people, but there were things in it that made one sit up: a clear, rich seam of invention, singular harmonies, a rhythmic temperament, in short all the signs of a gifted artist in the making – despite the striking Wagnerisms […].
>
> A man speaks [in this music] who is truly gifted, who does not shy away from honest, clear melody, who doesn't have a need to appear inventive through grotesque intervallic leaps. Of course this work is not wholly original – it shows a great love of Wagner and Bruckner, especially in the way the main theme is sculpted, which is derived from a triad. And the powerfully surging instrumentation and the rich ornamentation of the counterpoint betray a love of the *Meistersinger*. Flury's instrumentation is highly attractive

Solothurn and the Aare, watercolour by Franz Bözinger, Flury's friend in the 'Künstlerstübli'. Centre right: the Baroque Palais Besenval; behind and above it stands the Cathedral of St Urs.

> and original – the enchanting passage for harp and violins will remain long in our memory. [...] the man seems to be musical through and through.[3]

It is noteworthy that Renker reckoned Flury to be far superior – as a composer but especially as a conductor – to Luc Balmer, who conducted a symphony of his own in the same concert. Balmer, a former Busoni student, later made a notable career for himself as a conductor in Bern. Flury's First Symphony was also given its first complete performance by the Bern Orchestra, but this time in Solothurn, on 23 March 1924.[4] Renker reviewed this concert, too, and found the last three movements worthy of the first, summing up the work in the words: 'It is one of the best works to have been written in Switzerland for years'.[5] Not long after, Flury sent the score to Hermann Suter, who was more critical than Renker: he was not convinced by Flury's use of the harp, nor by his reliance on tremolo in the accompaniment to his themes, and he also objected to the close of the development section in the first movement and the re-use of its main theme elsewhere in the Symphony. But he congratulated him nevertheless on the 'symphonic breath' exuded by the work, and he found many of the thematic ideas in it good.[6] Suter was at the height of his powers – his spectacular oratorio *Le Laudi di San Francesco d'Assisi* had just received its world premiere (on 13 June 1924, in Basel) – and so the fact that he took the trouble to read carefully through a large-scale work by a young composer is proof enough that he took Flury seriously.

Flury subsequently dedicated the Symphony to 'The Solothurn Orchestra and its president Arthur Baumgartner', though the Orchestra never performed it, and the work was played only three more times before being placed on a shelf for the better part of a century. It was performed again in Solothurn in 2011, conducted by the composer's son Urs Joseph Flury, and a recording of it was released shortly afterwards.[7] Peter Palmer's review of the CD, noting the influence of Bruckner and Hans Huber, remarked that 'In a previous review of this composer, I suggested that his conservative output falls largely into the "light music" category. But the Symphony in D minor is an impressive prentice piece by loftier standards'.[8] It is indeed. For one thing, it's big – the first movement alone lasts for over thirteen minutes, and the other three movements bring the overall length to some 35 minutes. Formally it is conventional: the first movement is more or less in sonata form, the second movement is slow, the third is a scherzo, and

[3] Gustav Renker, 'Achtes Volkssymphoniekonzert', *Berner Tagblatt*, 12 September 1923.

[4] Letter from Flury to Joseph Marx, 30 December 1923.

[5] Renker, 'Konzertbericht' in the *Berner Tagblatt*, undated clipping in the Flury archives, presumably late March 1924, also quoted in *Lebenserinnerungen*, *op. cit.*, p. 130.

[6] Letter from Hermann Suter, Sils-Baselgia, 25 July 1924.

[7] Recorded, along with the Second Violin Concerto and orchestral extracts from the opera *Casanova e l'Albertolli*, by the Sinfonieorchester Biel on VDE-Gallo CD1385.

[8] Peter Palmer, 'Frank Martin *et al.*', *Tempo*, Vol. 67, No. 266 (October 2013), p. 117.

the finale also brings back material from the first movement towards the end. The orchestration is as good as Renker says it is. Novice composers can tend to overload their middle voices out of fear that they won't be heard (even the finest composers do it – witness the orchestration of Hugo Wolf or even of the young Brahms). But Flury manages to avoid such pitfalls, no doubt thanks to his extensive orchestral experience as a violinist and a conductor. His counterpoint is occasionally reminiscent of Mahler's in his symphonies, and the shadow of Bruckner certainly hovers in the background, as Palmer points out. So one can be certain that Flury had been studying his predecessors avidly. But his own melodic gifts come to the fore, and sometimes, when a melody seems about to descend into cliché, Flury brings a surprising twist that wrenches it back into originality. The first movement is the weakest – it is overly episodic – but its individual moments are themselves just about strong enough to bring it off. The first movement seems also to have been the first to be composed. It was Flury's first-ever large-scale movement, begun immediately after his intensive tuition with Marx, and it has the fascinating feel of a composer learning by doing. Listening to it is an experience not unlike leafing chronologically through his counterpoint exercises with Kurth (though on a more exalted level), as he seems to gain in confidence as he goes along. Ex. 3 gives the opening of the first movement (with all instruments notated here at sounding pitch). Its shimmering string accompaniment and main theme, with its emphasis on tonic and dominant, are clearly modelled on the opening movements of Bruckner's symphonies.

Flury did make several cuts to his score (as the manuscript reveals), and he could perhaps have revised it further to end up with a shorter, more concise result. But, as ever, he had other things on his mind, and other works to embark on. He conducted four performances of Gluck's opera *Iphigenie auf Tauris*, staged in the city concert hall in Solothurn in November and December 1923 (his brother Adolf sang the role of Pylades), and in 1924 he orchestrated several of his recent songs. He had already had experience of writing for voices and orchestra in his *Festspiel* of 1922, but his renewed interest might well have been because he was planning his first opera. The first proof of this intention comes in a letter from Kurth to Flury of 11 September 1924, in reply to a letter of Flury's (since lost) of 6 September ('It is a great joy to me to hear the news that you are writing an opera', Kurth wrote).[9] But Flury had probably been contemplating a move into opera for some time, given that he seems to have begun 'ticking off' one genre after another (a piano sonata, a symphony, now an opera, soon to be followed by a string quartet and a piano concerto).

[9] Kurth, *op. cit.*, p. 310.

Ex. 3

Allegro molto
Oboes
Bassoons
Allegro molto
div.
Violin I
Violin II
Violoncello

poco rit.
Ob.
Cl.
Bsn.
poco rit.
Vln. I
Vln. II
Vc.

a tempo
2.
Fl.
Ob.
Cl.
Bsn.
1.
Hn.
a tempo
Vln. I
mf espr.
Vln. II
Vla.
Vc.
Fl.
Ob.
Cl.
Bsn.
Hn.
Vln. I
Vla.
Vc.

Flury was at this time uncertain as to where his future lay in purely geographical terms. He was appointed the conductor of the Harmonie Mixed Chorus in Bern (the 'Gemischter Chor Harmonie') in the summer of 1924, with rehearsals due to begin later in the autumn. This position meant that he would now be dividing his time and his conducting duties between three cities: Bern, Solothurn and Zurich. Although his letter to Kurth of 6 September 1924 has not survived, from Kurth's reply one can easily discern what he wrote. Flury was afraid of festering in a small town such as Solothurn and hoped he might be able to establish himself more firmly if he moved to Bern, where he would in any case soon be busy with his choir. But Kurth made it clear that there was no guarantee that Flury would find enough pupils in Bern, and warned him that musicians in Bern who weren't in 'top ranking positions' tended to be looked down upon and got little opportunity to move up, however talented they were – 'festering' was then a real danger for them. Furthermore, Bern itself wasn't exactly a leading intellectual centre, Kurth continued, adding that he advised his other students to spend their holidays in real centres of activity such as Berlin, Paris, Munich or Milan, and to make the most of the time they had there.

Apart from his usual frustration at being an increasingly large fish in a very small pond, Flury had good reason to try and expand his professional activities: he was about to get married. His lack of luck in love had come to an end at some point in late 1923. He had written to Marx on 19 November of that year to tell him that he has now 'experienced love', and that his ambition is 'to live like other men, to have a wife, children, and no longer to have to brood over the meaning of life'. His wish would come true soon enough: in mid-1924 (presumably in August), his girlfriend, Lily Sollberger, became pregnant. By his own later admission, she was the first girl he had slept with, so perhaps his enthusiasm at finally casting off his virginity had got the better of a sense of caution. She was only nineteen at the time – nine years younger than Flury. Not surprisingly, given his Catholic upbringing and his sense of duty, Flury agreed to marry her before their child was born. His brother Adolf strongly advised against it, apparently convinced that the two were incompatible. It isn't known what Flury's mother thought, though she was probably more concerned about the potential scandal that it would have caused, had her youngest refused to do what was generally considered the decent thing. Lily's opinions on the matter are likewise unknown, as no correspondence seems to have survived (there is none in Flury's archives, and any letters he sent to Lily before or after their marriage seem to have been lost, too). Whatever their thoughts, hopes or fears might have been, the two of them probably had few options open to them, and so they married on 4 October 1924, and moved into an apartment together in Solothurn. In fact, they were married twice on the same day. Lily was Protestant, Flury Catholic, and so the first wedding took

Poster for Iphigenie auf Tauris, *conducted by Flury in November/December 1923*

The Gemischter Chor Harmonie of Bern on an outing with their families, mid-1920s. Flury is seated between the two men in the front row.

place in his church, the second in hers. He played a voluntary himself at the first wedding, leaving his bride at the altar to go across to the console; after finishing, he walked back to take his place beside her.

Whether or not Flury took on the chorus in Bern before he knew of Lily's pregnancy, they certainly needed the extra money in view of their imminent family life. But it also meant he was going to be away from home more often every week. Perhaps it was even this fact that made the job attractive to him. The tone of Flury's first letter to Marx after his wedding, dated 8 October 1924, does not bode well: 'I've been married for four days and setting up the household etc. [...] has cost a lot of suffering and money'. His wife remains otherwise unmentioned. He then promptly changes tack to say how much he misses Vienna, Graz and Salzburg. To say one misses a particular city is natural, especially if one is writing to someone who's living there. But to offer a list of places one misses suggests instead a desire to be where one is not. Brother Adolf had been right. The marriage was destined for disaster.

9
Needles and Knives

Almost as little is known about Lily after her marriage as before it. Flury mentions her only briefly in his memoirs and is honest enough to write of 'ugly and tragic scenes for which we were both to blame'.[1] He mentions that she earned money for them by sewing aprons for a shop in Solothurn, and that on one occasion he used her last five francs in earnings so that he could pay for a train ticket to go and conduct his most recent orchestral work in Bern.[2] Sewing – like spinning in the century before – was connoted as a feminine activity (not for nothing do most languages lack the masculine equivalent of the job-designation 'seamstress'). The opinions of Lily handed down among various branches of the Flury family and among the composer's friends concur in her having been unsuited to marriage with a gifted artist, and so it is striking that Flury's sole mention of her is of her manual labour that he in turn 'converts' into something more rarefied and aesthetic. But one must also beware of letting Lily's effective silence turn her into some kind of victim. In the years after their marriage fell apart, she reinvented herself as an entrepreneur, first running a souvenir shop for tourists and then working as a travelling saleswoman successful enough to own her own car by the 1950s. At least one of her grandchildren remembers her as strong-willed.[3] Her eldest daughter, Verena, once also mentioned to her half-brother Urs Joseph that her mother had been 'quarrelsome',[4] and a family anecdote (that has admittedly come down only via Flury's second wife) tells of how Lily's rage had on one occasion prompted her to throw a kitchen knife at her husband.[5] But as in so many other matters, one must assume that the original source of the story was Flury himself, and objective proof is lacking. Although Flury was hardly an easy husband to live with (as will be seen below[6]), Lily seems not to have been a weak-willed domestic type either. Had she been a meeker wife, perhaps those closest to Flury might not have found her so unsuited to him. But it is unlikely that much more will be known about her now.

[1] *Lebenserinnerungen*, *op. cit.*, p. 215.

[2] *Ibid.*, p. 215.

[3] Conversation with Fabio Zali, Lugano, January 2015.

[4] As related to the author by Urs Joseph Flury.

[5] *Ibid.*

[6] *Cf.* pp. 125–26.

What is known is that the physical side of their marriage seems to have continued to function even when the rest of the relationship didn't. Their first daughter, Verena, was born on 12 May 1925. She was followed by another, Eva, in 1927, and then another – Giovanna (also called Hanna or its diminutive form Hanneli) – in 1929, and finally by a son, Roger, in 1930. To get pregnant once unintentionally might be considered unfortunate, but four times suggests either intent, abandon, or both.

Flury and his wife settled down in an apartment on the Haffnerstrasse, a little up the hill on the north side of Solothurn, about ten minutes by foot from the old part of town where he taught (perhaps he found the Mozartian connection of the address attractive); the main railway station was an extra ten minutes away on top of that. At the end of the 1920s, Flury and his growing family moved to the Wengistrasse, not far outside the old city walls and much closer to his work and the station. But he was still wishing himself elsewhere. Two years after his marriage, he was again writing to Marx in the usual vein:

> I often yearn mightily for Vienna and would think myself lucky if I could be active like you in such a centre of musical life. Solothurn is a pretty, small, mediaeval town full of romanticism and poetry – a garden city like Graz – but for a young musician there's too little stimulation and I am afraid of festering and messing everything up, falling asleep in these small-scale surroundings. We only live once, and that's why I feel an inner urge and a duty to tear myself away, by force and with a rumpus if necessary, and move to Paris, Berlin or Vienna. If I were alone, nothing would stand in my way, but I have a wife and a one-and-a-half-year-old little daughter whom I love and whom I can't simply transport on a whim to a large city. These are the inner disagreements that oppress me increasingly as the years pass, and compromise a part of my joy in life. [...] My happiest hours are the ones when I am alone at my piano.[7]

Given that Flury had reached the age of 27 before being compelled to marry and had never taken the plunge and gone for good to Paris, Berlin or Vienna, it was somewhat disingenuous of him to say now that it was his family holding him back. But his predicament was remarkably similar to that of other Swiss composers in the 1920s. Marcel Sulzberger, the first-ever atonal Swiss composer, was writing to Busoni at this time of his longing for Paris and claiming that he was 'unable to breathe' in Zurich;[8] and even Othmar Schoeck, who enjoyed more international success in these years than any compatriot except Arthur Honegger, repeatedly complained about the smallness of his homeland – while making few efforts to move

[7] Letter from Flury to Marx, 28 October 1926.

[8] Chris Walton (ed.), *Marcel H. S. Sulzberger (1876–1941)*, Amadeus, Winterthur, 2010, p. 39.

anywhere else.[9] The economic turmoil in the surrounding countries had lessened in the mid-1920s, but the political turmoil had not ceased, which meant that Switzerland was acquiring its reputation as an island of stability that would stand it in good stead for the next century. No wonder Kurth was advising his students to stay where they were and use their holidays to enjoy the major music centres of Europe. It is clear that Flury hoped Marx might somehow procure him a job (as will have been clear to Marx, too). But he did not. Even if he had wanted to – perhaps he did – he would almost certainly have been unable to help. He must have realised that Flury's desire to be elsewhere was bound up with a less-than-happy marriage. And an unhappy marriage in Solothurn is likely to be unhappy everywhere else, something that Marx could never fix.

Flury gave up his job with the Zurich Academic Orchestra in October 1926, the month in which he unburdened himself to Marx. He kept his post with the Harmonie Mixed Chorus in Bern until 1927, conducting Handel's *Acis and Galathea* with them in April 1927 (Adolf sang the tenor solos). But he was also more active in Solothurn at this time: January 1927 saw him conduct thirteen performances of Weber's opera *Der Freischütz* at the Solothurn City Theatre (with Adolf in the role of Max). And in the summer of 1927, Flury also took on a job as a violinist in Eduard Favre's Kurorchester in Interlaken. He returned for the summer months every year up to and including 1931, during which time he also assumed more and more conducting tasks as a Second Kapellmeister to the orchestra, conducting a huge spectrum of popular repertoire, from Schubert's *Rosamunde* ballet music to Mendelssohn overtures, Sibelius' *Finlandia*, ballet suites by Delibes, lollipops by Chabrier, and swathes of Lehár, the Strauss family, Waldteufel and Offenbach. As a rule, Flury conducted the afternoon concerts and Favre took charge of the evening concerts, when the tickets were slightly more expensive, and when international soloists played more 'serious' works that were still easy on the ear, such as clarinet concertos by Weber or violin concertos by Wieniawski.[10]

Richard's marriage was not the only cause of friction in the Flury family: Adolf also took an active dislike to their brother-in-law Walter Jud, Rosa's husband. But while this aversion meant Adolf's relations with his sister became strained, his disapproval of Lily did not cause any rift between him and Richard. So when his younger brother needed money in 1928, Adolf provided it. Richard had been presented with the opportunity to buy a Blüthner grand piano, but having a wife, two children and only part-time jobs meant he could not afford it; and so, on 13 March 1928, he and Adolf signed a contract for a loan of 1,500 francs at two per cent interest,

[9] *Cf.*, for example, Chris Walton, *Othmar Schoeck. Life and Works*, Eastman Studies in Music, University of Rochester Press, Rochester, 2009, pp. 110, 165, 209 and 308.

[10] Flury's archives contain his Interlaken programmes, with the repertoire he conducted marked specifically by him.

Richard Flury in the mid-1920s

to be paid back in monthly instalments of 40 francs (Flury kept paying until 1935, when an inheritance from his mother allowed him to repay the rest[11]). In that year he also took a diploma in choral conducting at the Bern Conservatoire and signed up for a course in orchestral conducting at the Basel Conservatoire under its new director, Felix Weingartner – the same who several years before had recommended Flury to study with Joseph Marx. In a letter to Adolf of 6 November 1928, Richard writes: 'Don't forget to send me the 200 francs for the Weingartner conducting course *as soon as you can*' (his emphasis). The course lasted from October 1928 to June 1929, and Flury's fellow students included Paul Sacher, Carmen Studer (later to become the fifth Mrs Weingartner) and Erich Schild (1890–1975),[12] another Solothurn resident and a teacher at the Kantonsschule (Flury had competed unsuccessfully against him for the directorship of the local choral association, the Solothurn Cäcilienverein, seven years before).[13]

If Flury's wife had thought his decision to give up first the Academic Orchestra in Zurich and then his job with the Harmonie in Bern meant she would have him home more often to help with their growing family, she will have been disappointed, as everything else points to an undimmed ambition to establish a career as a conductor and composer beyond the confines of Biberist and Solothurn. Posterity can be grateful for it, for Flury's conducting activities will undoubtedly have exerted a positive impact on his already skilful orchestration. Perhaps his trips to Basel and his annual sojourn in Interlaken were to some degree also an excuse to get away from his wife and his duties as a father. But the trajectory of his marriage would soon mean that Lily found his career choices ever more incompatible with domestic harmony.

[11] The repayment in full after their mother's death is confirmed in Adolf's hand on the contract.

[12] The list of course participants is given in Musikschule und Konservatorium Basel, *Jahresbericht über den 62. Kurs 1928/29*, [Musikschule und Konservatorium Basel], Basel, [1929], pp. 41–42.

[13] *Lebenserinnerungen*, *op. cit.*, p. 152.

10
A Carnival Symphony

Flury's works of the mid-to-late 1920s display his continuing ambitions to establish himself in the major genres. In 1925 he wrote a short suite for orchestra, *Kleine Ballettmusik*, which comprises five dances-cum-character pieces: 'Arabesque', 'Melodie', 'alla Polacca', 'Valse pastorale' and 'Tambourin', all showing Flury's melodious, 'popular' vein (he later added a sixth movement, 'Chilbimarsch', a march taken from his earlier *Festspiel*). This same year saw him compose an attractive, four-movement solo sonata for the violin (only eight minutes in length).

The next year, 1926, brought something far more substantial in the form of his First String Quartet – 'first', if one discounts his student efforts in the genre. It is in the traditional four movements: an opening *Allegro moderato*, a tripartite *Andante*, a Scherzo with trio, and a closing *Allegro*. The key-scheme is not what one would expect from a quartet 'in D minor' (as the score labels it). The first movement opens with a genial, almost waltzing theme in F major, followed by what appears to be a second subject in G major – but then the opening theme returns, revealing the movement to be a kind of rondo form instead, of which the G major section is in fact the first episode; a second episode more or less in C major is followed by the opening material again, and a coda closes the movement. The slow movement has the key-signature of A major and ends in that key; but it is tortuously reached, for the opening of the movement (given here as Ex. 4) involves strangely winding contrapuntal lines that are in no real key at all. In fact, it is not until a cadence in B minor in bar 37 that one has a sense of being in any particular tonality. A quintuplet in the cello in bar 16 seems oddly reminiscent of the opening motive from Alban Berg's Quartet, Op. 3. And there is indeed something Bergian about this movement. Although Flury does not mention him, either in his memoirs or in the correspondence from this time, he must surely have looked at Berg's quartet, which had been published only six years before.

Flury's scherzo is a high-energy piece that also avoids any fixed tonality for much of the time. Its trio is in a bucolic mood reminiscent of Schubert or Bruckner, though it is most notable for its unusual harmonic shifts and its odd, hiccupping phrase lengths. The scherzo then returns and cadences in D major. The last movement seems to offer initial certainty where it was lacking before, for the opening theme in the first violin is in an unambiguous D minor, despite a chromatic accompaniment in the second violin. But

Ex. 4

again there are rapid shifts of key – most reminiscent of Prokofiev this time. Fugato passages seem to begin but dissipate before all the voices have entered. The form has something of a rondo about it but is more complex than that, for there are also references back to the thematic material of the first movement (to the second episode in particular). The movement ends in the 'proper' key of D minor.

This First String Quartet is in every way a major improvement on the achievement of the First Symphony. The string-writing is highly idiomatic, there is no sense of incongruity between the tonal material and the extended free-tonal passages, and both harmony and form play with the listener's expectations in a manner that is highly satisfying. It has few peers in the Swiss quartet repertoire of the late nineteenth or early twentieth centuries. Its first performance – according to Flury's own worklist – was in Solothurn on 11 September 1926, with the composer on viola, and it was broadcast the following year from the Bern Radio Studio by the Schiffmann Quartet, although Flury had to jump in to play the second violin at short notice because of the indisposition of the quartet member in question. The only known recording is a non-commercial release of a radio broadcast made over half a century ago by the Brenner Quartet on Swiss Radio. It is a shame; it really ought to be in the repertoire of at least the leading Swiss string quartets.

In 1927, Flury embarked on his first *concertante* work: his First Piano Concerto in B minor, which he originally called *Konzertstück* and which is in one large movement nearly a quarter-of-an-hour in length. The opening bars are for piano solo and two horns in an apparent reference to Brahms' Second Piano Concerto. But any expectation of Brahmsian nostalgia is soon dispelled: the biggest influence on the concerto – for both good and ill – is Rachmaninov. For good, because Flury seems to have studied his orchestration carefully – such as how, in his concertos, Rachmaninov is able to conjure up a full texture with only sparse lines of orchestral accompaniment. For ill, because Flury here aims at effect without taking into due consideration the architectural context in which Rachmaninov places his grand climaxes. Flury's thematic material is often beautiful – there are moments towards the end where it sounds as if he has whisked Rachmaninov off to a Viennese *Kaffeehaus* – but there is altogether too much climax and too little foreplay. The piano-writing alternates between scalic passage-work in octaves *à la* Prokofiev, and Romantic, Lisztian fistfuls. Where the First String Quartet manages to keep its material under control – the quartet, after all, was a genre with which Flury was intimately familiar as a performer – the First Piano Concerto is a splurge. If one does not trouble one's critical faculties too much, then it is a thoroughly enjoyable splurge, and a fine antidote to the dry, Neo-Classical *concerti grossi* that many of his Calvinist and Zwinglian Swiss contemporaries were churning out in the 1920s and '30s. The Concerto was first performed by Dino

Ghisalberti and the Solothurn Orchestra under the composer's baton in Solothurn on 27 November 1927, and then again two weeks later in nearby Lyss, in a concert that also included Beethoven's Violin Concerto, played by Paul Miche. Ghisalberti played the Concerto again on 27 March 1928 in Bern (in another of the Bern Orchestra's 'Peoples' Concerts'), and Grethe Gertsch was the soloist in a performance with the Interlaken Kurorchester the following summer, on 17 August 1928. The reception in the press was uniformly good: for the work, the conductor and the soloists (especially Ghisalberti). In the *Berner Tagblatt* of 28 March 1928, Renker wrote of Ghisalberti's 'consummate artistry' and praised Flury's melodic gifts and the economy of his orchestration. It was, wrote Renker, an 'impressive concert-piece that many pianists would take up if it were published and publicised by a big publishing company'. Regrettably, the work is still only in manuscript today.

Now that he had a concerto under his belt, Flury embarked on a symphonic poem – though he gave it the name of 'symphony': the *Fasnachts-Symphonie*[1] or 'Carnival Symphony' ('Fasnacht' being the Swiss-German term for the Shrovetide carnival that elsewhere in the German-speaking world is variously called 'Fasching', 'Fastnacht' or 'Karneval'). In Solothurn, the annual carnival begins on 'Schmutzige Dunschtig', the Thursday six days before Ash Wednesday ('schmutzig', today a word meaning 'dirty', actually derives from the word for 'fat', analogous to the 'fat Tuesday' – 'mardi gras' – by which carnival is known in other parts of the world). Before dawn on this particular Thursday, the youth of the city gather together, dressed in white nightgowns, wearing loud clogs and armed with rattles and bells. At the stroke of 5 a.m. they set off through town on what is called the 'Chesslete', making as much noise as possible to drive out the winter. Their exertions end in the assorted restaurants and pubs of the old town, where they eat traditional flour soup (which is far more delicious than it sounds to Anglo-Saxon ears, and is offered free in many establishments). Many of those over the minimum age are often already in a state of advanced inebriation and spend the later hours of the morning asleep with their heads slumped on restaurant tables until they are woken and cast out to make way for paying customers. In what to an outsider seems a delightfully cussed example of Swiss bureaucracy, all city schools are closed on the Thursday afternoon – but not in the morning, meaning that the young are expected to be present for a full morning of serious education before being allowed to sleep off their nocturnal exertions.

The programme behind the *Fasnachts-Symphonie* is a ballad poem by Carl Robert Enzmann (1888–1931), a Catholic priest originally from Lucerne who was appointed *Domkaplan* at the Solothurn cathedral during the First World War. His dialect poem ''S isch immer e so gsi' ('That's

[1] The title page of the first edition calls it the 'Fastnachts-Symphonie', but Flury consistently spells it the Swiss way, without the first 't'.

how it's always been'), an ironic comment on Solothurn and its traditions, has long become the unofficial anthem of the city (sung to a tune of Irish folk origins) and is learnt by everyone at primary school (it is also played daily by a glockenspiel outside the city walls; indeed, it is playing in the background as I write). Flury had got to know Enzmann while still at grammar school, and had on occasion accompanied his violin-playing at the piano. Enzmann one day showed Flury a new poem entitled 'Der Zeughausviggi und der Tod' ('Viggi of the Arsenal, and Death', 'Viggi' being a local diminutive of 'Viktor' – a popular name in Solothurn because of its association with one of the city patron saints). It tells of the dying hours of 'Viggi', the man in charge of the Zeughaus, the former city arsenal that has long been the resting place of booty won in the late-Mediaeval wars between the Swiss Confederacy and the Duke of Burgundy. In his death throes, Viggi imagines himself transported into the battle against the Burgundians, dying a hero on the battlefield; outside in the present day, the 'Chesslete' is making its racket throughout the town (Flury incorporates traditional carnival melodies here). Viggi awakes, is given the last rites, and dies. Flury was attracted by the contrast between the life-affirming youthful zest of the 'Chesslete' and Viggi's acceptance of death. Enzmann had envisioned his text as suitable for setting as a melodrama (that is, as a text spoken to music, along the lines of similar works by Franz Liszt, Richard Strauss and others). But Flury felt it would work better as a symphonic poem, and Enzmann consented. Flury finished the score on 21 May 1928 and conducted its first performance with the Kurorchester in Interlaken on 29 August of that year. It is cast in one movement lasting nearly twenty minutes, and was to become his most often performed orchestral work. It is highly effective and skilfully executed. There is a particularly lovely passage for solo violin with orchestral accompaniment in the centre of the work (the score does not have titles for the individual sections, so one can merely assume it is one of Viggi's pleasanter dreams); and when Flury's own radio recording of it from the 1950s was released on CD in 2012, Peter Palmer wrote that 'The contrast between the lonely death of an armoury custodian and a rowdy street carnival is richly exploited. The most gripping section evokes the old soldier's dreams of fighting in past wars'.[2]

The work that most occupied Flury in the latter half of the 1920s, however, was his first opera. He had informed Ernst Kurth back in late 1924 that he was planning an opera,[3] without giving further detail. A year later, in a letter to Joseph Marx of 3 September 1925, he names it as a setting of Oscar Wilde's *A Florentine Tragedy* (1894). This play is actually a fragment that was performed and published only posthumously. There are only three characters: Simone, a merchant in Florence; his bored wife, Bianca; and

[2] *Loc. cit.*, p. 117.

[3] *Cf.* p. 88, above.

Carl Robert Enzmann, priest and poet

Bianca's lover, Guido, the only son and heir of the ruler of Florence. Simone arrives home to find Bianca and Guido together. He soon realises that his noble guest has come for more than an inspection of his wares. Verbal sparring between the two men leads to a physical duel, with Bianca urging her lover to kill her husband. Simone overpowers his rival and kills him, and then turns to kill his wife too. But Bianca, astonished at the turn of events, 'comes towards him as one dazed with wonder and with outstretched arms', uttering: 'Why did you not tell me you were so strong?' at which Simone relents, cries 'Why did you not tell me you were beautiful?' and kisses her. The curtain falls.

Giacomo Puccini had apparently considered turning the play into an opera shortly after it was first performed, but Ricordi advised him against it. In 1911, while still a student, Sergei Prokofiev embarked on a one-act opera entitled *Maddalena*, Op. 11, to a libretto of his own based on a play by Magna Gustavovna Lieven-Orlov that was in turn based on Wilde's text.[4] The Italian composer Carlo Ravasegna (1891–1964) set Wilde's play to music during the First World War as *Una tragedia fiorentina*, using a libretto in Italian by Ettore Moschino.[5] Alexander von Zemlinsky also based an opera on the play at almost the same time, composing it in 1914–16. He used the then current German translation by Max Meyerfeld. The story reminded Zemlinsky of two love-triangles in his close circle – that of Alma Mahler, her husband Gustav and her lover Walter Gropius, and that of Arnold Schoenberg, his wife Mathilde (Zemlinsky's sister) and her lover Richard Gerstl. The first performance of Zemlinsky's opera took place in Stuttgart in 1917, and it was staged at several other houses in central Europe in the ensuing years.[6] Flury was also using Meyerfeld's text as his libretto, but seems to have been unaware of Zemlinsky's work – or at least unaware that it could have any consequences for his own plans. The reality had dawned at least by 28 October 1926, for it was on this day that he wrote in a letter to Joseph Marx that 'the performing rights [of *Eine florentinische Tragödie*] are regrettably only with Zemlinski [*sic*]'. But since the opera was finished by then, he presumably decided to go ahead and try for a local premiere anyway. Further details remain unclear until the business of who owned what rights resurfaced over two years later, as will be seen in the next chapter.

It is noteworthy that it is in this letter to Marx that Flury makes some anti-Semitic comments. He refers with distaste to the 'new composers' who are 'achieving prominence' at the international music festivals, despite the fact that 'these Jewish boys' are presenting their audiences with nothing but a 'swindle', while 'honest art' is being kept silent. Flury is angry at having written an opera that can't be staged because of Zemlinsky's apparently owning the rights, but he expresses it by resorting to a common trope of the time, mixing anti-Semitism with anti-Modernism (there is one more instance of this, also in a letter to Marx, in which Flury similarly links 'Jewishness' with an empty modernity). It is regrettable proof that not even Flury in little Solothurn was immune to the bourgeois anti-Semitism that one so often finds in the utterances of artists in the early twentieth century. To resort to racism to compensate for one's own lack of foresight is a cheap shot, and not a little ironic given that Flury's recent string quartet is stylistically close to the free atonal works of the Second Viennese School whose members are so obviously the target of his rage, not to mention the fact that Meyerfeld, his would-be librettist, was also Jewish. It is perhaps significant that Flury made his comments in a letter to Marx. Although

4 Prokofiev's unfinished opera was not heard until 1979, when Edward Downes conducted his own performing version for the BBC.

5 Rita Severi, '"Astonishing in my Italian": Oscar Wilde's First Italian Editions 1890–1952', in Stefano Evangelista (ed.), *The Reception of Oscar Wilde in Europe*, Continuum, London and New York, 2010, p. 120.

6 *Cf.* Chris Walton, 'Composing Oscar: Settings of Wilde for the German Stage' in Evangelista (ed.), *op. cit.*, pp. 222–23.

there is no anti-Semitic vocabulary in Marx's letters to Flury, Marx was already established as a conservative antipode to the Schoenberg school in Vienna – one commentator has even described him as the 'spiritual leader' of the anti-Schoenberg clique[7] – and he was regarded with suspicion by the Schoenbergians themselves: only a few months earlier, Alban Berg had criticised Marx's 'amateurism' in a letter to Schoenberg, calling a recent Marx performance a testament to 'the darkness of this musical winter'.[8] But even if Flury was merely fishing for sympathy, this is an explanation, not an excuse – and mercifully, this vocabulary disappears from Flury's letters as quickly as it arose; and in any case, his actions were henceforth also in stark contrast to his words. *Eine florentinische Tragödie* was in fact only the first of three stage works by Flury to a text by a Jewish writer, the last of which would be a collaboration with a Jewish *émigré* at the height of the Second World War, at a time when many of Flury's Swiss composing colleagues were hedging their bets on the outcome of the conflict by studiously avoiding anything that might antagonise the Nazis. When it really mattered, however, Flury never showed any such hedging in his dealings with his fellow human beings. A pity there hadn't been more men like him.

[7] Anton Haefeli, *Die internationale Gesellschaft für neue Musik (IGNM). Ihre Geschichte von 1922 bis zur* Gegenwart, Atlantis Musikbuch-Verlag, Zurich, 1982, p. 69.

[8] *Cf.* Berg's letter to Schoenberg of 13 March 1926, in Juliane Brand *et al.* (eds.), *Briefwechsel Arnold Schönberg – Alban Berg*, Vol. II, Schott, Mainz, 2007, p. 255.

11
The Flury Festival and *Eine florentinische Tragödie*

Switzerland may have been a confederation of assorted cantonal republics for several hundred years, but it still has the vestiges of a class system. The aristocratic prefix 'von' is not uncommon, especially in the patrician class of old Bern. And in Basel, the families of the *haute bourgeoisie* are to this day referred to collectively as the 'Basler Daig' (a word meaning both 'dyke' and 'pastry dough'), though they are perhaps now best known as snobbish figures of fun in TV and film comedies. They can in certain cases be recognised by specific spellings of otherwise common surnames (thus a 'Vischer' would belong to the 'Daig', whereas a 'Fischer' most definitely wouldn't; similarly, the Swiss telephone book lists over two thousand 'Burkhard', but only a couple of hundred 'Burckhardt', the 'ck/dt' being the signifier of the 'Daig'). Solothurn had its upper crust, too. Having long enjoyed special status as the residence of the French ambassadors to the Swiss Confederacy, it retained into the twentieth century the air of a genteel but slightly mouldy great aunt, keen to keep up appearances despite no longer entertaining the *crème de la crème* of Paris and Versailles in her parlour. Most of the old patrician villas have today passed into the hands of the local authorities or assorted foundations, but in Flury's day several were still inhabited by their founding families. One of the most prominent of these old Solothurn dynasties was that of Vigier von Steinbrugg, or 'de Vigier', as they call themselves, descended from a French aristocrat who had worked as an interpreter for the Ambassador of His French Majesty to the Swiss Confederacy. But unlike the stereotypical, untouchable aristocrats of other European countries, by the nineteenth century the de Vigiers were active in all aspects of local life. They achieved renown as judges and government ministers, they ran railway companies and even founded the first-ever Swiss cement company (still in existence today as Vigier Holding AG). The most prominent de Vigier of the twentieth century was Bill (1912–2003), who defied the wishes of his father by refusing to study law, did an apprenticeship instead, emigrated to London with none of Daddy's money, set up a workshop in the East End, and made his own millions by inventing, manufacturing and marketing steel scaffolding props. He also helped his adopted country win the Second World War by manufacturing engine frames for the air force and modular, portable harbours for the Normandy landings.[1]

Bill also took an active interest in music, in which he was very much the son of his parents. His father, Wilhelm, was a lawyer who loved music and had been appointed the President of the City Band in 1908 (a post he held in an honorary capacity until his death over 60 years later). Bill's mother, Berthe, was one of the best-known Swiss sopranos of her day, even singing in La Scala, Milan, and the Philharmonic Hall in Berlin. She was also one of Flury's earliest interpreters – she performed seven of his songs with orchestral accompaniment, under his direction, in a concert of the Bern City Orchestra back in October 1924, and sang six of them the following February in a concert of the Zurich Academic Orchestra, again under Flury. Berthe and Wilhelm were very wealthy and knew everyone who was anyone. So when they decided to do something concrete to promote Flury's career in 1928, he could have wished for no one better placed to help. Berthe gathered together a number of like-minded sponsors, engaged the financial help of the Canton and the City, and organised a 'Flury Festival' that took place in the Solothurn concert hall on Sunday, 13 January 1929. A chamber concert featured his First String Quartet, a suite for cello and piano (arranged from his Oboe Suite of 1926), piano pieces and songs (sung by Berthe de Vigier herself). Later in the day an orchestral concert featured the First Symphony, the *Fasnachts-Symphonie*, the First Piano Concerto (with Ghisalberti), the *Kleine Ballettmusik* and *Sapphos Tod*, a setting of Franz Grillparzer for soprano and orchestra composed the year before (sung by Berthe again). The Bern City Orchestra played under the baton of the composer. Both concerts were sold out (Wilhelm de Vigier had apparently pulled out all the stops to get as big an audience as possible) and the audience included prominent members of the Swiss music scene such as Fritz Brun, Gustave Doret, Josef Lauber and Paul Miche. After the concerts, the de Vigiers held a reception in their summer house that included a speech by a member of the 'Ständerat', the upper chamber of the national parliament. The Bernese critics were there, including Gustav Renker, and they were uniformly positive. *Der Bund*, the *Neue Berner Zeitung* and the Lucerne daily *Vaterland* all remarked on how composers usually have to wait until they're either ancient or dead to be celebrated thus, and were full of praise for the burghers of Solothurn for not having waited so long with Flury. Gian Bundi in *Der Bund* found the D minor String Quartet the most 'powerful' of the works performed, especially its second movement; Flury's friend Carl Enzmann, writing for *Vaterland*, also liked this movement and couldn't resist a poetic touch, saying it was like 'the Christmas blossoming of a rose of Jericho in the hoarfrost of a clear, sunny winter's day'. But even the French-Swiss press was positive. Edouard

[1] *Cf.* his obituary in *The Daily Telegraph*, 12 January 2004, and the exhibition brochure *100 Jahre Bill de Vigier*, W. A. de Vigier Stiftung, Solothurn, 2012.

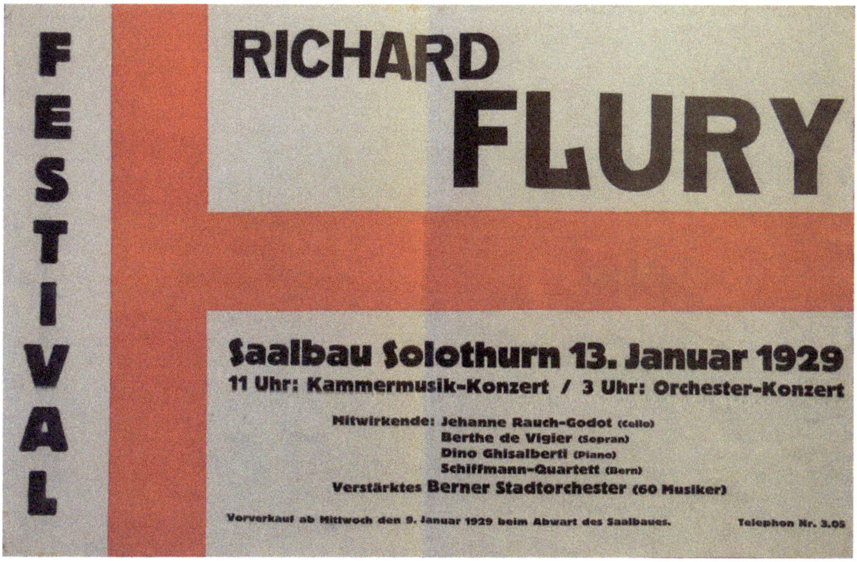

Poster for the Flury Festival, 1929

Combe in *La Tribune de Genève* preferred the *Fasnachts-Symphonie*, saying it showed how Flury had cast off a certain 'clumsiness' evident in his earlier work, and that he would not hesitate to recommend it to the Orchestre de la Suisse Romande for performance: 'The man who wrote it is perhaps not yet in possession of complete mastery, but he's not far from it', he wrote. And while Henry Reymond in *La Tribune de Lausanne* criticised a certain excess in Flury's textures, which he occasionally found 'congested', he was in no doubt that Flury was deserving of the attention devoted to him at the festival, and praised his 'fertile mind'.[2] Switzerland's national music journal, the *Schweizerische Musikzeitung*, brought a special report over a page in length by Kurt Joss of Bern, who offered a highly positive but also remarkably perceptive review of the Flury Festival. Flury was a 'lyrical composer', he wrote, but at the same he noted a discrepancy between Flury's claims to be a 'Romantic', composing only what he 'felt', and the fact that his music actually betrays a keen intellect in its formal structure. He also offered high praise for Flury's orchestration and suggested that passages in the *Fasnachts-Symphonie* and the D minor Symphony were more indicative of a born dramatist.[3]

All this positive publicity for the Festival helped to get further performances for Flury. Fritz Brun put the *Fasnachts-Symphonie* on the

[2] These various reviews were collected by Flury; they all date from shortly after the Flury Festival, but I have been unable to date them in every case. Enzmann's review in the *Vaterland* was published on 22 January, Reymond's in *La Tribune de Lausanne* on 15 January.

[3] Kurt Joss, 'Richard Flury-Konzerte in Solothurn', in *Schweizerische Musikzeitung*, Vol. 69, No. 3 (1 February 1929), pp. 88–90.

Felix Weingartner, photo from 1936 with a dedication to Flury

programme for his subscription concerts in Bern in the next season, as did the Lucerne Orchestra. Flury was now able to get a Solothurn businessman to pay for the publication of the score – Emil Brunner, owner of a malt factory, who was rewarded with the dedication of the work. Flury was still attending Weingartner's classes in Basel, and so he took the opportunity to give him, too, a copy of the *Fasnachts-Symphonie* (it is held today by the Basel School of Music, and the dedication bears the date '17 March 1929'). Weingartner took his time to look at it, then wrote to Flury on 22 September 1929 to tell him that he was putting it on his concert programme in Basel in the 1930–31 season; he kept his word, too, conducting it in a subscription concert on 14 March 1931.

Flury's local success continued only a few weeks after the festival with the premiere of his *Eine florentinische Tragödie* at the Solothurn City Theatre on 9 April 1929. The Solothurn Theatre had been reorganised two years earlier, as the 'Städtebundtheater Biel-Solothurn' (the 'theatre union of the cities of Biel and Solothurn'), in which the same ensemble performed the same repertoire, with the same cast and sets, at the theatres of Biel and Solothurn, alternating between them. The idea was not new, and a similar structure exists today. It is the most practicable means of providing the population of two cities with live theatre without the cost of each supporting its own ensemble. What made the Solothurn Theatre in 1927 different from the ensembles that had gone before it was the person of its director, Leo Delsen. Born 'Samuel Leiser Idelson' in 1888 in Russia, he had studied at the Munich Conservatoire, was thereafter engaged at assorted German theatres, and had the good fortune to be on tour in Zurich in 1914 when the First World War broke out. He spent the War singing at the Zurich City Theatre, and then moved to the Bern Theatre in 1918, where he sang all the staple bass roles until his elevation into theatre management in Solothurn nine years later.[4] The new Städtebundtheater was able to afford a small orchestra, which meant it could programme operas on a regular basis – an art form that had hitherto enjoyed only irregular appearances on the boards of Solothurn. The first opera Delsen staged was Mozart's *Die Entführung aus dem Serail* in September 1927, and soon music theatre would constitute over a third of the annual theatre performances at the Städtebundtheater.[5] The Solothurn theatre itself was renovated in 1928, the old Baroque, Jesuit edifice now being overlaid with red velvet and plush.[6] Flury was the first Swiss composer to have a work performed under Delsen's direction. Oddly, Flury's operatic tale of lust and murder was paired in a double bill with *Die Maienkönigin*, an innocent pastoral *Singspiel* concocted from Gluck's music by Max Kalbeck in the late nineteenth century. Since it is tuneful and easy on the ear, it was perhaps chosen as an audience-pleaser to entice those who might have baulked at a whole evening of modern music – although it was first on the bill, which meant that anyone coming for tunes could leave in the interval.

It is unclear who had the foresight to engage Gottfried Kassowitz from Vienna to conduct the production of *Eine florentinische Tragödie*, but it was probably Delsen. It was not the first time that Kassowitz had conducted the Solothurn ensemble – he had even gone on tour with them the previous winter, taking their production of Mozart's *Marriage of Figaro* as far as Geneva.[7] Kassowitz (1897–1969) was a former student of both Alban Berg and Arnold Schoenberg and was already making a name for himself – even *The Musical Times* in London had noticed him, remarking on this 'talented pupil of Alban Berg' in a brief notice on events in Vienna in February 1925, the occasion being a performance of Mahler's version of Weber's opera *Die drei Pintos*.[8] And Kassowitz was much more than merely being Berg's pupil. Berg had even asked him to make the piano vocal score of *Wozzeck*;

[4] *Cf.*, for example, Hans Rindlisbacher (ed.), *Nachlass Delsen, Leo (1884/88–1954)*, Zentralbibliothek, Solothurn, 2003, p. 1.

[5] *Cf.* Anon., *50 Jahre Städtebundtheater Biel-Solothurn 1927–1977*, [Städtebundtheater Biel-Solothurn], Biel, 1977, pp. 20–21.

[6] At its most recent renovation, completed in early 2015, the process was reversed, with the old Baroque decorations revealed and restored.

[7] This *Figaro* was given a good review in the *Gazette de Lausanne* on 21 November 1928.

[8] Paul Bechert, 'Vienna', *The Musical Times*, Vol. 66, No. 984 (1 February 1925), p. 172.

Poster for the world premiere of Flury's Eine florentinische Tragödie *at the Solothurn City Theatre*

lack of time had made Kassowitz decline the offer, but he was then tasked instead with correcting all the orchestral parts before the rehearsals for the opening run of the opera in Berlin under Erich Kleiber, and Kassowitz was himself present on the opening night. His collaboration with Flury for the premiere of *Eine florentinische Tragödie* was probably the very first time that Flury had become properly acquainted with someone so close to the inner circle of Viennese musical Modernism. All the more pity, then, that there is no record of their conversations.

It might seem odd that Kassowitz, a man at home in Vienna and Berlin, a trusted colleague of one of the best-known contemporary composers, should come to little Solothurn to conduct an unknown opera by an unknown local only three years after having collaborated on an operatic success at the Berlin State Opera. Aspects of the Solothurn set-up were undoubtedly amateur – the sets for Flury's opera, for example, were the responsibility of Dr Johannes Kälin, Cantonal Archivist and a keen musician in his spare hours.[9] But the circumstances of the time come into play here: Switzerland was not yet the rich country it is today, but it had nevertheless stayed politically and economically stable since the First World War. To be sure, fascists and communists alike had their supporters there and occasionally even won seats in local and regional assemblies over the coming years. And the far-right Swiss 'National Front' would become ever louder when Hitler's assumption of power across the border brought it an upswing in financial support. But the political extremes of the rest of central Europe never acquired more than marginal importance in Switzerland in these inter-war years. Austria, by contrast, remained turbulent. In 1927 – the same year in which the city of Solothurn was able to place its theatre on a firm artistic and financial footing – the venerable Volksoper in Vienna went bankrupt. Political riots between left and right were also the order of the day, and in July 1927 the Viennese police opened fire on protestors, killing over 80 people. So while Flury could curse his provincial shackles and still hanker after a life in the old imperial capital, men such as Kassowitz, who were personally acquainted with its vagaries, were probably more than happy to get paid work in sleepy Solothurn. And what's more, it's clear he really liked Flury and admired his music: only a year later he would conduct the *Kleine Ballettmusik* on Viennese Radio, and after the Second World War he performed Flury's *Waldsymphonie* on Austrian Radio.

The feeling was mutual – Flury liked and admired Kassowitz too. And, given Flury's hankering for everything Viennese, one can assume that on his extended visit to Solothurn in early 1929 Kassowitz brought him up to date with musical developments beyond the more conservative circles in which Flury's former master Marx lived and worked. Kassowitz was an embodiment of the same modern school that had prompted Flury to a fit of

[9] *Lebenserinnerungen*, *op. cit.*, pp. 170 and 203.

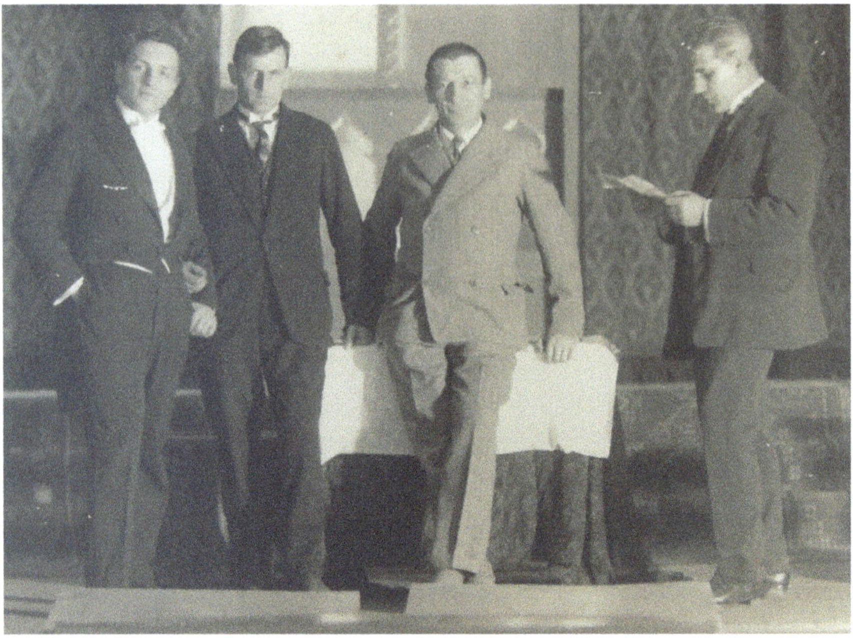

From left to right: Gottfried Kassowitz, Richard Flury, Leo Delsen and Johannes Kälin on the set for Eine florentinische Tragödie

rage in his correspondence with Marx back in 1926, and so their friendship presumably helped Flury to realise the absurdity of his opinions. And Flury's works over the next few years were to testify to a certain stylistic rapprochement with Viennese modernity. He and Kassowitz remained close for the rest of their lives.

The premiere of Flury's *Eine florentinische Tragödie* did not generate much attention outside the region, but the reviews, at least, were enthusiastic. The *Neue Zürcher Zeitung* was the closest the work got to attracting international attention, but its review was only 100 words long at the bottom of a column entitled 'Brief chronicle'. All the same, it praised Flury's 'dramatic power', his 'eye for what works on stage' and the 'exquisite beauties' of the score.[10] The Basel and Bern papers brought brief but similarly positive notices, with Gustav Renker in the *Berner Tagblatt* the most erudite and also the most effusive. He noted that 'the time of those Italian Renaissance operas is really past. They enjoyed their climax in royalties with Schreker's *Die Gezeichneten*, Korngold's *Violantha* [*sic*] and Schillings' *Mona Lisa*', but he went on to praise Flury's stagecraft and the manner in which he had conceived the entire score as a dramatic crescendo. He declared that *Eine florentinische Tragödie* was worthy of being placed alongside the operas of

[10] '-dm-', *Neue Zürcher Zeitung*, midday edition, 12 April 1929.

Othmar Schoeck – and since Schoeck's most recent opera, *Penthesilea*, had recently been given its premiere at the renowned Dresden State Opera, this was high praise. Delsen's stage direction and Kassowitz's conducting were also singled out. Renker seemed confident that it marked the beginning of a major operatic career for its composer.[11]

The story of Flury's *Eine florentinische Tragödie*, however, was almost over before it had properly begun. After Flury's letter to Marx of 28 October 1926 there was no more mention of problems with the rights to Max Meyerfeld's text – Flury claimed to have written to Zemlinsky to ask his permission to go ahead with his own setting, and when he got no reply, he seems to have assumed that all was well.[12] It wasn't. Zemlinsky heard of Flury's opera only in April 1929 – perhaps via Kassowitz, whom he knew as one of the Schoenberg circle.[13] (It is probably safe to assume that Kassowitz knew nothing about any possible problems with the rights – apart from the unlikelihood that he would to risk conflict with a senior Viennese colleague, any such legal problems could have torpedoed the production and jeopardised Kassowitz's fee.)

Zemlinsky had himself endured immense problems getting permission to use the German translation of Wilde's play and had assumed that all rights to it had long been acquired by his publisher, Universal Edition. So when he heard about Flury's run of performances, he informed Hans Heinsheimer, the Head of Opera at Universal. Heinsheimer in turn wrote to Flury, 'demanding all royalties from me and wanting to forbid any further performances of the opera', as Flury wrote in horror to Joseph Marx on 7 June 1929. Zemlinsky had meanwhile written a brief, conciliatory note to Flury.[14] He stressed his own inability to act because he, too, was bound by contracts – though to his credit he also wrote to Heinsheimer to insist that Flury should not be penalised.[15] In the end it was all a storm in a teacup. Universal suddenly realised that they did not possess any exclusive rights to Wilde's text at all. With no legal basis to demand anything of Flury, they backed down straight away.[16]

Flury had sent Ernst Kurth a copy of the vocal score of his *Eine florentinische Tragödie* almost three years before the first performance. Kurth played through it carefully and wrote back in warm terms, specifically mentioning Flury's ability to merge the lyrical and the dramatic. But he wasn't wholly convinced by the cuts Flury had made to Wilde's text, and felt that the dramatic shift towards the close, where the banter between the

[11] Newspaper clippings in Flury's archives, all from mid-April 1929, though individually undated.

[12] Flury writes this in a letter of 7 June 1929 to Joseph Marx.

[13] The story of Zemlinsky, Universal Edition and Flury is told in Antony Beaumont's foreword to his new edition of Zemlinsky's opera. *Cf.* 'Andere Vertonungen' in Zemlinsky, ed. Beaumont, *Eine florentinische Tragödie: Oper in einem Aufzug op. 16 (1916)*, Universal Edition, Vienna, [2012], pp. xxiv–xxvi.

[14] Undated, presumably April or May 1929, in Flury's archives.

[15] *Cf.* Beaumont, *op. cit.*, p. xxv.

[16] *Ibid.*, pp. xxv–xxvi.

The final scene of Eine florentinische Tragödie *in Solothurn, 1929. From left to right: Hans Skrivanek (Guido), Otto Jenk (Simone) and Annie Christiansen (Bianca)*

characters turns serious, could have been better managed. He furthermore regretted the lack of any orchestral prelude or interludes (though he also added a nice anecdote, saying that he had seen a copy of the play on Gustav Mahler's desk in 1908, when his piano and his table were otherwise covered in sketches for *Das Lied von der Erde*).[17] Not surprisingly, Kurth's criticism is highly astute. The opera is sung more or less from start to finish in a highly conversational style that seems prescient of the later Richard Strauss. The opera lasts only three-quarters of an hour, so the rapid musical dialogue helps to maintain the dramatic tension. But the ear still occasionally longs for a moment of repose. In his review, Gustav Renker wrote that he found the close of the opera – the scene where the married couple come together over the dead body of the wife's lover – to be the finest part of it. It is easy to agree with him. Here, Flury at last lets the orchestra speak as the husband moves towards his wife with the intention of killing her. Diatonicism gives way to glittery, almost Bergian harmonies over a slowly moving bass before the two remaining characters resolve their differences in an ecstatic C major (Ex. 5).

It would take a fine director and a gifted conductor to pace the work properly so that the long dialogues do not tire the ear, but *Eine florentinische Tragödie* certainly deserves to be staged occasionally, and ought to have been recorded long before now. Yet it has been performed only twice since its premiere. It was given another brief run in Solothurn in 1933, this time

[17] Schmid and Hinden, *op. cit.*, pp. 312–13.

Ex. 5

[Grave ♩ = 54]
Simone
rit.
A - men! Und jetzt zu dir!
Poco più mosso
Simone erhebt sich und sieht Bianca an. Sie kommt auf ihn zu,
Sehr ruhig ♩ = 60
wie geblendet von einem Wunder, mit ausgebreiteten Armen.
poco accel.
rall.
Primo tempo

Sehr ruhig und verklärt
Bianca
Wa - rum hast du mir nicht ge - sagt, dass du so
Sehr ruhig und verklärt
stark? Dass du so stark, Du so stark,
Simone
Wa - rum hast du mir nicht ge - sagt, dass du
dim.
rall.
Largo
so stark?
Er küsst sie auf den Mund
so schön?
molto cresc.
Der Vorhang fällt!

coupled with Mascagni's *Cavalleria rusticana*, and the Bern Radio Studio broadcast it in 1944 with a fine cast comprising Siegfried Tappolet (Simone, baritone), Annie Weber (Bianca, soprano) and Willy Frei (Guido, tenor), with the Bern City Orchestra conducted by Christoph Lertz (1888–1961). An archive recording has survived that makes one wish all the more that the work could be performed again.

12
Spreading his Wings

Flury's third daughter, Giovanna, was born in May 1929. It probably did not improve marital harmony that Flury left for Interlaken only a few weeks later, when his summer employment in the Kurorchester now entailed more conducting duties. Lily was thus left at home for the summer with three young girls. Was Flury taking the path of least resistance? It is true that the little money he earned in Interlaken will have been useful to the family finances. But he seems to have preferred to keep his distance from the hands-on business of small children. His correspondence with Marx retained its confessional aspect – but in his next letter to his old teacher, of 7 June 1929, he mentions his daughter's recent birth almost as a footnote to a discussion of his musical activities. And a postcard to Marx from Interlaken on 9 August 1929 even refers to his job there as his 'summer holiday'. Flury adds that he is using his spare time to work on his Second String Quartet. The other musicians in the Interlaken orchestra this year included as concert-master the violinist and composer Heraklit Nestoroff – a fascinating but murky figure who was an almost exact contemporary of Flury's. Born in France in 1896, he was half-Austrian (like Flury) and half-Bulgarian. His mother, the writer Elsa Asenijeff, had been a sometime lover of the artist Max Klinger, and Nestoroff himself studied in Vienna with Émile Jaques-Dalcroze.[1] He also knew Joseph Marx, and added a postscript to Flury's postcard: 'A pity you're not here. There's a whole host of charming girls'. In his autobiography, Flury mentions Nestoroff as a man who was 'brutally' obsessed with the erotic. He also says that another of his Interlaken musician colleagues, one Ernest Schmidt, was a gourmet chef who took as much delight in dining sumptuously as he did in preparing sumptuous dinners. So it does not sound as though Flury practised any monastic asceticism during his Interlaken summers. And if he was unwise enough to tell Lily about his friends – presumably after she had spent July and August mopping up after her babies – it can't have made her very happy. All the same, whether out of duty or in an endeavour to find meaning when it was otherwise absent, their physical relationship continued. Shortly after Flury's return from Interlaken in the summer of 1929, Lily became pregnant again.

[1] *Cf.*, for example, www.leipzig.de/jugend-familie-und-soziales/frauen/1000-jahre-leipzig-100-frauenportraets/literatur/literatur-portraets/, accessed March 2016.

Flury (centre, with violin case) caught by chance on a tourist postcard of the Kursaal in Interlaken, 1931

Flury's teaching and conducting commitments in Solothurn continued as before. He also remained active on the chamber-music scene. For several years he had been performing in local concerts together with Dino Ghisalberti (who alternated between the piano, the viola and violin), Otto von Tobel (cello), Heinrich Wydler (viola) and others, and their programmes included large-scale works such as Schubert's 'Trout' Quintet and his A minor Quartet (in November 1928 in the Solothurn Concert Hall, on the centenary of Schubert's death), and Mendelssohn's Octet and Brahms' First Sextet, Op. 18 (in January 1930 in the same venue). Given all these professional and private commitments, it is hardly surprising that Flury composed little in the year-and-a-half after the premiere of his first opera. And his Second String Quartet, written in 1929, is not a very satisfying work. It is dedicated to the Schiffmann Quartet of Bern, which gave its first performance. There are promising moments, but overall it conveys a desire to be more than it is. The opening of the first movement, with a vague triplet accompaniment in the middle voices, looks more like the start of a neo-Brucknerian symphony than a string quartet; there is some attractive augmented harmony in the second movement, but it lacks the contrapuntal interest of the First Quartet; and the jocular passages in the first, third and last movements do not seem to lie easily with the rest. The score looks like a work for large string orchestra that has been reduced less than skilfully for smaller forces. It seems that Flury at some point indeed tried it out with

Poster for the Vienna performance of Flury's Fasnachts-Symphonie *on 1 June 1930*

more players, as a part for double-bass has survived in his archives. But he never published it in any form; perhaps he too realised it was not his best effort.

Towards the end of 1929, Flury was invited to participate in the First International Congress of the 'Welt-Musik und Sangesbund' in Vienna, which was to take place during the Vienna Festival in the first week of June 1930. He was asked to give a short lecture on modern Swiss music and was also offered the chance of having his *Fasnachts-Symphonie* performed – though on condition that he pay for the rehearsals. He agreed, but decided to conduct the work himself, and notified the relevant authorities that he would manage with a single rehearsal. Flury had apparently joined the Sangesbund through the offices of Joseph Marx, and so he was perturbed to hear through the grapevine in March 1930 that Marx had meanwhile fallen out with the people running it. He seems to have felt he ought to show solidarity with Marx, but then sensibly decided not to withdraw and lose the chance of performing his work in Vienna. He stayed with a relative from the Gamohn side of his family[2] in the capital, and conducted the Vienna Symphony Orchestra in his work on Sunday, 1 June. The second half of the programme was taken up by a performance of Beethoven's Ninth Symphony conducted by Martin Spörr. One could hardly have imagined a more

[2] *Cf.* p. 22, above.

daunting programme for the Viennese debut of an unknown composer. At least one newspaper, the *Arbeiter-Zeitung*, did not even bother to mention Flury's contribution in its announcement of the programme for the day. With so much else happening at the time, the concert seems not to have been given much attention in the press – but at least the *Reichspost* of 2 June took note and praised Flury more than the music of the rest of the evening. Its reviewer wrote that the Beethoven performance had been 'very nice', whereas the *Fasnachts-Symphonie* 'gripped one on account of its original invention, its modern harmonies, finely spun voice-leading and motivic workings in a *Tristan* style'.[3]

There is an odd postscript to this Viennese performance. The opening of Flury's *Fasnachts-Symphonie* (Ex. 6(a)) bears an odd resemblance to the Mahlerian coda in the First Act of Alban Berg's *Lulu* (Ex. 6(b)), which it seems Berg only composed several weeks after Flury's symphony was performed in Vienna.[4] And yet Berg can hardly have attended the concert, for that same week saw him travel to Königsberg for the premiere of his concert aria *Der Wein*. The possibility that Berg saw the score cannot be excluded, and in fact the publication of the *Fasnachts-Symphonie* was advertised by Hug that same summer in the Viennese new-music journal *Melos*[5] (although only as one of many new works). Even so, there is no reason to suppose that Berg had any more interest in Richard Flury than in the other Swiss composers on Hug's books. Nor does Berg's library today hold a copy of Flury's score.[6] Nevertheless, Kassowitz probably told Berg of his experiences in Solothurn, and since he will have received a copy of the *Fasnachts-Symphonie* (Flury always made sure to send copies of his scores to conductor acquaintances and friends), it is possible that Kassowitz might have shown it to Berg. Flury was certainly in Kassowitz's thoughts at this time, because he conducted Flury's *Kleine Ballettmusik* on Viennese Radio in a concert broadcast on Monday, 8 September, along with works by Korngold, Schreker, Kodály, Bittner, Strauss and others.[7] It may never be known whether Berg saw or heard the *Fasnachts-Symphonie*, let alone whether it had any influence on him. But the resemblance is just close enough to make it worthy of brief mention here.

The day after Kassowitz's broadcast, Flury wrote to Marx in Vienna to express regret that they hadn't managed to meet during his visit to the city. He went on to announce the birth of a son, Roger. In fact, Roger had already been born on 25 May 1930, only a day or so before Flury had left for Vienna.

[3] 'A.R.' in the *Reichspost*, 2 June 1930.

[4] Patricia Hall, 'The Progress of a Method: Berg's Tone Rows for "Lulu"', *The Musical Quarterly*, Vol. 71, No. 4, 1985, p. 518, and Hall, *A View of Berg's 'Lulu' through the Autograph Sources*, University of California Press, Berkeley, 1996, pp. 39–40.

[5] *Melos*, Vol. 9, No. 7, July 1930, p. 336.

[6] Communication from the Berg Foundation via the kind offices of Thomas Leibnitz of the Austrian National Library.

[7] Listed in *Radio Wien*, Vol. 6, No. 49, 5 September 1930, p. 34.

Ex. 6
(a)

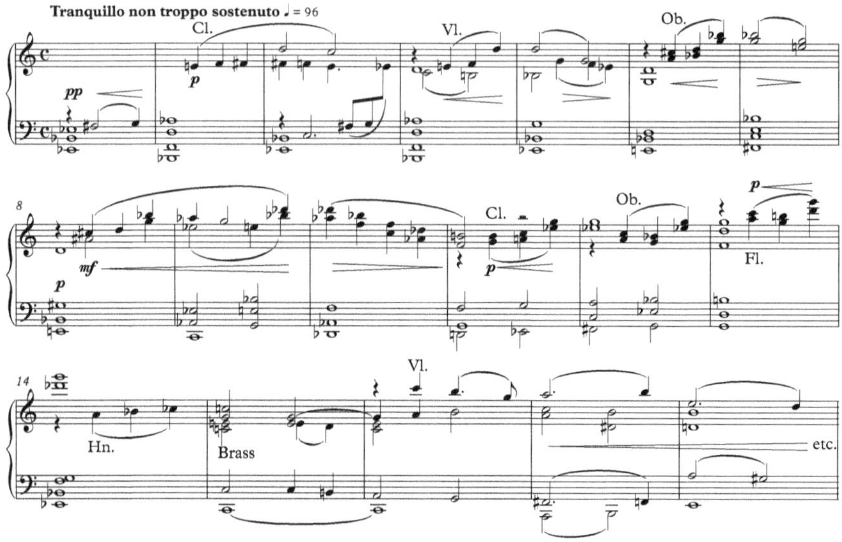

Having three girls and a boy, he wrote, 'brings much joy but is bound up with just as many worries'. He continued with an odd horticultural metaphor in a convoluted passage:

> I still go into raptures about young buds that are just opening up, even though I am aware that a mature woman is worth much more. I often curse the calamitous urge that threads its way through our lives, determining our fate, and yet that tender scent, those fabulous charms of untouched beauty, that sweet yearning and everything that is bound up with the urge to love, the ideal and symbol of life itself, that primeval mystery (the unconscious will of nature to reproduce) is also what drives us on to achieve in art and to endure. How would life be bearable otherwise? [...] the older I get, the more I'm beginning to appreciate the enjoyment of food and drink – things that I did not know earlier.[8]

It sounds like Flury's hedonistic colleagues in the Interlaken orchestra were having an impact on his worldview. But it was one shared by Marx, who wrote back three weeks later, on 29 September 1930, to assure Flury that he was

> completely correct. A man must seek emotional, adventurous, beautiful experiences in every form; he has to seek them. Ultimately, that's his right

[8] Letter from Flury to Marx, 9 September 1930.

(b)

> and his privilege [....] we need the indescribable magic that young women exude, their mysterious scent [...].

Presumably emboldened, Flury continued in a similar vein in his next extant letter to Marx, written on 2 March 1931:

> I would often like to step out of the fetters of the physical [...]. I feel entangled in a paradoxical problem that seems to have no way out [....] the whole world turns around this one, naïve type of love that I detest when I have enjoyed it, but seek time and again when I have got over my 'hangover'. There is no means of putting aside this drive radically, and you can't put some higher, holier power in its place. For 7 years [actually six-and-a-half] I have been subject to a kind of constraint through marriage. My wife does not comprehend that a man can also love other women. She believes in marriage as if it were a single, correct algebraic formula, a + b = c or x + y = z.[9]

Flury does not mention who 'b' or 'y' might have been – it would have been typical for him for there to have been several, meandering infatuations – but in his memoirs, he does admit that he was at this time already 'undyingly' in love with Rita Gosteli, one of his violin pupils in Solothurn[10] (there is also a 'Gavotte' for violin and piano from 1930 that is dedicated to her). In a much later letter to Rita's mother and stepfather, he admitted to having fallen in love with her right from the start, in 1928, when she was not yet fourteen (and he already over 30), though he assured them that he had undertaken nothing immoral at the time.[11] It seems he managed to keep his libido in check when teaching her, though that same letter to her parents admits that he had 'kissed and embraced' Rita in about 1931, when she was no longer his pupil. So perhaps she was one of those 'young buds' to which he referred. Several years later, Rita would become his second wife – although she was not the last teenager with whom he would become infatuated. By contrast, though, his later loves were well over the age of consent; and since in those later cases – by their own admission – Flury retained a respectful

[9] Letter from Flury to Marx, 2 March 1931.

[10] *Lebenserinnerungen*, *op. cit.*, p. 215.

[11] Flury to 'Mr & Mrs Frigerio-Gasparini', 18 April 1939.

distance, it is not unreasonable to believe his protestation of distant love in the case of the under-age Rita.

Flury's marriage was obviously falling apart. Perhaps his wandering eye was also intended (subconsciously or not) to bring on the inevitable. His resort to algebra, ostensibly to characterise his wife's rigidity, suggests more an attempt to objectify his own non-exclusive desires. But while his private life was disintegrating, his public profile was improving considerably. His old violin-teacher Heinrich Wydler at the Kantonsschule had retired the previous year, and Flury was keen to replace him. It would mean teaching older school students, up to the age when they leave for university, which was both better paid and more interesting to him than his job at the music school. Applying for the job meant going through a selection process in autumn 1930, performing and giving test-lessons before a committee. By Flury's own admission, none of the candidates played to the full satisfaction of the committee, but his pedagogical abilities and his competence as a composer made up for what he apparently still lacked on his instrument. The committee included Fritz Brun, the Bern music director and conductor of the City Orchestra, who was well acquainted with Flury's music and (according to Flury[12]) gave him much support in the appointment process. Other members of the committee, by contrast, were keen to appoint another leading Solothurn musician to the post, namely Max Kaempfert, who was already 59 years old, and had been running a private music school since arriving in the city in 1923.[13] A compromise was decided upon: the post was accordingly divided between the two men, though Kaempfert resigned only a few years later on account of ill health, at which point Flury was appointed to the full position.[14]

The following year, 1931, brought performances of the *Fasnachts-Symphonie* in Basel under Weingartner (on 14 March), and in Kobe in Japan (on 24 January) under Josef Reitinger-Laska, who had attended Flury's own performance of it at the Congress in Vienna in 1930 – it was Laska who first introduced the Austro-German orchestral repertoire, including the symphonies of Anton Bruckner, to Japan. But the biggest event of this year for Flury was the annual festival of the Swiss Musicians' Association, held in May 1931 in Solothurn. This was the centenary year of the Cäcilienverein in Solothurn, the main choral association of the city. Its conductor, Erich Schild, had married into an important Solothurn family, so he had intimate connections to people with money and influence. In order to celebrate its jubilee in an appropriate manner, the Cäcilienverein had invited the Swiss

[12] *Lebenserinnerungen, op. cit.*, p. 210. Also letter from Flury to his brother Adolf of 19 September 1930, in Flury's archives.

[13] Max Kaempfert, violinist, composer and conductor, born in 1871 in Berlin, studied violin with Charles Dancla in Paris, thereafter active in Munich and Frankfurt. Moved to Solothurn in 1923, and died there in 1941.

[14] *Cf. Lebenserinnerungen, op. cit.*, pp. 209–11.

Musicians' Association to hold its annual festival in Solothurn at the same time as its own festive concerts. The board of the Association apparently had reservations about this conjunction, fearing that they would merely be a useful marketing tool for the Cäcilienverein, and that their own concerts would be sidelined.[15] Nevertheless, they agreed to hold a joint festival, which accordingly took place from 2 to 4 May 1931. Its biggest event was the world premiere of a new oratorio by Arthur Honegger written especially for the Cäcilienverein: *Cris du monde*, which was performed on the afternoon of Sunday, 3 May, conducted by Schild, and with the Bern City Orchestra imported for the occasion. On that Sunday morning, Schild also conducted the same choir and orchestra in the premiere of a new work by Flury: a Mass in D minor, which he had written over the course of the previous year and which was his first religious choral work for a decade. He dedicated it to the memories of his father and of Richard Spiegel, his father's friend and his own early mentor. It requires a large chorus, four soloists and a medium-sized orchestra (strings, double woodwind, two trumpets, four horns, three trombones, tuba, timpani and harp). Although all eyes and ears will have been focused on the performance of Honegger's oratorio later in the day, the list of soloists for Flury's work makes it clear that it wasn't simply a sideshow. Besides the local soprano Paula Adam-Girard, these were Ilona Durigo (a Hungarian-Swiss contralto with an international career who premiered songs by Béla Bartók and Othmar Schoeck), Ernest Bauer and Felix Loeffel (tenor and bass respectively; both were preferred interpreters of Othmar Schoeck, too).

The Mass is a work that seems to take one step forwards and sometimes two or three back. It aims to be grandiose, but this ambition prompts Flury into a default, pseudo-ecclesiastical imitative choral style, the Neo-Classical allusions of which do not always sit well with his expanded harmonic vocabulary, even if his choral entries are at times a semitone apart instead of the traditional fourth or fifth. There are mitigating moments: the 'quoniam tu solus' passage in the Gloria is attractive (sung in octaves over slowly moving harmonies: Ex. 7), there is a charming, almost Griegian G major passage over a pedal point in the Sanctus, and then a somewhat startling *chinoiserie* in the orchestra at the 'Osanna' in the Benedictus that evokes Puccini's *Turandot*.

These all suggest that Flury's imagination soars when he puts off the shackles of his Catholicism and abandons his imitative counterpoint. The vocal writing is not always happy – some of the lines cannot be any easier to sing than those of his Kyrie of a decade before – and many of the choral melismas are neither wholly tonal nor completely atonal either. The score looks like the work of a proto-modernist trying to burst out, but held

[15] *Cf.* Schweizerischer Tonkünstlerverein (ed.), *Der Schweizerische Tonkünstlerverein im zweiten Vierteljahrhundert seines Bestehens. Festschrift zur Feier des 50jährigen Jubiläums 1900–1950*, Atlantis Verlag, Zurich, 1950, p. 40.

Ex. 7

back by the traditionalist Flury thought he wanted to be. Its shortcomings notwithstanding, Gottfried Kassowitz praised the work at length in his letters to Flury – more than would have been required by mere politeness: 'both spiritually and technically it is a great success', he wrote, further praising the 'expressive power' of 'both the lyrical sections and the mighty fugues'.[16] But in later years Flury had his own doubts about it, admitting in his memoirs that he 'did not really think much of it'.[17]

[16] Kassowitz to Flury, 15 August 1935, letter in Flury's archives.

[17] *Lebenserinnerungen*, *op. cit.*, p. 206.

The film of a reception held that weekend shows Flury and other Swiss composers such as Fritz Brun alongside major patrons like Werner Reinhart from Winterthur. The most prominent figure in the film is Honegger, for he was, after all, the best-known Swiss composer with an international reputation. But the festival was a major success for Flury. It also provided him with an opportunity to get to know the painter Cuno Amiet (1868–1961), who along with Friedrich Hodler was one of the leading Swiss artists of the early twentieth century. He had been born in Solothurn, and had his studio in the little village of Oschwand just across the cantonal border in

Flury in 1934, lithograph by his friend from the 'Künstlerstübli', Franz Bözinger

Bern. Several years later, Amiet painted several portraits of Flury (one of which is on the cover of this book).

Besides the allure that Honegger brought, there was another composer featured at the festival who, in his own way, would prove significant to the history of music in Switzerland: Erich Schmid (1907–2000), whose Sonatina for violin and piano, Op. 1, was performed on Monday, 4 May. Schmid was from Balsthal in Canton Solothurn and had attended the Kantonsschule in the mid-1920s, before Flury was appointed there. He had taken lessons with Max Kaempfert and Erich Schild before going to study in Frankfurt. In 1930, Schmid moved to Berlin to study with Arnold Schoenberg. The Sonatina was written shortly before Schmid's lessons with Schoenberg and is not yet dodecaphonic, but its free atonality was enough to have him branded the 'enfant terrible' of the Festival by the *Bund* in Bern and to prompt laughter during its performance.[18] Schmid's subsequent music was no better received in Switzerland, so he abandoned composition and concentrated on conducting (in which field he played a major role on the Swiss scene after the Second World War). If Flury had attended the chamber concert on 4 May – as he probably did – then he might well have suspected that Schmid's work was the shape of things to come. But his encounters with Modernism over the coming years would only cause him to retreat further into his self-appointed bastion of Romanticism.

It seems for the moment, however, that Flury was uncertain as to where his compositional future lay. Besides those strange moments in the Mass when a Modernist seems to want to break out, he also kept his 'popular' side ticking over: 1931 saw the composition of his *Viennese Waltz* for orchestra No. 1, dedicated to Eduard Favre of the Interlaken orchestra, which is a deliciously tuneful and unarguably conservative waltz. But then there are five short Preludes for piano from this year that are harmonically more adventurous once again. They also feature a 'Valse' (the French spelling is deliberate: Flury uses the German term 'Wienerwalzer' for his Viennese pieces). It, too, is tuneful – but the harmonies keep slipping out of one's grasp, and the melody itself now and then veers off, as if forgetting the rules of tonality. It ends with a seventh chord on E flat that sounds uncertain as to whether it has indeed arrived or not. It offers fascinating proof that the gap between Flury and the Modernism of Schmid and Schoenberg was not so vast after all. Perhaps it was this potential proximity that made him all the warier of it.

The success of his *Fasnachts-Symphonie* in Basel and elsewhere, the grand event that was the world premiere of his Mass and his confirmation as a teacher at the Kantonsschule with all the financial security it brought meant that Flury could approach his 35th birthday with no little satisfaction at his growing reputation. But this public recognition was now paired with private

[18] *Cf.* Kurt von Fischer, *Erich Schmid*, Hug, Zurich, 1992, pp. 16 and 39–40.

chaos. In early late 1931 or early 1932 – the precise date is not recorded – Flury's wife decided she had had enough. Whether something specific had happened to prompt her is not known. And although his letters to Marx and others have survived to confirm his wandering eye and his indiscretion, the blame may not be his alone: his wife remains a blank slate. There is rarely a wholly innocent party when two people find that continued coexistence is no longer possible. But regardless of who might have done or said what to whom, the fact remains that Richard arrived home from teaching one lunchtime to find no one in their apartment. Lily had gathered her four children together, packed her bags and boarded a train. It is not even sure that she bothered to buy a ticket. According to family lore, she was asked by the train conductor where she was going. She told him she was going to start a new life and wanted to go to Locarno. 'Lugano is a nicer place', he is supposed to have replied, 'Why not go there instead?'. 'Alright', said Lily, and so she bought a ticket for Lugano and, once there, took a room for her and the children in the Hotel Pestalozzi, not far from the lake and across the road from the main park (chosen, no doubt, for the opportunities it gave for the children to play). She stayed there for two months until she had found her feet and was able to move into her own place – all at Richard's expense for the moment. She would never go back to live in Solothurn again.

13
Life without Lily

> I would have to tell you a long, tragic story, profound, beautiful and ugly, full of intimate tenderness and brutality all at the same time, as changeable and contrary as life itself and as the women who for the large part determine our lives for us. The result is this: my wife is living with her [*sic*] 4 children in Lugano (Canton Ticino), separated from me as we have agreed. It seemed to be the only way out for both parties, because I refused a divorce on account of the children and because I still love my wife and the children and because I can't condemn our almost 8 years of marriage despite all the misery and because the suffering we have borne together has bound me closer to my wife than a so-called 'happy marriage' would have been able to.
>
> I'm now living with my aunt again, like I used to, I visit my family now and then and otherwise feel very lonely. [...]
>
> Most of all I'd like to come to Vienna for good, even as a boot-polisher in these bad times [...].

Thus wrote Flury to Joseph Marx on 17 May 1932. But he was better off in Switzerland. Only three days after Flury's letter, Engelbert Dollfuss assumed the Chancellorship in Austria, and within a few months he would seize power in a *coup d'état* and turn Austria into a one-party fascist state following Mussolini's example in Italy. Like everywhere else, Switzerland was suffering under the Great Depression, but its impact remained relatively mild. In 1932 unemployment was still rising, but even at its peak in about 1936 it was still only a little over six per cent. By contrast, unemployment in Austria reached almost 22 per cent at this time. Viennese composers were financially no less precarious than other professions in Austria unless, like Marx, they had a permanent teaching or conducting post. Alban Berg was one of the most successful of contemporary composers – his *Wozzeck* had brought him fame and a lot of money – but his correspondence from the time makes it clear he was still short of cash, especially after the Nazis banned his works and Germany fell away as a source of royalties.[1] (Richard Strauss was also resident in Vienna throughout the 1930s, but remained ever the exception to the rule, as the international earning power of his operas and orchestral works never diminished.)

[1] *Cf.*, for example, Herwig Knaus and Wilhelm Sinkovicz, *Alban Berg. Zeitumstände – Lebenslinien*, Residenz, Vienna, 2008, pp. 391–95.

From left to right: Lily, Flury, unknown, on Monte San Salvatore above Lugano, 1934

Flury's letter to Marx makes it evident that he and Lily had found some arrangement to keep a semblance of 'family' alive, albeit on a part-time basis. But there seems to be no indication of when she let him know where she had gone – although soon enough, one imagines, for him to send the money for her hotel bill (as he did). Over the next few years, Flury would generally spend his summers in Lugano, visiting his wife and children. They remained married, though Flury's above claim to Marx that he refused divorce 'on account of the children' is something of a simplification. It seems it suited both him and Lily for the moment; divorce only became necessary later, when he wanted to marry again, and in any case he continued paying maintenance until Lily herself remarried in the late 1940s. But absence seems not to have made the heart grow any fonder. According to their eldest daughter, Verena, whenever Richard came to visit them in Lugano, he and Lily would start arguing even before they had left the train station. It must have been distressing beyond belief for the children.

Flury's desire to spend as much holiday time as possible with the children was complicated in this first year of their absence by what was otherwise a heartening sign of his increasing reputation, namely a commission for a new *Festspiel*. This time it was to commemorate the centenary of the Swiss National Gymnastics Association, to be held in Aarau in the summer of 1932, and for which his friend the poet Bernhard Moser (1897–1959) wrote the libretto. Their earliest surviving correspondence dates from 1929, but they had known each other for several years, having first met when Flury was playing in his regimental band over a decade before.[2] Moser came originally from Hägendorf in the easternmost part of Canton Solothurn and earned his living as the head of the music collection at the Basel University Library. But his main calling, he felt, was as a poet and dramatist. And although today he is forgotten outside the confines of Solothurn, he enjoyed a degree of success in his lifetime with works in both High German and Swiss dialect. His text for the Aarau Gymnastics Festival is in both languages. He wrote in the *Zürcher Illustrierte* at the time that the subject of the *Festspiel* had been prescribed by the festival committee. The first act celebrates the Unspunnen Festival of 1808 – a kind of Swiss national proto-Olympics featuring various sports from wrestling to shot-putting and even including a competition for alphorn players. The second act was to commemorate the first-ever Gymnastics Festival, held in Aarau in 1832; and the third and final act was dedicated to 'the youth of today'.[3] Regrettably, no correspondence between Flury and Moser about their collaboration on the *Festspiel* has survived; indeed, since Moser was based in nearby Basel, perhaps they met whenever there was anything to discuss or simply rang each other on the phone. But because Moser had been given precise instructions for the work that also constrained Flury's role in it, perhaps there wasn't really much to discuss anyway.

Flury wrote 29 musical numbers for this work, which was entitled *Schweizer Turner* ('Swiss gymnasts'). It would be impossible to perform this or Flury's other *Festspiele* today, for their subject-matter is so dated. *Schweizer Turner* is full of hearty, pious, patriotic Swiss men singing of freedom and the glories of physical exertion and of the Swiss Alps. It also features Swiss women, beavering away in the kitchen for their men while the latter are busy with their hearty, manly exertions out in the countryside; then there are Swiss girls aspiring to grow up to have the privilege of beavering in the kitchen while their men are out being manly; and Swiss boys all aspiring to become hearty, manly men. On the positive side, this is actually all terribly innocent when compared to the superficially similar but dreadfully fascist dross that would soon be popular on the northern side of the border. And while Flury's music is necessarily straightforward and popular, given that the performers were largely amateur, there are still some charming numbers, such as the 'Aufmarsch der Kadetten' featuring fifes, drums and trumpets, or the yodelling passages that occur in certain of the numbers.

Flury himself wasn't too happy with his *Schweizer Turner*, however, because the musical numbers were performed as a backdrop to gymnastic exercises that held the attention of the audience. These exercises were not coordinated to begin and end precisely with the music, meaning that they

[2] *Cf.* Bernhard Moser, 'Offener Brief an Richard Flury zum 60. Geburtstag' in *Oltener Tagblatt*, undated newspaper clipping in Flury's archives, presumably from March 1956.

[3] Bernhard Moser, 'Meine "Schweizer Turner"', *Zürcher Illustrierte* 1932, No. 29, p. 917.

Poster for the Swiss National Gymnastics Festival of 1932

repeatedly prompted applause in the middle of the latter, drowning it out completely. And Flury was well aware of the limitations of *Festspiele* in general:

> Even though these occasional *Festspiele* carried my name out far and wide, I have to regard them as thankless tasks because they were one-day wonders with a brief existence, and their texts were only relevant for a specific event [....] *Festspiele* have to appeal to broader circles, so when writing them I always had to make compromises between a popular style and the free flow of my imagination. The biggest disadvantage of my festival performances lay in the fact that I always had to forgo having a professional orchestra and the choirs were usually mediocre or hadn't even been prepared properly [...].[4]

All in all, though, the *Schweizer Turner* is a fine utilitarian piece. On further inspection, it strikes one as a shame that Flury was apparently never asked to write film music. Had there been a Swiss 'GPO Film Unit' such as employed the young Benjamin Britten in these years, Flury would have been an ideal choice for its house composer. But the Swiss film industry would not take off for a few years yet. And he seems never to have considered reusing any of his *Schweizer Turner* music either. He was too busy composing new things.

It is not known how often Flury managed to visit his children in Lugano in these initial months of the separation, given that the *Schweizer Turner* will have occupied much of his summer. With the absence of any correspondence between him and his first wife, detailed information appears to be lacking altogether. Flury writes in his memoirs of having spent three months every year in Lugano,[5] and since the school summer holidays are not much over a month long, it seems he must have visited whenever he could at other times.

Judging from Flury's extant (later) letters to his daughter Eva and the reminiscences of his family, he made a concerted effort to play an active role in the lives of his children beyond providing financial support, despite their geographical distance. The only story handed down about him in his first family, however, is of how he once nearly set himself on fire when lighting the candles on the Christmas tree. His first wife told the story gleefully to her grandchildren into her old age. Whether he had found it as funny, or whether it brought her a degree of schadenfreude, remains a matter of speculation.

Richard's first opera, *Eine florentinische Tragödie*, was scheduled for new performances at the Solothurn Theatre in the 1932–33 season. Perhaps it was this prospect, coupled with his renewed experience of musico-dramatics in Aarau, that prompted him to start work on a new opera, *Die helle Nacht*. It was composed – according to Flury's own work catalogue – partly in

[4] *Lebenserinnerungen*, *op. cit.*, p. 202.

[5] *Ibid.*, p. 215.

Richard and Dino Ghisalberti with (left to right) Roger, Verena, Giovanna and Eva in Lugano in 1934

Solothurn, partly in the Lugano suburb of Viganello, where he finished the piano score on 8 October 1932 (the printed vocal score gives 'La Santa' as its place of completion, which is the name of a street and of a pension in Viganello). It is a setting of a play of the same name by Paul Zifferer, published in Berlin in 1912 (Zifferer calls it a 'Gedicht', a 'poem', though it is in fact a drama). Zifferer (1879–1929) was a well-connected Viennese journalist and writer in his day. He edited the cultural section of the *Neue freie Presse* in Vienna before and during the First World War and was close to Hugo von Hofmannsthal, whose works he helped to publicise in France, and whom he even accompanied on a trip to North Africa in 1925.[6] Since Flury's 'librettist' was already dead, there is naturally no correspondence to explain how the opera came about. It is not known how Flury came across Zifferer's work in the first place (though it was presumably through Marx or Kassowitz), nor is there any record of why he decided to set the drama to music. His choice of text also demonstrates a certain insouciance – laudable in itself – towards his career prospects as an opera composer. At the time he sketched the opera, in mid-1932, he might well have had hopes of its being performed abroad. But by the time he set about orchestrating it (which took until 1935) he will have known that there was no hope that it

[6] *Cf.* W. E. Yates, review of Hilde Burger (ed.), *Hugo von Hofmannsthal: Paul Zifferer: Briefwechsel*, *The Modern Language Review*, Vol. 79, No. 4 (October 1984), p. 987.

might be performed in Germany, because Zifferer had been Jewish. Already during the First World War, Zifferer had been the victim of vicious attacks in the Austrian press that linked his Jewish descent with his Francophile tendencies and his refusal to kowtow to the jingoistic tenor of the times.[7] Although one cannot be sure just how much Flury knew about this vitriol, his close contact with Vienna through Marx and Kassowitz means he cannot have been unaware of Zifferer's controversial status in right-wing circles.

Flury made numerous cuts in Zifferer's text and divided it into two acts, though without altering its substance. The plot of *Die helle Nacht* is as follows. It is Paris in 1514, on the night after Princess Mary Tudor has married the aging King Louis XII of France. The main character is a world-weary doctor whose only delight in life is his wife, Solange. He is obsessed with controlling her every movement because of a single night she spent away from him several years before. Here, Flury brings his first act to a close. The second opens with a crowd bringing the corpse of a knight to the doctor, for purposes of dissection. But once alone with him, the doctor realises that the man is still alive. He uses his arts to revive him, and they talk. The knight is a hedonist and the complete opposite of the cynical doctor. The doctor slowly realises that the knight had slept with Solange several years previously, on that night when she had been away from him. He resolves on revenge. He poisons the knight, who collapses, unconscious. But the doctor suddenly realises that the act of murder will not set his mind free, so hurriedly administers an antidote and sends the knight on his way. Solange returns; the doctor's immediate intention is to punish her for her infidelity, now long past. But he relents and says nothing of what he knows, for he has come to a realisation that his obsessive questions about the past have prevented him from achieving true happiness in the present. As the morning bells of Notre Dame sound, they exit the stage together (Ex. 8).

In a brief obituary of Zifferer in 1929, *The Modern Language Journal* had noted that *Die helle Nacht* had been 'a great stage success',[8] though since it enjoyed neither a prolonged stage career nor any edition beyond its first, that was perhaps an exaggeration. Given that the drama is effective, not long (that first and only edition runs to 100 pages), requires only a few characters and seems well suited to operatic treatment (the closing scene with the bells of Notre Dame almost cries out for music), it is surprising that no one among Zifferer's Viennese contemporaries seems to have thought of setting it to music. After all, plots of jealously and infidelity in the Renaissance were very popular at the time: witness Korngold's *Violanta*, Schillings' *Mona Lisa*, Schreker's *Die Gezeichneten*, Zemlinsky's *Eine florentinische Tragödie*, etc. Zifferer's verse does not have the polish of a Hofmannsthal, but as literature it is much better than many libretti of the day.

[7] *Cf.*, for example, Anon., 'Paul Zifferer und der Kosmopolitanismus', *Ostdeutsche Rundschau*, 20 November 1917.

[8] Anon., 'Foreign Notes', *The Modern Language Journal*, Vol. 14, No. 1 (October 1929), p. 66.

Ex. 8

Solange
mf
Wie selt - sam fremd Ihr heu - te blickt, als hät - tet Ihr mich
mf
3
f
nie ge - schaut.
f
Arzt
p
(lässt den Arm schlaff herunterfallen
und schüttelt traurig den Kopf)
Ei - tel Gau - kel - spiel wie man durch's
(mit plötzlichem
Entschluss)
Le - ben pil - gert Hand in Hand und hält doch jeder un - ver wandt ein süss Ge - heim-nis fest,
pp

(mit Frau Solange ab.)
ein süss Ge - heim - nis. Bis in den Tod.
Die Glocken von Notre Dame rufen zur Frühmesse.
Glocken
cresc. poco a poco
rall.

The subject-matter of *Die helle Nacht* is not far removed from that of Flury's first opera. Here, too, there is a love triangle and an adulterous wife (but at least no one here is killed to bring about a happy end). In spite of Flury's seeming preoccupation with adulterous women, there is no proof that this was a result of any such behaviour by his own wife. One could claim that he might be working through his own adulterous desires by projecting them onto his operatic (anti-) heroines, but such an assertion would mean drawing a conclusion from an assumption based on a supposition. (According to a later confession on his part, Flury remained now – and later – 'adulterous' only in thought, never in deed.[9]) But the topic of 'marriage' and what constitutes a happy one certainly seems to have been uppermost in his mind during these years of his own unhappy union. Regardless of what might have triggered his choice of libretto, what one can say unequivocally is that the music of *Die helle Nacht* is a big step forward from his first opera. The idioms of the Italian and German composers of *verismo* and proto-Expressionism seem to have come naturally to him and he was also able to draw on his experiences of staging his *Eine florentinische Tragödie*. Composing for opera seems to have freed Flury to indulge in the more advanced harmonies that are hitherto found *in ovo* in passages of his First String Quartet and in his occasional piano pieces. The opening of the Second Act, for example, is atonal; and this music returns later in extended form, after the doctor administers the antidote to the knight. The vocal parts are written in a declamatory style similar to that of *Eine florentinische Tragödie*, and Flury later admitted in a letter to Marx that *Die helle Nacht* perhaps lacks the necessary 'lyrical breadth'.[10] Although there are times when one indeed wishes that the music were more expansive, there are several beautiful *arioso* passages in this opera that offer the kind of respite absent from *Eine florentinische Tragödie*, such as when the knight recalls his brief affair with Solange. The contrast between the revels taking place out on the streets and the human drama of betrayal and forgiveness is cleverly managed – Flury had already experimented with something similar in his *Fasnachts-Symphonie*. And there is an especially effective musico-dramatic moment when the doctor realises the truth about the knight and so goes to lock the doors and windows in order to wreak his revenge, unheard to the world. The close, when the doctor and Solange depart to the sound of the early morning bells, is more luscious in its harmonies than almost anything Flury had yet written. *Die helle Nacht* is through-composed, with no discernible attempt at a leitmotif technique (again, like his *Eine florentinische Tragödie*), although the occasional return of music already heard ensures a sense of unity, and the action is more or less framed by an offstage aria from one of the unseen revellers.

[9] Flury told his son in later years that his physical relationships had been confined to his two wives.

[10] Letter from Flury to Marx of 3 July 1935, after the first performance of the work.

Flury organised a subscription over the coming months to get enough money together to publish the vocal score. He had neglected to have the vocal score published for *Eine florentinische Tragödie*, but he must have realised that being able to send a printed piano reduction to assorted theatres was the only way to have a chance at getting performances (perhaps Kassowitz had told him how Berg had done so with *Wozzeck* a decade earlier – although in that case Alma Mahler had provided the necessary funds). The vocal score of *Die helle Nacht* was accordingly published by Hug in autumn 1934, and Flury set about distributing it everywhere he could. But getting theatres to put on his new opera proved more difficult than he had ever imagined. 'To tell of the fortunes and the wanderings that *Die helle Nacht* endured with Swiss theatre directors, opera dramaturges and conductors would mean writing an "odyssey"', he noted in his memoirs over a decade later.[11] He wrote to his brother on 26 August 1934 that Kassowitz was going to conduct his opera in the theatre of Baden (outside Vienna) in the coming year – but the little correspondence surviving between Flury and Kassowitz from this time makes no mention of any such promise. Flury succeeded in getting it on the season programme for the Solothurn opera in the 1934–35 season, but it was dropped before rehearsals began. Felix Weingartner had meanwhile moved back to the Vienna State Opera and showed an interest in the work, although he asked Flury to submit it in another two years – by which time Weingartner had left Vienna again.[12] The conductor Christoph Lertz managed to programme a concert performance with the Bern City Orchestra and assorted soloists, which was broadcast from the Radio Bern studio on 17 May 1935. This performance was the only one it has ever had, and the recording – which was broadcast more than once – has not survived. Moreover, because the opera received only a radio broadcast, the reviews were perfunctory, though generally positive.[13] Most Swiss composers of Flury's generation composed opera, though none had any lasting success – with the notable exception of Othmar Schoeck with *Penthesilea*, and not even this work was very successful during Schoeck's lifetime. If anything, the main Swiss theatres have for several decades seemed even less keen to stage Swiss operas than have theatres abroad. But when *Die helle Nacht* is rediscovered – as it surely will be – then it will be revealed as one of the best examples of the genre to have been composed in Switzerland in the first half of the twentieth century.

Flury's correspondence in the years after his separation in 1932 is notable in making little reference to the turbulent events happening out in the world. Only two months after Hitler's assumption of power in January 1933 – and five days after the German Reichstag voted itself out of existence with the

[11] *Lebenserinnerungen*, *op. cit.*, p. 204.

[12] *Ibid.*, p. 204.

[13] There are assorted press clippings in Flury's archives, undated but clearly from late May 1935, from newspapers including *Der Bund* in Bern and the *Basler Nachrichten*.

Nazi 'Enabling Act' of 24 March 1933 – Flury wrote to Joseph Marx to tell him about a forthcoming radio broadcast of *Eine florentinische Tragödie* in Solothurn. He makes no mention of the tumultuous events happening elsewhere – but then Marx, too, ignores politics in their correspondence of the mid-1930s.

Hitler's seizure of power in Germany was mirrored by the success of the Austro-fascists, who banned all elections the following May and henceforth allied themselves with Mussolini. In July 1934, the Austrian chancellor Dollfuss was assassinated by the Nazis, after which his right-hand man Kurt Schuschnigg became the *de facto* dictator of Austria until Hitler annexed the country in March 1938. Any notion that the music world might be spared major changes must have been quickly dispelled. Arnold Schoenberg lost his professorship in Berlin in 1933, at which he emigrated first to France and then to the USA. Alban Berg's music was soon effectively banned in Nazi Germany, although Erich Kleiber managed to premiere the *Lulu Suite* in Berlin on 30 November 1934; Kleiber then resigned his position and left Germany. In the same week as that concert, a public spat began between Wilhelm Furtwängler and Joseph Goebbels that led to Furtwängler's enforced resignation from all his posts, including that of chief conductor of the Berlin Philharmonic. And half-a-year later, in June 1935 (a month after the first broadcast of Flury's *Die helle Nacht*), the premiere of Richard Strauss' opera *Die schweigsame Frau* resulted in even Strauss becoming temporarily *non grata* on account of his having worked with a Jewish librettist, Stefan Zweig. By this time, a host of major writers, musicians and scientists had left Germany to escape the Nazis and headed for Switzerland, Britain, North and South America, South Africa, even Australasia. Many – such as Bruno Walter and Otto Klemperer – left because they were Jewish and had lost all career prospects. Some left for political or personal reasons, Thomas Mann, Paul Hindemith and Bertolt Brecht among them. Others, such as Kurt Weill, were unpalatable to the Nazis because they were both Jewish and left-wing. When the Germans invaded Austria and Czechoslovakia in 1938 and 1939, yet more people were forced to flee.

This exodus was both a human tragedy and also the most significant event ever to have occurred in the artistic and scientific life of central Europe. There was no precedent in the modern era for a leading nation state depriving itself willingly of so many of its finest minds – and yet there is not a syllable on this upheaval in Flury's correspondence. With hindsight, this omission may seem astonishing, but it should be remembered that almost everyone around him, in Switzerland and abroad, assumed that life would sooner or later return to 'normal'. And there had already been so much economic and political turbulence in central Europe since the end of the First World War that 'normal' was already a very broad category. Hindemith was only one of many who assumed that he would find a *modus vivendi* with the new regime in Germany; Alban Berg toyed with the idea of taking up a professorship in Berlin even after his friend and former teacher Schoenberg had been sacked there (in the end, he was not offered a job).[14] Given that few musicians earned high salaries, most of them – like Flury or Berg – were muddling by, too concerned about trying to pay the bills to worry much about politics. Even Gottfried Kassowitz's letters to Flury are mostly about work. He, too, mentions nothing of attempted Nazi coups, the Austro-fascists, the persecution of political opponents and the reintroduction of the death penalty in Austria; instead, he complains about the intrigues among the Viennese music fraternity and the parlous economic state of musicians in general, himself in particular. He lost his job as Kapellmeister in Baden in late 1936 when it was temporarily abolished to save money and the second concert-master was assigned his tasks. When the economic situation deteriorated further in 1937 and it transpired that the theatre could function without him, Kassowitz's job was cancelled permanently, and he had to get by with *ad hoc* work.

Flury had the good fortune to live in Switzerland, which was increasingly alone in central Europe as an island of peace and liberality. But his main worries were still about money. In mid-1934, he wrote to Marx that he was earning so little that he was unable to get to Lugano as often as he wanted to see his children. At least his productivity as a composer seems to have increased after his separation. All the sources suggest that he truly missed his children, but given that his output accelerated, perhaps he was finding that spending his evenings alone was conducive to work: without toddlers around him, without marital squabbles, but with his aunt there to see to his everyday needs such as cooking and washing. He wrote his First Violin Concerto in 1933, and conducted the premiere that summer in Interlaken, with Luigi Valerio accompanied by the Kurorchester. It has some sumptuous, one might say Korngoldian, moments, but comes across as slightly forced. It feels somewhat formless, perhaps because its thematic material, for all its loveliness, is not quite distinguished enough to sustain interest over its considerable length (the first movement alone, in the currently available recording, lasts almost twenty minutes). It feels as though Flury is straining to write a big Romantic concerto in the mould of Brahms and Bruch, and the grittiness of *Die helle Nacht* has evaporated. But soon he was to write for the stage again – and would be forced to keep his 'grittiness' in check, as he was now commissioned to write yet another *Festspiel*. This time it was for the Bernische Landwirtschafts-, Industrie- und Gewerbe-Ausstellung ('Bernese Agricultural, Industry and Commerce Exhibition') – or LIGA, as it was known – of 1935.

This exhibition was held in August and September in Zollikofen, a little town to the north of the city of Bern. Flury's libretto was by one Hans

[14] *Cf.* my *Lies and Epiphanies: Composers and their Inspiration from Wagner to Berg*, University of Rochester Press, Rochester, 2014, p. 73.

Zulliger (1893–1965), who acquired an international reputation as a child psychologist and was active as a writer and poet, especially in Bernese dialect. His *Festspiel* for the LIGA was entitled *Der Scholle treu* – 'Faithful to the clods [of earth]' – and reading it makes one wish he had stuck to child psychology. As was typical of the genre, it is without any real narrative thread, but is instead a series of scenes that elucidate the significance of the land to the Swiss, and how 'the blessings of work are given only to those who stay faithful to the earth' (thus the *Berner Tagblatt* in its summary).[15] Speculators try to get the Swiss peasants to sell their land (the text even features a 'Dance and chorus around the Golden Calf'), but are thwarted just in time, and the blessed peasants remain – as the title states – faithful to their clods, and happy for it. The text is partly in Bernese dialect, partly in High German, and is even more a product of the times than was Moser's libretto for the Gymnasts' centenary in 1932. These were the years when the fascists abroad were stressing their bonds of blood and earth, so to counter their influence there was a concurrent, not dissimilar, trend in official Swiss art in the 1930s. By stressing the importance of the (Swiss) Alps, cows, lakes and pink sunsets, it was hoped to forge a sense of national pride to keep the country distant from the ideologies that were dominant to the north, south and east of the country. The subject-matter of *Der Scholle treu* is superficially very close to Nazi art in its ghastly obsession with the soil. But the differences are as important, for nowhere here is there any call for a 'leader' to save the people from chaos (such as is found in Nazi cantatas), nor is anyone demonised, singly or collectively. There are choruses for happy huntsmen and for jolly Swiss peasants mowing their fields, there's a hymn to Bern itself, and there's yodelling again (as in the 1932 *Festspiel*). But apart from the naughty speculators, everyone in it comes across as rather nice and decent, and the overall impression is of a slightly embarrassing quaintness. It is astonishing that Flury somehow managed to compose music for this nonsense that is actually attractive. He couched it in a popular, occasionally neo-Griegian idiom. There were ten performances of *Der Scholle treu* during the LIGA, starting on 31 August and continuing until 29 September. They were all sold out, despite the hall being big enough to seat 2,000 people at a time. Some 800 performers were involved, including a host of male, female and mixed choruses and gymnastics associations from around Canton Bern; they were accompanied by the Bern City Band under the baton of one Ernst Ruprecht, who was a 'Music director' in Zollikofen itself. Real horses onstage helped to provide some extra local colour, though surviving photos of the scene show that the singers had to tread carefully across the boards. Being 'faithful to the clods' doesn't mean you want to step in them.

Flury received the commission for *Der Scholle treu* at the time that he was busy scoring *Die helle Nacht*, and although he wanted the money for

[15] Review of *Der Scholle treu* by '-nn-' in the *Berner Tagblatt*; undated clipping in Flury's archives.

Cover picture for the libretto of Flury's Festspiel Der Scholle treu, *summer 1935*

Scene photo from Der Scholle treu, *with horses and (below) happy Swiss peasants*

the commission (and the publicity it would bring), he was sensible enough to realise that he could not possibly do both at the same time. He therefore asked Eduard Favre, his old friend from the Kurorchester in Interlaken, for help. Favre was no longer employed in Interlaken and was living out his final years in Lausanne on very little money. So he agreed both to copy out the orchestral parts for the opera and to score Flury's draft for *Der Scholle treu* for the required wind and brass band. Flury's real hopes lay in his opera, whereas *Der Scholle treu* was another of those 'one-day wonders' that would never be performed again. He was paid 2,000 francs for *Der Scholle treu*, and gave half to Favre.

Der Scholle treu was reviewed by all the main papers, with Flury's tuneful music praised by all of them – though, of course, newspapers do not as a rule send their most discerning music critics to agricultural exhibitions.[16] The success of *Der Scholle treu* must have pleased him, but it perhaps helped to cement a picture of him as a composer of 'lighter' music. And although there is no proof of it, he must surely have been stung by the irony that *Der Scholle treu* was covered so widely and so positively, whereas his opera, which was in every way the superior work, had been neither staged nor even properly acknowledged.

[16] Flury's archives have a host of press clippings with reviews of *Der Scholle treu*, from the *National-Zeitung* in Basel to the *Berner Tagblatt*, the *Tribune de Genève*, the *Neue Zürcher Zeitung* and others. Everyone seems to have liked the work.

14
Enter Rita

'The problem of woman has retreated somewhat into the background for me', Flury wrote to Marx on 20 June 1934. This state of affairs did not last for long. In 1935 he came into contact with his former pupil Rita Gosteli, who was living in Bern and studying the violin at the Conservatoire there. He was now separated from his wife, with no clear prospect of reconciliation (although he still spent several weeks a year with her in Canton Ticino). His mother died on 1 March 1935, and this confrontation with the hard facts of mortality might well have encouraged him to re-evaluate with whom, and in what circumstances, he intended spending the rest of his own life. Or perhaps a couple of months in the Ticino every year were simply inadequate to the needs of his hormones. Whatever his reasons, he now began to court Rita, and his pursuit of her would occupy the next four years of his life.

Rita's side of the correspondence has not survived, and Flury's extant letters start only in April 1936 – a year after he began his attempts to establish a relationship with her. There are over three dozen surviving letters from him to her from now until their marriage in September 1939, some dated, some not. They document a relationship characterised by stark mood-swings as Flury sees his feelings reciprocated, rejected and then reciprocated again. He was not the only man wooing Rita. In one letter – apparently from 1936 – he complains how 'This business with E is crazy for me, I'm suffering incredibly because of it. You may not write to him again'; in another undated letter, probably from about the same time, he tells her: 'Your heart belongs to another. I won't complain about that now' – though he goes on to complain about it for another one-and-a-half pages (the identity of 'E' remains unknown). In late October 1936, his competition is now one 'Heinz Müller', and Flury writes to Rita to tell her he that loves her so much he is ready to give her up if it makes her happy – though he adds that he's going to write a violin sonata for her. Five days later, he writes to tell her that he has visited her mother, confessed his love for her daughter, and then adds reproachfully '*I don't believe* [underlined] that you were only in Müller's room three times and that you never kissed. I can forgive you this [...]'. On another occasion he complains about a 'Rinaldo' who has supposedly wormed his way into Rita's affections. When Rita tells him on the phone she is going dancing at the Metropol (presumably the hotel of that name in Bern[1]) he is consumed by jealousy and cannot sleep that night. She is 'unreliable', he tells her, and one of his letters asks a question, though – tellingly – without a question mark at the close: 'And where did you sleep from Saturday to Sunday'. He repeatedly tells her how much he loves her, then apologises for his intense jealousy, and has crises of conscience about his children in the Ticino. His letters are dotted with hearts in red pencil, the initials 'R' twice entwined in them. The violin sonata he wrote for her – his fourth – also offers compelling proof of his feelings. The violin almost never stops playing – the first movement alone has only two-and-a-half bars of rests in a total of 295 bars. The piano does nothing but accompany, there is an over-use of sequence, and one has the feeling that Flury is trying his hardest to be ecstatic. The result sounds forced, and the work as a whole is simply not very successful.

In view of Rita's position, it seems perfectly natural that she should have been hesitant about committing herself to her former teacher. What from Flury's perspective seemed like her toying with him was probably only a clash of expectations. She was twenty when Flury began his serious endeavours to woo her, and he was nearly twice her age. She was a student, surrounded by others her own age, among whom there were several young men as keen to pursue her as was Flury. Flury had a failed marriage behind him and wanted certainty and commitment; she was much younger and wanted fun. What's more, Flury spent a good part of his holidays throughout the year in Lugano with the woman to whom he was still legally married. Although he would assure Rita that his heart belonged to her alone, it cannot have comforted her that he was not yet contemplating divorce and was perhaps, for all she knew, discharging his physical obligations in the marital bed whenever he returned to Canton Ticino. (Although Flury was a Catholic, his faith does not seem to have been a prime hindrance in his hesitation to bring his marriage to an end.) In an undated letter to Rita from around late 1938 he mentions that Lily knows of Rita's existence and of his feelings for her, and that it makes things awkward when he visits her in Lugano. And how could it not? Lily's feelings in the matter are not known, but since she kept receiving Flury into her home during his holidays, and since he had until now refused divorce, she must have assumed that he was now being openly adulterous and living out his fantasy of playing the field. Although Flury for his part was torn between his desire for Rita, his love for his children and – it seems – residual feelings for his wife, he apparently did not hide his situation from either woman. 'I don't know what to do. I often pray through half the night to try and find out what is right. [...] I can only attain happiness by causing unhappiness to others, and yet I can't give up your love', he wrote in despair to Rita in a letter dated only '28.II' (probably 1938, but possibly the year before or after). Rita's relationship with Flury

[1] There was a popular hotel/restaurant of that name in Solothurn, too, near the main station; but since Rita was mostly in Bern, it was probably the 'other' Metropol to which she referred.

Rita after performing Beethoven's Romances *under Richard, 3 February 1938*

also opened up professional opportunities for her; thus she performed Beethoven's two *Romances* for violin and orchestra under Flury's direction in a concert on 3 February 1938 to celebrate the twentieth anniversary of the Solothurn Orchestra.

It wasn't only Flury's emotional life that was in turmoil. In 1936, the same year that he was so desperately pursuing Rita, his professional situation became suddenly more complicated when his colleague and rival Erich Schild founded the Solothurn Chamber Orchestra.[2] According to Alban Roetschi,[3] Flury was devastated by the news, as the pool of musicians available in Solothurn was small, and he feared Schild would poach all his best players. In time they managed to achieve a *modus vivendi*: Flury played violin in the Chamber Orchestra on occasion, and Schild programmed Flury's music now and then; and the two orchestras had to share many wind-players over the coming years. But back in 1936, coming on top of his family problems, Flury saw it 'as a catastrophe. He wept when he heard about it', Roetschi recalled.

Given that Flury was juggling two women in his life for the second half of the 1930s, there is no little irony in the fact that he was now commissioned

[2] *Cf. SKO. 50 Jahre Solothurner Kammerorchester 1936–1986*, no publisher given, [Solothurn, 1986].

[3] Conversation with the author, Solothurn, 11 January 2013.

to write a stage work about Casanova. There is a brief pre-history to the tale that has to be told. During his regular visits to Lily in Canton Ticino from 1932 onwards he had established contact with the people in charge of music at Radio Svizzera italiana (which itself was founded only in 1932, initially under the name of Radio Monteceneri). These were first and foremost Leopoldo Casella (1908–72), who was the first conductor of the Orchestra of Swiss Italian Radio when it was founded in 1935, and Guido Calgari (1905–69), a writer and active anti-fascist who worked at the radio in Lugano from 1933 onwards; after the Second World War, Calgari would be appointed to the chair in Italian at ETH Zurich. In 1936 Flury wrote a new symphony – officially 'No. 2', as he had not numbered his *Fasnachts-Symphonie* – and was invited to conduct it with the Orchestra of Swiss Italian Radio on 1 August, the Swiss National Day. It is in four movements. The first is based on the chimes of the church of Pazzolino on the outskirts of Lugano. These chimes were used as the call sign for the radio, meaning that the listeners at home would hear the call-sign twice – once between programmes and then again at the start of the Symphony, played by the orchestra. The other movements are based on Ticino folksongs. The slow movement uses the barcarolle/love-song 'Vieni sulla barchetta' ('Come into the little boat'), the scherzo another love-song, 'Quattro cavai che trottano' ('Four trotting horses') and the last movement 'Addio la caserma' ('Farewell to the army barracks'). The work is colourfully orchestrated and the use of folksong gives Flury ample opportunity to indulge his more 'popular' leanings. There wasn't much of a critical response to the premiere on the radio, but the few reviews were all positive. The only recording is of an old, crackling radio performance in Zurich, conducted by the composer, although the work really ought to be available in a polished performance in modern sound.

Casella and Calgari were impressed with Flury, and now arranged for him to write a large-scale *Festspiel* for Lugano. The occasion was to be the 1938 Expo in Lugano. The Expo had begun in 1933 and was both a trades fair (not unlike the LIGA in Zollikofen in 1935) and a cultural event intended not least to strengthen the sense of 'Swissness' in Italian Switzerland at a time when Mussolini was endeavouring to exert an influence on the Italian speakers north of the Italian border. *Casanova e l'Albertolli* might have been designated a *Festspiel* by the Expo organisers, but its dramatic trajectory really makes of it an opera. In fact, it was the first *Festspiel* since the Ticino Expos began to be conceived as a drama, not as a non-narrative, musico-visual spectacle. The action takes place in Lugano in 1769 – the First Act on 10 August, during an annual festival in honour of the Swiss cantons, the Second three months later. There are pageant-like scenes for the various representatives of the cantons, but the main story is Casanova's failed attempt to seduce Lucia, a local girl who is also loved by Albertolli, a Ticino sculptor. The latter is based on the historical figure of Giocondo Albertolli

The poster for the premiere of Casanova e l'Albertolli

(1743–1829), but Calgari states in his brief preface that this character is really only a symbol representing the best human qualities that the Ticino has to offer. The historical Casanova was indeed in Lugano in 1769, but the details about him in the plot are Calgari's invention. Given the tenor of the times and Calgari's anti-Mussolini stance, one could justifiably interpret the drama as the failed attempt by a charismatic Italian to woo the Ticino – represented by Lucia – who all but succumbs and yet in the end decides in favour of the honest, homely Swiss virtues symbolised by Albertolli. But the drama eschews overt politicising, and can also be read simply as a love-story. Flury finished sketching the work in 1937, at which the vocal score was published by Hug (he sent a copy to Rita on 27 November 1937, telling her he expected her to study it carefully). Flury again employed Favre as his orchestrator. The reason handed down in the family is that Flury was too busy orchestrating *Die helle Nacht* to manage this further task, but in fact he had already finished the latter by the time he began work properly on *Casanova e l'Albertolli*. Perhaps his other commitments did not allow him the necessary time, or perhaps he had little inclination to spend a large part of the year scoring yet another *Festspiel*.

There does not seem to be any other instance of a Swiss-German composer writing an Italian-language opera before Flury or after, and it is proof of the high regard in which his colleagues held him that the commission to write *Casanova e l'Albertolli* was not given to a local composer. It is also proof that Flury had acquired more than a working knowledge of the Italian language back in high school. His children were going to Italian-speaking schools and playing with Italian-speaking friends, and so it was probably important for family harmony that Richard, too, was able to communicate with everyone around him in the long weeks he lived in Lugano every year. *Casanova e l'Albertolli* was given its first performance in Lugano on 1 October 1938 and ran for a further four showings over the days thereafter. The Orchestra of Swiss Italian Radio was conducted by its new music-director, Otmar Nussio (a former Respighi student), who would in future remain as faithful to Flury as did his colleagues Casella and Calgari. (In fact, Nussio and Flury had first met back in Bern in 1928 when the former's *Poemetto* for orchestra was given its world premiere on the same programme as Flury's First Piano Concerto, each under the direction of its composer.)

Casanova e l'Albertolli was a very different work from Flury's previous *Festspiele*. Apart from actually having a real story-line, it was performed by professionals and was in general far more ambitious. Stylistically it lies somewhere between the popular idiom of the LIGA *Festspiel* and Flury's late-Romantic manner, but without any sense of strain between the two. No recording of the work exists except for the overture and a few brief numbers (it seems the radio recording made at the premiere was destroyed several years later).

A scene from Casanova e l'Albertolli, *October 1938*

The reviews of *Casanova e l'Albertolli* were overall very good; the *National-Zeitung* in Basel praised its melodiousness, the crowd-scenes and the manner in which Flury had 'missed no opportunity that the musical comedy offers', although it did find the opera at times a bit too 'serious' for a festive occasion. 'A.B.' in *Der Bund* in Bern thought that *Casanova e l'Albertolli* was a 'significant work' that enriched the Swiss opera repertoire. Only 'To.'[4] in the *Neue Zürcher Zeitung* on 3 October was really critical, finding that Flury hadn't really understood Italian diction, that his *Sprechgesang* was too Wagnerian, and that the ensemble numbers were weak. He went on as follows:

> the decisive question [is this]: Is Calgari-Flury's 'Casanova e l'Albertolli' a festspiel, a singspiel, an opera, a music drama or an operetta? It's none of them – and yet a little of all of them. It's too concise for a large festive hall, the music too subtle and the plot – while schematic – too individual. On the operatic stage or as a musical chamber drama, the music would come across far better – but the drama would then have to be motivated very differently, better developed, more fully imbued with humanity and 'filled with flesh and blood'. The music isn't relaxed enough for an operetta, it's too weighed down by Wagnerian music drama.

Flury's memoirs make it clear he generally felt he got a raw deal from the *Neue Zürcher Zeitung*, and it is true that – with the exception of Willi Schuh, who had joined it a few years before – its critics had long been turning up their noses at what was happening out in the provinces; indeed, in spite of what he might have felt, Flury wasn't being singled out, for others were

[4] Possibly Ernst Tobler, though his abbreviation was otherwise 'E.Tb.'

treated far worse.[5] But while I disagree with the above reviewer's overall assessment of the music, the work does indeed fall between several stools, and that is its main weakness. The pageantry in *Casanova* would probably preclude its ever being staged again – it is the one aspect that truly makes it seem dated – and the sheer number of soloists and chorus members needed will probably mean that concert performances will be rare. But it is a shame, for there are melodious numbers – solos, duets and choruses – that suggest an affinity with the more popular 'classical' Italian styles as practised by the song-composer Paolo Tosti, or even Puccini on occasion. And the overture, which was released in a modern recording on the Gallo label in 2012,[6] ought to be on the programmes of orchestras everywhere. It is perfectly proportioned, has a witty fugal section, and a 'big tune' to sweep one along.

There is a banal irony in that it was during the preparations for his *Casanova e l'Albertolli* that Flury realised he would have to cut his ties with Lily and commit himself to Rita if he were to have any hope of a new life – even though the 'moral' of the work is really that multiple dalliances don't work out. So he finally filed for divorce. Since he had effectively been separated for six years, and since he seems to have accepted on principle that he would have to pay alimony for a long time to come, the courts granted the divorce without much ado. Divorce, however, did not simply open up the gates to a second marriage, and it seems there was still much convincing to do – both with Rita and her parents. There is an odd letter of 18 April 1939 from Flury to Rita's mother and stepfather that is obviously intended as a reply to assorted accusations (no longer extant). He confesses to having loved Rita for over ten years, but assures her parents that he did nothing immoral at the time, has done nothing immoral since their re-acquaintance in 1935, and wants only to make her happy. He even writes that '2½ years ago, in reaction to a case of slander, Rita proved her innocence by means of a doctor's examination and a medical certificate'. By the summer of 1939 at the latest, Rita had agreed to marry him. In all these years, Flury's letters are full of desperate professions of love, jealousy, willing renunciation and yet more protestations of 'eternal' love.[7] But in a letter to Rita of 8 August 1939, a little over a month before their planned wedding, Flury suddenly changes his tone:

> I have suffered much, though I know today that suffering is also necessary for an artist. But I desire especially from you as my wife that you will *help* me to deal with all obstacles and overcome them, and you may calmly trust my guidance in all matters.

[5] As was Marcel Sulzberger, for example; *cf.* my *Marcel H. Sulzberger*, *op, cit.*, pp. 107, 109 and 112, for various awful, unfair reviews of his music from the *Neue Zürcher Zeitung*.

[6] Richard Flury, *Orchesterstücke aus 'Casanova'* (coupled with the First Symphony and Second Violin Concerto), Urs Joseph Flury conducting the Orchestre Symphonique Bienne, Gallo CD-1385, Lausanne, 2012.

[7] The declaration of 'eternal' love is in an undated letter written in the train on his way back from Lugano, presumably from 1937 or 1938.

He tells her that it is time to put away all childish things and become a 'mature, beautiful wife, in whose reliability and discipline one can have a rock-like trust in all things'. He praises her for having meanwhile rejected all 'external frippery' and for the fact that she doesn't go dancing any more, as these are 'things I find repugnant'. He continues: 'I know that you love me and that you have the good will to bring sacrifices, otherwise you would not want to marry me'.

There is no record of how Rita reacted to this letter, nor whether it was presaged by a similar change of mood in their conversations. But the shift is striking. Perhaps this letter was a unique occurrence, perhaps it did not say anything that Rita did not know already, or perhaps it gave her second thoughts that she had to dispel, with preparations for the wedding having already advanced so far. Maybe even the bleak mood of the times played a role in her decision-making – for between their engagement and marriage, war again broke out in Europe. Germany invaded Poland on 1 September 1939, Britain and France declared war on Germany two days later, and Switzerland was now manning its borders to try and repel any potential invaders. Flury was bound to be called up again soon – as indeed he was – and so perhaps Rita thought committing to a joint future was the sensible thing to do at a time when there soon may not be a future for anyone at all.

Whatever doubts might have lurked in Rita's mind in August and September 1939, she married Flury in the Protestant Church in Biberist on 30 September – St Urs' Day, a holiday in the city of Solothurn. The music was provided by pupils of Flury's: by Charles Dobler on the organ and by a schoolboy string quartet. Dobler was primarily a pianist – he would later have an extended concert career, performing Swiss music all over the world – and had not bothered to practise his final voluntary, a movement from a Mendelssohn organ sonata, beyond the first couple of pages. During a rehearsal in the church, he got three members of the quartet to play out the end of the service, one of them taking the part of the priest, the other two the happy couple, and they timed how long it would take for Flury and Rita to conclude the ceremony, walk the length of the church and go out of the main door. Dobler accordingly practised just enough for the purpose – but, to his horror, Flury and Rita decided to sit down and enjoy the performance at the end. Dobler kept playing beyond his self-appointed pages and somehow managed to improvise his way to a halfway-satisfactory close.[8]

This marriage would last until he died, but Flury would soon enough find that the 'reliability and discipline' he desired from Rita would be conditional on reciprocity, and therefore a very fragile commodity.

[8] As told to the author by Charles Dobler (interview on 12 July 2012) and Max Reber (20 May 2012); Reber was a member of the schoolboy string quartet.

15
Politics Intrude

Politics had already begun to intrude into Flury's life more than a year before war finally broke out. Gottfried Kassowitz had remained in and about Vienna during the 1930s, and it seems that he and Flury had barely been in touch since Kassowitz's last extant letter, dating back to 1934. Flury had kept him on his mailing list, however, and had been sending him his new scores whenever they were published.

In March 1938, Germany annexed Austria in a near-bloodless coup, and the Jewish population of the latter was immediately subjected to all manner of repression. Many of them fled this new, enlarged German Reich (for which privilege the Nazis charged exorbitant fees wherever possible). But many stayed, as did Kassowitz. He wrote a long letter to Flury on 16 April 1938, only a month after the *Anschluss*, and after apologising for his long silence he went on to sketch out all his problems. He was not Jewish, he explained at length, for he had a Catholic mother and had been raised a Catholic and sent to a Jesuit grammar school. But having a Jewish father meant he was now classed as a 'half-Aryan', he wrote.

Kassowitz's terminology was telling; when he was mentioned in the notorious Nazi *Lexikon der Juden in der Musik* ('Dictionary of Jews in Music') two years later, he was not listed as 'half-Aryan', but as a 'half-Jew'.[1] In official Nazi terminology he was a 'Mischling ersten Grades' (a 'person of mixed blood to the first degree'). He did not yet know that this 'semi' status would help to spare him from later deportation and murder, and for the moment his prime concern was that he was not allowed to practise his profession as a conductor. He explained his situation to Flury over six densely typed pages, and asked if there were any way Flury might be able to help him find work. He also mentions that he is writing to Leo Delsen, the director of the Solothurn Theatre, to see if he can assist. Flury's reply has not survived, since Kassowitz's archives were all inadvertently thrown away after his death. But in Kassowitz's next letter, written two weeks after the previous one, on 30 April 1938, he thanks Flury for writing back so promptly and reports that Delsen has already given him a 'completely definitive negative reply'. One should not interpret this apparent rejection as cold-heartedness on Delsen's part, for he made the Solothurn theatre a second home to many

[1] Theo Stengl and Herbert Gerigk (eds.), *Lexikon der Juden in der Musik*, Bernhard Hahnefeld, Berlin, 1940, col. 131.

German-speaking exiles from the Nazis and his anti-fascist credentials are in no doubt. But the financial and organisational opportunities offered by a tiny theatre in a small Swiss town were limited, and Delsen could hardly assist everyone who asked for help. Flury, however, was more forthcoming, as Kassowitz's letter of 30 April 1938 confirms:

> I offer my warmest thanks to you for your truly kind efforts on my behalf. The fact that these efforts were without hope was something I more or less already knew precisely in advance, for I had heard reports by word of mouth that meant I was in large part properly informed. But the fact that you even wanted to pass on your orchestra to me shows you to be truly *the* friend that I have always seen in you, but I assure you that I would not ever have accepted such a sacrifice on your part because I feel towards you just the same way that you feel towards me.

No further details of Flury's offer have survived in any of the sources, and it is not even certain that the position would have sufficed to get Kassowitz a work permit. Conducting the Solothurn Orchestra did not pay a living wage, a fact of which Kassowitz will have been aware. Besides, the prospect of moving from Vienna to an amateur set-up in Solothurn must have still seemed slightly absurd to him. Only the previous February he had conducted the Austrian premiere of Janáček's *Věc Makropulos* in the Theater an der Wien, and although hindsight affords the knowledge that things were only going to get far, far worse, Kassowitz had not given up hope that circumstances might yet change in Austria. Conducting was now forbidden to him, but he was still allowed to work as an accompanist for singers and so probably felt he did not yet have to grasp at straws. He also had a sister living in Zurich; Flury was thus not his only potential lifeline.

Nonetheless, Flury's offer was remarkable by any measure. The Solothurn Orchestra did not pay a lot, but he already needed every cent he could get. He was supporting a family, trying to save enough for his train fare to see his four children as often as he could, and was now contemplating remarriage. His letters to Rita during their courtship even mention how he would cycle to Bern to see her (a round trip of nearly fifty miles) because he did not have the money for a train ticket, or how on occasion he had to choose between buying milk and a train ticket to visit her.

The next letter from Kassowitz in Flury's archives is dated 30 January 1940. It seems they have not corresponded since spring 1938, and Kassowitz relates how things have only been getting slowly worse. He is not, it seems, the object of active measures of repression, but his letter reveals exactly how insidious was the Nazis' 'passive' repression. He is still not allowed to conduct, and as much as he is trying to occupy himself with learning English, practising the piano and suchlike, his sheer lack of hope for month after month is making him spiral into depression. At least, however, he is currently spending two months in Italy as the guest of friends – he is staying at the Villa Jeanette in Abbazia (today Opatija in Croatia), where Gustav Mahler had once vacationed. His next letter, dated 26 February 1940, is written from Abbazia just before his permit runs out and he has to return to Vienna. Kassowitz's next extant letter – apparently the last for nearly six years – is dated 22 March 1940. He is now getting desperate and begs Flury to intercede with Delsen at the Solothurn Theatre to give him a job. Flury obviously replied to Kassowitz's letters at this time because Kassowitz thanks him profusely for writing. But after this letter of March 1940, there is nothing more from Kassowitz until after the War, and it is not known whether Flury tried to contact him or what measures he might have taken to try and help him out. Since their friendship resumed as soon as the War was over and they remained close thereafter, it is probably safe to assume that it was circumstances that interrupted their correspondence, not any lack of concern on the part of the one for the other. After the War, Flury managed to procure a permit for Kassowitz to leave war-torn Austria and stay with him for several weeks to regain his strength, and he also stayed with Kassowitz when visiting Vienna in the post-War years. Kassowitz managed to survive financially during the War by editing choral music that had been composed for Nazi propaganda purposes.[2]

Kassowitz wasn't the only friend in need during the War. Eduard Favre was eking out an existence in Lausanne. His letters to Flury continued sporadically until late 1944. He thanks Flury now and then for sending a packet of cigarettes, and Flury still sends him works to copy (with Favre meticulously listing what he has done and what is owed). On one occasion (28 August 1941) Favre apologises for the increase in price, but it's because manuscript paper has become so expensive (no doubt because of paper shortages during the War). His handwriting begins to deteriorate, and in what appears to be his last letter – though undated – each line slopes off at the end. He complains bitterly about a 'Johannot' maltreating him, and asks if he couldn't come and live with Flury for a while instead. Flury's reply is not known, but for all his generosity to friends, he was hardly in a position to take in anyone, let alone a man at the end of his life – Favre died in 1946 – who, to judge by this letter, was suffering from something akin to a persecution complex. Flury's family, moreover, had grown in the meantime, and money was tight.

Rita's and Richard's only child, Urs Joseph, was born on 25 August 1941. The three of them lived in the early 1940s in a rented apartment on the Wassergasse in Solothurn, a couple of hundred metres south of the railway station, near the city border with Biberist. The tin roof had holes in it that meant Rita had to place buckets across the floor when it rained.[3] Flury was also still paying maintenance to his first family. In a letter written to Rita

[2] As told by Kassowitz to the Flury family, and to me in turn.

[3] *Lebenserinnerungen, op. cit.*, p. 233.

Flury's children Urs Joseph, Giovanna and Roger in Solothurn, c. 1942

on 26 May 1943 on his way back from seeing the children in Lugano, he complains that Lily has presented him with bills for CHF 2,589.55 (he even spells it out in words): for a child's bicycle, a radio, doctor's bills, taxes, food, electricity, wood, water and so on. He tells Rita he's going to check with the local authorities to see exactly how much he will legally have to pay (how this matter worked out is not recorded). There were other costs, and he seems to have done his best to be a father despite the distance. On several occasions in the early war years he sent various of his children the money for train tickets so that they could come and visit him and Rita. In October 1941 he writes to his daughter Eva that the shoe ration-card is ready and he'll buy her a new pair of her choosing. When she gets a job in a factory in 1943 he isn't happy, suggests she does a commercial apprenticeship instead, and even offers to employ her as an *au pair* at 60 francs a month to help with Urs and around the house until she manages to find a job as a telephonist.[4] Then there's an angry letter a few weeks later telling her he *really* isn't happy about her *still* working in the factory,[5] followed by a relieved letter two weeks later when she changes job, and in which Richard also asks about Giovanna's planned apprenticeship. His eldest daughter Verena is also a worry – there is an undated letter from 1944 in which Richard urges her to stop an affair she is having with a married German teacher in Geneva, because she should know all too well how families suffer when there is a divorce (it's not until three years later that Richard mentions the end of this affair in a letter to

[4] Richard to Eva, 6 September 1943.

[5] Richard to Eva, 22 January 1944.

Rita – 'thank God', he comments[6]). The children – who were by now hardly children any more – visited as often as Richard could have them, and both family anecdote and the warm tone Rita adopted in her greetings appended to Richard's letters make it clear that she made a big effort to make them feel welcome. To judge from Richard's letters to Rita when he was away from home, that wasn't easy for her. It must have been awkward that her eldest stepdaughter was only ten years younger than she. Nor had the wider Flury family abandoned its dislike of Lily; according to family anecdote, whenever the children arrived from Lugano they were dirty and unkempt and had to be put straight in the bath. Perhaps they were; or perhaps this says more about their opinion of Lily's supposedly deficient parenting skills than about the actual degree of cleanliness of the children themselves.

Richard was also away for several weeks at a time during the War, as he was still of an age when military service was compulsory. For much of the War, Switzerland feared invasion from Germany – especially after the German authorities discovered early on that supposedly neutral Switzerland had been exchanging military information with France. The national myth at the time (and for long after) was that the strength of the Swiss Army, manning its borders and ready to repel any attack, had succeeded in deterring Hitler from invading. As with every myth there was an element of truth to this assertion, though it is known today that Switzerland had also quietly demonstrated compliance, exporting both munitions and electricity, hoarding Nazi gold and allowing the use of the Gotthard Tunnel for the transport of vital supplies to and from Italy. Numerous morally dubious deals were done which, with hindsight, were even more compliant than would actually have been necessary. But there were no certainties at the time, and when the German eastern front finally collapsed and Europe descended into chaos, there was still a danger that the Nazi High Command might find an invasion of Switzerland a tempting distraction. For all their wheelings and dealings with the Nazis, the Swiss succeeded in keeping out of the War without sacrificing their democratic institutions.

For the duration of his military service, Flury was assigned purely musical duties away from the border. His cards and letters home to Rita and Urs are usually stamped 'Im Feld' (literally 'in the field', i.e., on military service), but it is clear from their content that he was on more than one occasion based in Stans in Canton Nidwalden in central Switzerland. There he was responsible for conducting his regimental band in assorted public concerts, these duties being occasionally interspersed with marching up and down an alp. Quite how performing in a town with some 4,000 inhabitants was intended to strengthen the Swiss war effort remains as much a mystery today as it was to Flury then. But little Stans was of military significance, being situated in a natural defensive position south of Lake Lucerne, with

[6] Richard to Rita, Interlaken, 23 July 1947.

military airfields to the east and west. It was one of the outermost points of the 'réduit', the fortifications set up around central Switzerland early in the Second World War to which the Swiss army was to withdraw in the case of a massive attack from Germany. If there had been an invasion, then, Flury would have found himself on the front line. But he seems not to have feared any such eventuality, and spent his time composing military marches again to keep himself occupied. His periods of army service in any case never lasted longer than a few weeks at a time, twice a year. On 27 May 1943, he wrote to his brother Adolf that he was having a 'pleasant' time in the army. But a year later, his opinion had changed – or perhaps he had been hiding his real feelings because Adolf was an enthusiastic army officer. Richard's letters from the military were presumably subject to a censor's approval, but he still openly called his commanding officer a 'donkey' ('Esel') in letters to both Eva and Rita, and on 25 June 1944 he wrote to his wife that 'The purpose and point of the military is as *un-Christian* as it possibly can be'. It is chastening to think that the expression of such sentiments across the border at the time would have resulted in capital punishment.

The War also had an impact on the Solothurn Orchestra, because its members – like Flury – kept being called up. There were even discussions in the early stages of the War about whether the Orchestra should cease all activities until it was over. But since large parts of the army were demobbed when the European situation stabilised into an uneasy peace after the fall of France in 1940, most Orchestra members, like Flury, were absent only for short periods. Flury's pupil Alban Roetschi helped out by conducting rehearsals when Flury was away with the military, and Flury's commanding officer, Lieutenant Colonel Max Schilt, gave him leave to go back to conduct the concerts themselves.[7] A major fundraising drive with tombola also served to fill the depleted coffers of the Orchestra.

The War had a major effect on cultural life in Solothurn in two other aspects – both of them beneficial. Leo Delsen was unable to help Kassowitz, but was already busy gathering some of the finest exiled talent to his little theatre. The Swiss author Hermann Ferdinand Schell (1900–72) had enjoyed a successful career in Vienna in the 1930s with novels and plays; he was one of the first Swiss playwrights to be performed at the famous Burgtheater, but after the *Anschluss* of 1938 he and his wife, the actress Margarethe von Noé, fled to Switzerland with their four children, where Schell was able to continue his career. Delsen's fondness for programming his works did not always go down well with other local writers: Cäsar von Arx complained to Delsen in 1941 that he felt he'd been 'replaced' by Schell in his affections.[8]

[7] *Lebenserinnerungen*, *op. cit.*, p. 167.

[8] *Cf.* Thomas Blubacher, '"Sorge in Freude und Leid in Vergessen wandeln!" Das Städtebundtheater Biel-Solothurn unter der Direktion von Leo Delsen 1927–1954', in Simone Gojan and Elke Krafka (eds.), *Theater Biel Solothurn – Théâtre Bienne Soleure. Geschichte und Geschichten des kleinsten Stadttheaters der Schweiz*, Chronos, Zurich, 2004, p. 35.

A playwright who owed his discovery to Delsen was Fritz Hochwälder (1911–86), who had also fled Vienna after the *Anschluss* and had reached Switzerland by swimming across the Rhine. His *Das heilige Experiment* was given its world premiere at the Biel-Solothurn Theatre in 1943 and after the War became one of the best-known modern German plays. The director for its first performance was Peter Lotar, an *émigré* writer/actor/director from Prague and a former student of the Max Reinhardt Schule in Berlin. He, too, had fled to Switzerland, in 1939, and in the immediate post-War years would be partly responsible for discovering Friedrich Dürrenmatt. Other *émigrés* at the theatre included Egon Karter (1911–2006), also originally from Czechoslovakia, who had founded a Jewish theatre group 'Klavier Vier' in Amsterdam in 1940 and managed to flee to Switzerland as late as 1942. Many years later, he recalled that 'at least a third of the members of the ensemble [in Biel-Solothurn] were Jews or so-called half-Jews'.[9] Delsen's daughter used to accompany her father on his trips to the *Fremdenpolizei* (the 'aliens police' responsible for all matters pertaining to residence and work permits for non-Swiss citizens), and she remembered him telling her that 'for every foreigner I want to employ I have to engage two Swiss'.[10] There were also immigrants from Nazi-occupied Europe who came to Solothurn for personal rather than political reasons. Foremost among these was Richard Kauffungen (1854–1942), one of Vienna's leading sculptors, whose statue of Thucydides still stands outside the Austrian Parliament on the Ringstrasse. Shortly after the outbreak of the Second World War, Kauffungen decided to join his son Friedrich and his family, who had been living in Solothurn for several years. Previous visits to Solothurn had already brought Kauffungen into contact with Flury, who naturally delighted in his tales of old Vienna, since Kauffungen had known just about everyone of importance up to the Kaiser himself. Kauffungen's last work, completed shortly before he died in 1942, was a bust of Flury.[11]

German and Austrian theatres had become *de facto* inaccessible to up-and-coming Swiss talent, unless they had excellent connections and were devoid of compunction about working with the Nazis, and so the Biel-Solothurn ensemble was also able to attract fine young Swiss performers – it was here, during the War, that the soprano Lisa Della Casa and the conductor Peter Maag began their careers. But as the only neutral country with hard currency in central Europe, Switzerland was also now attractive to the best performers from the surrounding countries. It is ironic, then, that once Flury's Solothurn Orchestra had survived the initial uncertainty of the first months of war, it was able to start engaging some of the finest soloists

[9] *Cf.* Thomas Blubacher, 'Egon Karter und Charlotte Sender', in Gojan and Krafka (eds.), *op. cit.*, p. 72.

[10] *Cf.* Thomas Blubacher, 'Leo Delsen und Elisabeth Delsen', in *ibid.*, p. 65.

[11] *Cf. Lebenserinnerungen*, *op. cit.*, p. 196, and Olga Stieglitz and Gerhard Zeillinger, *Der Bildhauer Richard Kauffungen (1854–1942): Zwischen Ringstraße, Künstlerhaus und Frauenkunstschule*, Peter Lang, Frankfurt, 2008, p. 326.

Flury in 1942: the last bust made by the Viennese sculptor Richard Kauffungen (1854–1942)

in the world – a practice that continued into the years immediately after the cessation of hostilities. Wilhelm Backhaus (1942), Erna Sack (1943), Beniamino Gigli (1943), Georg Kulenkampff (1945) and Walther Gieseking (1945) all performed with the Solothurn Orchestra under Flury, but the biggest impression on everyone was made by Pablo Casals, who played three times in Solothurn and astonished everyone equally by his musicality and his modesty. Given a choice of staying with a friend of Flury or in the villa of one of Solothurn's *grandes dames*, he chose the former; when the only dais to be found for him to sit on when performing was a wooden box for beer bottles, he accepted it without demurring; and to Flury's relief Casals was quite unconcerned by the rainwater dripping from the ceiling when invited to lunch at his house.

Flury was even more impressed by Casals the musician than by the man. In his first Solothurn concert (6 November 1941), Casals played only solo works or ones with piano (Bach's solo Suite in D minor, BWV1008, then Brahms' E minor Sonata, Op. 38,[12] and pieces by Beethoven, Granados and others). The orchestra began the concert with a movement from Beethoven's Second Symphony, and played Mozart's overture to *Figaro* after the Brahms sonata. Such a mishmash programme, without any musical interaction between orchestra and soloist, was not uncommon when big names came to visit. But at his second and last concerts (9 May 1942 and 31 March 1946), Casals played Haydn's D major Concerto and Boccherini's Concerto in B flat respectively. Rehearsals were a delight, Flury recalled in his memoirs, for Casals somehow did not have to interrupt or talk to get his wishes across; the occasional nod of his head and the sheer warmth of his personality were sufficient to communicate to Flury and his players alike what he desired and intended.[13] 'I had difficulty in holding back my tears as I conducted',[14] wrote Flury, recalling their Haydn Concerto together. 'The audience was jubilant such as I have never before experienced in the concert hall of our city'.[15] They would remain in touch throughout the years to come, and whenever Flury sent his latest published scores to Casals, the cellist always wrote a cordial reply. The last time they met was in 1960, when the Flurys drove all the way to Prades to attend the Festival that Casals organised, and were invited to tea by the old man himself.

[12] The concert programme lists the Sonata in F, but this was an error, as is evident from the correspondence between Casals and Flury in the latter's archives.

[13] *Lebenserinnerungen*, *op. cit.*, p. 168.

[14] *Ibid.*, p. 233.

[15] *Ibid.*, p. 233.

Pablo Casals rehearsing under Flury's direction in the Restaurant Schwanen in Solothurn, 1946

16
Of Forests and Chambers

After writing *Der Scholle treu*, *Die helle Nacht* and *Casanova e l'Albertolli*, Flury had returned to non-dramatic genres. It was not simply a matter of choice. He had written to Cäsar von Arx in early 1936 to ask for a libretto, only to be turned down because von Arx had already promised an opera text to the composer Werner Wehrli (1892–1944) – although in fact no such collaboration came about.[1] A Te Deum for Erich Schild and the Cäcilienverein in Solothurn gave Flury an opportunity to write a quasi-dramatic, large-scale work for soloists, chorus and orchestra, and it was given a successful first performance in Einsiedeln – as part of Solothurn's contribution to the Swiss National Exhibition of mid-1939 – shortly before Flury married Rita. It received several further performances, and delighted Ernst Kurth when he was sent a copy of the vocal score a few months before the premiere. Flury's letter enclosing the work has not survived, but it must have mentioned his worry that it might be too Brucknerian, since Kurth reassures him about it.[2] It is intentionally imposing, and Flury seems to have imagined the resonance of a large church as he was writing it. It is more successful than the Mass of eight years before, and its choral writing is friendlier to the voices. But it, too, seems to fall between several stools. The harmonic adventurousness of *Die helle Nacht* has evaporated but, unlike *Casanova e l'Albertolli* with its Italianate tunefulness, there is little to compensate for it here. The powerful opening gesture in octaves keeps returning, but it comes across less as a structural signpost than as an inability to think of what to bring next. The bass-line is strangely static – did Flury perhaps worry that the booming, ecclesiastic acoustic would make anything more active too muddy to come across properly? Too often the music sounds like an improvised doodling over a slow-moving, largely stepwise bass. There are many imitative passages, but only one fugato in the work – towards the end – and it peters out quickly after the entrance of the fourth voice. Its countersubject, oddly, never appears again after its first occurrence.

Apart from the Te Deum, Flury's *œuvre* at this time is marked by a return to chamber music, prompted at least in part by the fact that he was courting a fellow violinist. His dedications – now as in later life – also reflect his

[1] Letter from von Arx to Flury, Nieder-Erlinsbach, 26 March 1936.

[2] Letter from Kurth to Flury, Gümligen, 9 May 1939.

Poster for the world premiere in Einsiedeln of Flury's Te Deum, July 1939

shifting affections. He had dedicated a Gavotte to Rita in 1930 (thus some five years before declaring his love for her). His first work for violin after he began courting her was a Gavotte dedicated, not to Rita, but 'To my dear Lily for Christmas 1935'; it was his first piece for violin and piano in five years. In the same year, 1935, he wrote a *Träumerei* for two violins, which he dedicated to the memory of his mother. There are six 'album leaves', also dedicated to 'My dear Lily', in 1936, but his next Gavotte for violin is this time for Rita, being one of Three Pieces for Violin and Piano dedicated to her as a Christmas present in 1939 (though the last movement was the Serenade from the *Suite Pastorale* for oboe and piano of 1926). These are all in Flury's lighter vein, as are other occasional works he wrote for Rita after their marriage, such as the *Suite for Two Violins* of 1942, similarly dedicated to her as a Christmas present for them both to play. It includes two movements inscribed to their little son Urs Joseph, 'Ursli's Gavotte' and 'Ursli's Cradle Song' ('-li' being the Swiss-German diminutive suffix; the latter piece has the alternative title 'Ninna-Nanna'). *Three Little Pieces* for two violins followed in 1943, a *Dance Suite* for two violins in 1944 and another *Christmas Gavotte* for Rita in that same year.

Rita also inspired Flury to more 'serious' music. The violin sonata he mentioned in his correspondence with her in late 1936 is his No. 4 in C major: although he had consigned the three early violin sonatas written in 1918 to his archives, never to be resurrected, he retained the numbering they occasioned. No. 4 was dedicated to Rita, as were No. 5 in F major in 1940, No. 6 in B minor in 1943 and No. 7 in C major in 1948. A *Romantic Song* of 1937, for cello or violin and piano, is similarly dedicated to her. Flury wrote his Second Violin Concerto in 1940, dedicating it to Rita on her birthday, 1 March – although he never got around to orchestrating it, and in his lifetime it was performed only with piano accompaniment; his son Urs Joseph orchestrated and performed it after Richard's death. Nor did Flury restrict himself to violin works at this time. He wrote his First Cello Sonata in 1937, a Second in 1941 (dedicated to his brother, Adolf, who played the cello) and a First Piano Trio (that is, for piano, violin and cello) in 1941 (dedicated to Rita on her birthday in 1942). Flury also wrote his Third String Quartet (in C major) in 1938, and his Fourth (also in C major) in 1940. This last work was dedicated to Ernst Kurth, whose fondness for Bruckner perhaps prompted Flury to start it with a long-held tremolo in the middle strings, like a Bruckner symphony. Flury sent Kurth a copy of the Third and Fourth Quartets. Kurth accepted the dedication with delight in a letter of 23 April 1941, and praised both works, noting their 'unconstrained textures' and the 'unified overall impression' that they left on him, 'which is the most essential sign of true art'.

Kurth's letters – which became more sporadic as he grew older – were ever more focused on reassuring Flury that his 'Romantic' aesthetic 'has not outlived itself' (as Kurth wrote on 14 March 1944). Kurth and Flury were apparently united both in their dislike of Modernism in music, and in a belief in what they both held to be the age-old virtues of traditional tonality and form. Flury was not the only composer afraid of seeming behind the times: in Zurich Othmar Schoeck was becoming ever more obsessed with appearing out of date. Different composers reacted in different ways to the shifting aesthetic of the day. Some adopted the new techniques – thus Frank Martin adopted a free version of twelve-note music (so free that one can often hardly call it dodecaphony) and negotiated a skilful transition into the post-War world. Others, like Schoeck, retreated further and further from the modern, watering down their style in the process until there was little left at all.[3]

Flury's case is reminiscent of Schoeck's, though not as clear-cut, and he does not demonstrate a decline similar to that of Schoeck's last years. Flury's music from the mid-1930s through the years of the War offers many lovely things. The slow movement of the First Cello Sonata is luscious and tuneful, and the 'lighter' works, often *à la* Kreisler, are as delightful as ever; the Three Pieces for Violin are among his works most often broadcast, not least because they feature on a CD released by Swiss Radio International. But the chamber works of these years often give a sense of *déjà entendu*, their melodic material not always being distinctive enough for the large-scale sonata and *Lied* forms that they have to carry. Flury had admitted in his letter to Rita announcing his Violin Sonata No. 4 that 'It's getting too long (almost 60 pages). But one can always cut and shorten';[4] but cutting and shortening was, it seems, all too often abandoned in favour of writing yet another work instead. It is at times almost as if Flury felt he could justify his aesthetic by composing as many works as possible in the traditional genres. If he had not already composed works that were so much stronger, this trend might not perhaps be so noticeable. The impression left by his one-movement *Waldsymphonie* ('Forest Symphony') of 1942 is also mixed. As with the *Fasnachts-Symphonie*, Flury did not include this work in his numbered symphonies, and it is really a symphonic poem (perhaps he had Richard Strauss' *Eine Alpensinfonie* ('Alpine Symphony') in mind, which is similarly programmatic despite its title). There is no 'official' programme for Flury's *Waldsymphonie*, but a few months before he died, Flury mentioned that its content was 'Birdsong – storm – the mysticism of the forest – epilogue'.[5] The orchestration is skilful (by now one has come to expect nothing less from him) and at times unusual – such as a passage for the first violins accompanied by three trombones and tuba before the storm. But Flury too often resorts to sequence, and the thematic fragments one hears at the beginning never seem to coalesce properly. Nevertheless, others have been more positive about it. Ernst Kurth was very impressed

[3] *Cf.* my *Othmar Schoeck. Life and Works*, *op. cit.*, p. 314.
[4] Flury to Rita, Solothurn, 15 December 1936.
[5] Information provided by Urs Joseph Flury.

when he heard the first performance of the work on the radio, writing to Flury on 8 November 1942 that

> Your *Waldsymphonie* is quite wonderful, full of original beauty, poetic and unique. It would be unjust were it not to lead to your breakthrough and your fame. So I do not doubt that we will soon be hearing your work everywhere [....] I have every reason to be proud of my dear student.

The *Waldsymphonie* did indeed prove popular elsewhere after the War. Ricard Lamote de Grignon conducted it in Valencia in October 1947, and Kassowitz on Viennese Radio in that same month; and in July 1948, the Dresden Mozart Orchestra performed it under Erich Schneider in Dresden in the Soviet Zone of Germany.

Flury's increasing insistence on the virtues of tradition does not mean he cannot still surprise. His Second Piano Concerto, composed in 1943, takes up where his First Piano Concerto left off. It, too, is Rachmaninovian in spirit, though without the freshness of the earlier work. It shares many of the faults of Flury's recent music, namely an over-reliance on sequence and on grand Romantic gestures, compounded by a refusal to give free rein to his melodic imagination. The second movement, however, is very different from the outer two. It is only 49 bars long and lasts for under four minutes. But its harmonies keep shifting, leading frequently to unexpected dissonance, and even where the score looks as though the textures ought to be muddy, the orchestration shines. There is an odd moment (in bar 24) where the only wind instruments playing are two bassoons in their low register and a dissonant flute three octaves above them. On paper it looks like a miscalculation, but in performance it sounds lovely.

The premiere of the Second Piano Concerto was given on Swiss Radio on 5 November 1943 by the Swiss pianist Paul Baumgartner (1903–76), with Flury conducting the Zurich Radio Orchestra. Baumgartner had previously taught in Cologne, moving back to Switzerland in 1935 because of the political climate in Germany. He accompanied Casals when the cellist visited Solothurn, and later recorded Bach's gamba sonatas with him, and his own students included Alfred Brendel and Karl Engel. But he also remained a faithful friend of Flury and was given the dedication of this Second Piano Concerto. He performed it again in Zurich and Winterthur, and also played assorted smaller piano pieces by Flury on Swiss Radio in the coming years. Because its premiere was on the radio, there was not much of a critical echo except for a hymn of praise from Josef Remenyi, who wrote the concert reviews for the *Solothurner Zeitung*.[6] But Flury did not wait long to write another concerto. His next was a highly virtuosic Third Violin Concerto, which was finished in draft form in mid-1943. When the violinist Georg Kulenkampff visited Solothurn to perform with Flury's orchestra in 1945,

[6] Review by 'yi', i.e. Josef Remenyi, in the *Solothurner Zeitung*, undated clipping in Flury's archives.

a private get-together was held at which Kulenkampff played Flury's Fifth Violin Sonata perfectly at sight, and expressed enthusiasm for the music. So Flury offered him the world premiere of his Third Concerto. Kulenkampff accepted, Flury scored the work, and the first performance took place in Bern in February 1946. Flury's Second Violin Concerto, however – dedicated to his wife Rita, as mentioned – remained unorchestrated. The story of the one concerto is closely bound up with that of the other. These two works would prove both a symptom of circumstances and a catalyst of others, the ramifications of which would extend far beyond Flury himself.

17
Three Saints in One Act

Flury's *œuvre* in the early 1940s was dominated by chamber music and orchestral works, but he still had not given up his theatrical ambitions. In 1941, Delsen's Director of Plays, Vasa Hochmann (a left-wing Czech *émigré*),[1] asked Flury to write the incidental music for a production of Gerhart Hauptmann's *Hanneles Himmelfahrt*. Since Flury finished the score on 7 December, and the first performance took place only a week later, on the 14th, the amateurs of the Solothurn Orchestra who were engaged to play cannot have had an easy time of it, even though its eight numbers last only about 25 minutes. Flury had apparently anticipated the active involvement of a harpist, but there was none, so Charles Dobler played this part on the piano. Hochmann complained that the music was too long. That might well have been the case from his perspective as the director, but in fact this music is some of Flury's most attractive, with none of the long-windedness that often afflicts his more 'serious' works of absolute music. The idiom is pitched perfectly – harmonically sumptuous enough for a sophisticated theatre audience (Richard Strauss and the later Mahler seem to pop their head round the corner occasionally), but pithy and popular enough to suit this sentimental tearjerker of a play: the topic is the protracted death of little Hannele, a girl abused by her nasty stepfather. The instrumentation – despite the modest forces – is masterly. It makes one wish once more that Flury had turned to film music, for working under time-pressure and under strict conditions seems to have brought out the very best in him.

The actors involved in *Hanneles Himmelfahrt* included Peter Lotar, one of Delsen's many *émigrés* from Nazi-occupied Europe.[2] It was presumably through this production that Lotar got to know Flury. The music for *Hanneles Himmelfahrt* must have appealed to him, for a few months later he began to ponder a possible theatrical collaboration. Lotar was an author himself, and his diary for mid-1943 records how he was looking for a new topic for a drama. He initially intended it to be 'about the persecuted Jew, about the opportunists and scaremongers, down to Quisling and traitors. But to write for my desk drawer again? Then I'd rather leave it for later'.[3]

[1] *Cf.* the entry on Hochmann in the *Theaterlexikon der Schweiz online*, http://tls.theaterwissenschaft.ch/wiki/Vasa_Hochmann, accessed April 2016.

[2] *Cf.* p. 165, above.

[3] Peter Lotar, manuscript diary, 20 May 1943. Held by the Swiss National Library in Bern, shelfmark: SLA-Lotar, C-3-a.1.

Then he thought about turning the story of Karl Stauffer-Bern and Lydia Welti-Escher into a drama. Lydia was the daughter and daughter-in-law of the two most powerful Swiss families and had run off with the artist Karl Stauffer in 1889. Theirs had been Zurich's most scandalous love-triangle since Wagner and the Wesendoncks in the 1850s. But thanks to their money and political influence, Lydia's in-laws had her captured and placed in a mental asylum, while Karl was arrested for kidnapping and rape. They were both set free again, but committed suicide some eleven months apart in 1891. Then Lotar decided against this topic too, for fear of the influence of the Welti and the Escher families: Lydia's estranged husband had died only in 1940. Then he finally decided to write a drama featuring the two Solothurn saints, Urs and Viktor, and carried out extensive research. From the start, Lotar seems to have wanted to write a play with music, the latter to be provided by Flury. Lotar wrote in his diary:

> If this summer allows me the time, I want to do it if only because I've promised it to the Solothurn composer Richard Flury, who's full of enthusiasm about it, and is an exceptionally upright, decent fellow. Just to have got to know him is a good thing in itself.[4]

It took Lotar over another year to finish his text. It is dated 'Solothurn, 27 September 1944', and is inscribed 'Dedicated in great friendship to the dear citizens of Solothurn, with cordial feelings of gratitude and solidarity, in particular to Richard Flury, my collaborator and encourager'.[5]

Lotar's intention was to create a kind of *Festspiel* specific to Solothurn that could be performed in the open air by the old city walls and that might serve to bring the whole community together. It is cast in eight scenes and a prologue that is metaphorical in character, featuring 'Science' and 'Faith' personified and a dialogue between the devil and an angel. Only then does the play proper begin. It tells the story of the martyrdom of the two Roman soldiers and Christian converts Urs and Viktor – although in Lotar's retelling, they are saved by a miracle from being burned at the stake. At the end, Lotar even brings on a third saint, Verena, who is said to have lived as a hermit in a tiny picturesque valley outside Solothurn (today called the 'Verenaschlucht').

Flury promptly set to work on the music. There are many passages of melodrama, for Urs and Viktor only speak and do not sing, and here Flury made precise notes in the typescript as to the number of seconds of music required for each section. Besides these melodramas, his score features a prelude and a postlude, songs for the Devil and the Angel, several choruses and smaller numbers. He finished the sketch in piano score on 6 March 1945 and the orchestration a month later. Stylistically, this *Festspiel* is close

[4] Lotar, diary, 20 May 1943.

[5] Lotar, *St. Urs und St. Viktor. Ein Solothurner Mysterienspiel*, copy of the typescript in the Zentralbibliothek Solothurn, shelfmark R I 88.

to its predecessors for Zollikofen and Aarau (though without the yodelling), but one does get the impression that Flury's heart was more in this work than was the case with the previous two. Its choruses are clearly intended to be sung by amateurs and are a bit foursquare, and yet Flury seems to feel he can make fewer compromises than he had found necessary in his earlier *Festspiele*: amidst folksy passages for amateur performance there are slithery, more chromatic interludes for orchestra, though nothing on a par with his harmonic experiments of the late 1920s or early 1930s. The orchestra is not large (single woodwind, two each of horns and trumpets, one trombone, percussion, harp and strings), but the scoring is felicitous – perhaps a little too felicitous for open-air performance. Being neither for a gymnastic anniversary nor for an agricultural expo, *St. Urs und St. Viktor* was not intended as a one-off venture. And although the local setting affords the piece a mildly patriotic air, Lotar's text is devoid of the dreadful, earthy-peasant symbolism of Zollikofen, and seems to have been conceived as an event suited to repeated performance over the years.

But no performance came about. *St. Urs und St. Viktor* was not heard until 1996, when the composer's son gave a concert performance in which – with Lotar's permission – the spoken texts were assigned to a narrator (a solution that works well; it is a pity that Lotar and Richard had never thought of it themselves). Why the work failed to get off the ground is easy to see. Lotar's position at the Biel-Solothurn Theatre did not provide him with the far bigger forces, infrastructure and funding that are required to put on a *Festspiel*. Working on their own, Lotar and Flury were always going to find it difficult to get backers, and it would have been sensible to have done so before embarking on the project in the first place. But outside events were the main factor. Nazi Germany surrendered on 8 May 1945, Europe lay in ruins and, although Switzerland remained a little island of tranquillity in the midst of chaos, Swiss society also now began to adjust to the post-War situation in Europe. The economic and political situation was simply not conducive to putting on a large-scale *Festspiel* by a late-Romantic composer and a Czech *émigré* in Solothurn in the spring of 1945.

In spite of his failure to get his *Festspiel* off the ground, Flury did have one success in the Solothurn Theatre in the early 1940s, in a genre at which he had never yet tried his hand. He had written a *Little Ballet Music* back in 1925, but that was a title that seemed apt only for a small group of dances. On 14 December 1945, his first of two 'real' ballets was given its world premiere at the Solothurn Theatre: *Die alte Truhe*, to a story by Bet Hauschild-Sutter (1914–2016), who had studied dance under Jaques-Dalcroze and later became known for developing a dance-therapy that has since become established at assorted clinics in German-speaking central Europe.[6] She also designed the costumes and devised the

[6] *Cf.* 'Pionierin der Bewegungsschule hat ihren 100. Geburtstag gefeiert', *Der Landbote*, 29 October 2014.

choreography. The orchestra at the first performance was not the Theatre's own, but made up of members of Flury's Solothurn City Orchestra. The dancers were (so the poster announced) the 'amateur dance group' run by Hauschild-Sutter herself, and they included Flury's wife Rita. The story is this: two children (a boy and a girl) discover an old chest full of toys and dolls in the attic, and by magic they come to life – a jack-in-the-box, a gypsy girl, a creole girl, a knight, and so on. Flury wrote some twenty short musical numbers for them, including several minuets and waltzes, with a tarantella, a tango and suchlike tossed into the mix. Such popular *Gebrauchsmusik* was the kind of thing that he did extremely well, and it seems to have come more naturally to him than the large-scale sonata forms he was nevertheless assiduously cultivating. His dances are both tuneful and nicely scored. The critics were admittedly very few – an amateur dance performance in Solothurn in the middle of winter was not the kind of thing to attract major reviewers from the big cities – but they were very positive all the same. The *National-Zeitung* in Basel at least published a review by a Solothurn correspondent, praising the 'impulsively lovely music' and calling Flury himself 'a modern Romantic', which no doubt pleased him.

Very few prominent Swiss composers emerged with much credit after the Second World War. Othmar Schoeck was briefly ostracised for having written an opera, *Das Schloss Dürande*, to a libretto by a Nazi sympathiser, Hermann Burte;[7] Heinrich Sutermeister enjoyed his breakthrough success with the opera *Romeo und Julia* under Karl Böhm in Dresden in 1940, and wrote another opera to a commission from Dresden before the War ended; Arthur Honegger enjoyed much success as a composer in Paris under the German occupation, and even attended the Nazi-sponsored Mozart Festival in Vienna in 1941;[8] and as President of the Swiss Musicians' Association from 1942 to 1946, Frank Martin was jointly responsible for hampering the careers of *émigré* musicians in wartime Switzerland.[9] None of these men ever supported the Nazis, and their actions can be explained as an attempt to prolong a supposed *status quo ante* in which relations between composers and their patrons (both private and public) were considered above politics. It is arguably unfair to condemn them today simply because they – and many like them – were unwilling to acknowledge that the world around them had changed. Nor were the Swiss alone in harbouring such sentiments. Even Ralph Vaughan Williams, who did much in England

[7] *Cf.* my *Othmar Schoeck. Life and Works*, *op. cit.*, pp. 252–56.

[8] *Cf.*, for example, Roman Brotbeck, 'Prekäre Ambivalenzen. Arthur Honeggers Anpassungen nach 1941', in Andreas Eichhorn (ed.), *Kurt Weill und Frankreich*, Waxmann, Münster/New York, 2014, pp. 9–23.

[9] *Cf.*, for example, Thomas Gartmann, 'Der Schweizerische Tonkünstlerverein 1933 bis 1945. Ein Berufsverband, der sich nicht mit politischen Fragen befasst (?)', in Chris Walton and Antonio Baldassarre (eds.), *Musik im Exil. Die Schweiz und das Ausland 1918–1945*, Peter Lang, Bern, 2005, pp. 39–58.

Flury, Gottfried Kassowitz and the latter's sister, Eleonora Helgers, after the War. To the right are the Eiger and Mönch.

to aid refugees from Hitler, was afraid that the influx from abroad would 'entirely devour the tender little flower of our English culture'.[10]

Nevertheless, the fact remains that the leading Swiss musicians accommodated themselves to the reigning political situation for reasons of personal and professional advancement. Flury, by contrast, had offered a job to Kassowitz when the Nazis' anti-Semitic laws made him unemployed. Flury's first two operas were unperformable in Nazi Germany because his librettists (though dead) were *non grata* there, and his *Casanova e l'Albertolli* would have been equally unpalatable because its libretto was by a committed Swiss anti-fascist. Yet instead of hedging his bets during the War by avoiding the company of those who might compromise him should the Nazis invade – which at the time seemed a real threat – Flury did not hesitate to work with men such as Leo Delsen, Vasa Hochmann and Peter Lotar. And although Flury made no overtly political statements before or during the War, neither did he try to publicise or profit from his anti-fascist connections after it.

Kassowitz survived the War in Vienna, and after the Nazi surrender, Flury straight away began efforts to get him to Switzerland so that he might recuperate. It seems – to judge from Kassowitz's letters – that it was also Flury who helped Kassowitz's sister in Zurich to re-establish contact with her brother. In a letter of 3 February 1946, Kassowitz thanks Flury

[10] Letter of 16 August 1942 from Vaughan Williams to Friedrich Rauter, quoted in Hugh Cobbe, 'Vaughan Williams, Germany and the German Tradition: A View from the Letters', in Alain Frogley (ed.), *Vaughan Williams Studies*, Cambridge University Press, Cambridge, 1996, p. 95.

for his efforts to get him an entry visa to Switzerland. The application was successful, as Kassowitz's next letter confirms, for on 22 June 1946 he wrote from Vienna thanking Flury and his wife for having had him as their guest, saying that he felt 'renewed in body and soul'. In the summer of the next year, 1947, Flury invited Kassowitz for a longer visit so that he could come and conduct the Solothurn Orchestra, although he had to get brother Adolf to intervene with the aliens police in Bern to smooth over getting a permit. The friendship between Kassowitz and Flury continued for the subsequent years as if nothing had happened. Kassowitz resumed his career conducting at the Vienna Radio and elsewhere, occasionally programming a work by Flury in the process, and Richard stayed with Kassowitz when he visited Vienna in the post-War years.

For all the vicissitudes of the times, Flury's old friendships were proving rather more constant than his marriage. One of his early post-War letters to Marx reveals the current state of the Flury household. On 19 August 1947, he wrote to him as follows:

> I'm happier ['glücklicher'] in my second marriage. My wife graduated on the violin but is now studying in the Theatre Department of the Bern Conservatory and wants to train to become an actress. So for two days of the week I'm a bachelor and our 6-year-old Urs-Josef [*sic*] is looked after by my mother-in-law. It's important to me that my wife, who is 20 years younger than me, can pursue her artistic ambitions and doesn't feel that her talent is being swamped by the household.

There are details here that are worth teasing out. The comparative – 'happier' – almost serves as an antonym of 'happy'; for by assigning gradations to the emotion Flury implies a knowledge that his attainment of it is insufficient. In German, as in English, to talk of being a 'bachelor' during the absence of one's spouse can be a banal, throwaway joke; but in concrete terms, being a sometime bachelor suggests that the state of marriage – and the duties it involves – is now something to be switched on and off. And when Flury says he doesn't want his wife to feel that her talent is swamped, it sounds like an accusation she has already cast at him. This is a far cry from what Flury had imagined back on 8 August 1939 in his letter to Rita before their marriage, in which he spoke of her future 'sacrifices' for him, trusting in her 'discipline'. She had since then disobeyed his *de facto* ban on dancing, despite his having declared it 'repugnant' – but since it had been in his own ballet in late 1945, he could hardly have said 'no'. Back when they were engaged, Flury had felt sure that Rita would accept his 'guidance in all matters'. Well, she wouldn't any more.

18
Forever Young?

This letter from Flury to his wife is undated, but presumably from the latter half of the 1940s:

> I put up with your infatuation for the actor, though it pained me, because I didn't think it went very deep [....] it is distressing and humiliating for a husband if his desires are refused when he wishes to unite with his wife. You have done that often and it was difficult for me to try and approach you again in the knowledge that I might once again be met with such coldness [...]. Your jealousy of my girl pupils was always completely unfounded.

'The actor' was the Viennese actor Johannes von Spallart, who arrived in Switzerland with his family in late 1944 and worked as an actor and director at the Biel-Solothurn Theatre for the next ten years. No details of the affair between him and Rita Flury seem to have survived, except that it took place; nor is it known whether von Spallart was the first lover she took after her marriage, though he was not the last. Flury's insistence in the same letter that Rita is needlessly jealous of his girl pupils suggests some causality between their respective infidelities. In purely physical terms, Flury was right: Rita did not need to be jealous, since it is reasonably certain that he never embarked on a physical relationship with any of them, to judge from the reminiscences of his students and according to his own admission, late in life. But he freely admitted to infatuations from afar, even referring to them openly in the autobiography that he published in 1950. And Rita well knew that he had once venerated her thus too, before pursuing her doggedly into marriage and divorcing his first wife. Flury seems to have assumed that an avoidance of penetration exonerated him from any guilt. As the letter above suggests, Rita seems to have thought otherwise, and through her actions confirmed that she felt no longer bound by any marital vows of constancy. Richard's serial infatuations and Rita's affairs were known to each party, and soon became an open secret among family and friends. Such behaviour was not uncommon among the Solothurn upper crust: one of Flury's friends, a leading Solothurn doctor, kept a mistress in Biel who was an actress at the theatre.[1]

Rita's theatre connections not only provided her with a lover; they also led to Richard's first major crush since his marriage. Rita's teacher at the Bern

[1] This information is based on assorted local conversations in Solothurn.

Flury in 1944, modelled by his friend from the 'Künstlerstübli', Walter Peter (1902–97)

Theatre School was Margarethe Schell-von Noé, the wife of the dramatist and poet Ferdinand Schell. Their daughter Gritli Schell (1926–2005) was an up-and-coming young actress who had already played in the Swiss film *Steibruch* in 1942, even before having had any theatrical training (her name, the Swiss diminutive of 'Margarethe', was later abandoned for 'Maria' when her international career began). She afterwards joined her mother's class at the Bern Theatre School, where Leo Delsen saw her in 1944, recognised her talent, and promptly gave her a contract at the Biel-Solothurn Theatre.

Maria Schell became a regular visitor to the Flury household, presumably because of the connection between her mother and Rita. She even helped out with Urs Joseph, feeding him when Rita had to see to other household matters. Maria's looks and charisma were such that schoolboys would steal photos of her from the local shop windows in which the Theatre advertised its new productions.[2] Richard Flury, too, was soon head over heels in love with Maria, though he initially expressed it in a rather odd fashion: from late January to early February 1946 he set twenty poems to music (mostly love poems, beginning with one entitled 'He loves me'), all to texts by Maria's father, Ferdinand.

[2] Told to the author by Urs Joseph Flury.

Kulenkampff gave the first performance of Flury's new Third Violin Concerto at the Radio Studio in Bern on 2 February 1946. Flury invited Maria Schell to accompany him to the event, and they travelled together by train from Biel, where she lived in digs. Flury presumably hoped that the performance would impress her. It did, but not after the manner he had anticipated, for she fell in love with Kulenkampff as he played, went to meet him afterwards and was about to accompany him to his hotel room for the night when Flury insisted that he take her home instead, as he had given his word to her landlady that he would bring her back (Maria had turned twenty only four weeks earlier). Although Maria relented, she remained sullenly silent in the train all the way back to Biel. By the time Flury had deposited her at home he had missed the last train back to Solothurn – and Maria took the first train back to Bern and Kulenkampff in the morning anyway. Consumed by frustration at his thwarted passion, Flury walked all the way back to Solothurn – which must have taken five or six hours altogether. When he arrived, he set about making himself a rice soup. His wife was well aware of his infatuation with Maria, found out what had happened, and asked whether eating soup was maybe not the best cure for lovesickness. He replied 'My feelings have nothing to do with my stomach'. He did say, however, that he felt like tearing up all the songs he'd written for Maria.[3]

A little over a month after Maria Schell had rebuffed him and bestowed her affections on a rival, Flury celebrated his 50th birthday. There were congratulatory articles in the press, and he presumably enjoyed all the attention. But at the same time, 50 is a turning point, and Maria's rebuttal must have also brought home to him that he was now getting too old to expect any returns on his erotic pursuit of the young. It was around his 50th birthday that the Flurys also moved for the last time, this time to a rented house on the Alte Bernstrasse in the south-west of Solothurn near Biberist, close to where the houses peter out and farmland begins. Their new house was higher up than the rest of the city, affording them a splendid view out towards the Jura mountain range. A couple of hundred yards away (though on the Biberist side of the city boundary), Flury rented an old half-run-down apartment to use as his composing study. A sense of having reached a caesura in life also seems confirmed by Flury's decision, apparently made that year, to embark on his memoirs.[4]

There is a postlude to the story of the Third Violin Concerto, for Maria now embarked on a long-lasting affair with Kulenkampff. He was over twice her age (the fact that he was only three years younger than Flury must have rankled all the more with him). Apparently all too aware of the gap and in an effort to roll back the aging process, Kulenkampff followed the advice

[3] Family reminiscence.

[4] He mentions this plan in a letter written in Solothurn to his daughter Eva on 8 November 1946.

Maria Schell, c. 1950

of Wilhelm Furtwängler and others and underwent a so-called 'live cell cure' in the summer of 1948, a procedure that involved being injected with cells from the brains of young animals (usually lambs) in the belief that they would bring about physical rejuvenation. But there was no adequate screening process for the cells used, and Kulenkampff was one of several patients who received infected cells. He died of encephalitis some weeks later, on 4 October 1948.

After two years in Solothurn, Maria moved on to more prestigious stages in Vienna and elsewhere, and in 1948 she was given her first leading film role (in *Der Engel mit der Posaune*). She moved to England in 1950, starring in films with Robert Donat, Laurence Olivier and Trevor Howard, then set off for Hollywood, where her leading men included Yul Brynner and Gary Cooper. By the end of 1957, her photo had graced the covers of *Time*, *Life* and *Paris Match*. Contact with the Flurys dwindled to a minimum but remained cordial, as her two extant letters in Flury's archives confirm; the last, written in 1963 on letterheaded paper that states simply 'MARIA SCHELL', closes with 'lots of love to you and yours, Maria'. At a chance meeting with Urs Joseph Flury outside the Burgtheater in Vienna several years later, Maria

Flury (right) at his 50th-birthday celebrations, with Josef Remenyi of the Solothurner Zeitung

reminisced how Richard had so plied her with chocolate mousse whenever they met during her years in Solothurn that she had never been able to eat it since.

After his disappointment with Maria, Flury transferred his affections elsewhere within only a few weeks. In mid-1946, the Solothurn Orchestra gave a concert in Mühledorf – about six miles south-west of Solothurn – to raise money for a new organ in the local church. At the little reception afterwards, there was a young girl helping to serve the guests. Her name was Maria Bangerter. For Flury it was love at first sight. He admits it in his memoirs, writing that 'her facial features had something of an inward warmth, something Madonna-like about them, and her being exuded an elegant reserve that captivated me from the first moment'. They danced together, and for Flury, 'that prosaic room opened up to the heavens before me'.[5] They became friends. Maria found him very charming, enjoyed the stories and anecdotes he told, and learnt a lot from him. He recommended that she read Gotthelf, suggested music she should get to know, and occasionally provided her with tickets for the theatre. Sometimes he joined her there, but mostly she went with a girlfriend. Flury writes in his memoirs that 'there was no erotic passion burning within me', which sounds a bit disingenuous. Maria lived on a farm in the village of Tscheppach, not far along the road from Mühledorf. Flury now began making long walks through the woods to where she lived, picking flowers for her along the way. Once, after a concert, he walked to her farm late in the evening so as to leave her the bouquet that he'd been given; but he knocked over a pile of firewood stacked outside, which woke everyone, and he had to hand over the flowers in person. Her parents were quite unconcerned about Flury's attentions, she recalled.[6]

The area where Maria lived is known collectively as the 'Bucheggberg'. In spite of the suffix 'berg' it is not mountainous but a hilly, undulating region of which about a third is covered in forests. Flury loved walking here, writing in his memoirs:

> Even as a child I loved the little hills and dales of the Bucheggberg, which, untouched by railways and factories, left their mark on my soul as an ideal landscape [....] charming, ever shifting images surprise the wanderer: idyllic villages can appear in the midst of giant trees and forests, or you can come across an old mill in a valley floor.[7]

Flury already had friends in the Bucheggberg: Martha and Alexander Stuber, who ran a restaurant in nearby Lüterswil. His adoration for Maria Bangerter now intensified his love for the area:

> I felt happy to wander the roads of the place she called home, to warm myself under the same sun [...] and to dream at the edge of the forest under the same mysterious moonlight that shone through the windows of her bedroom.[8]

The prose in Flury's memoirs is nowhere more purple than when he writes of Maria Bangerter. She and the place inspired him to his Third Symphony, in 1946, the *Bucheggberg Symphony*, which he dedicated to her. It is a vast thing, some 50 minutes in length, and despite its fine orchestration it suffers somewhat from the same tendency to sprawl as the one-movement *Waldsymphonie*. The best movement is also the shortest – the Scherzo. Maria Bangerter and her region also inspired the *Bucheggberger Ländler* for small orchestra in 1947, a ländler-cycle reminiscent of the waltz-cycles of

[5] *Lebenserinnerungen*, *op. cit.*, p. 227.
[6] Interview with Maria Böhlen, *née* Bangerter, Solothurn, October 2013.
[7] *Ibid.*, p. 225.
[8] *Ibid.*, p. 227.

Mühledorf, in the rolling hills of the Bucheggberg, c. 1970

Johann Strauss (it lasts roughly a quarter of an hour). They also exist in an alternative piano version that is no less delightful. In spite of the geographical location in their name, these ländler show Flury's Viennese side again, and are so tuneful that one wishes Flury had put some of their tunefulness into his *Bucheggberg Symphony*. Also inspired by the Bucheggberg was the *Sketchbook from the Bucheggberg. 50 Romantic Pieces* for piano from 1949, a series of character pieces with often Schumannesque titles such as 'Kinderspiel' ('Children's Game'), 'Ringel-Reihn' ('Round Dance') and 'Schulpause' ('School Recess'). There are also character sketches in it; thus No. 16, 'The Schoolmaster', and No. 38, 'The Organist', are both about Alexander Stuber, and No. 29, 'The Lovely Farmer's Daughter', is inspired by Maria Bangerter.

As with his violin pieces of the 1930s, Flury's shifting affections can be observed in his dedications. He published a selection of his songs in 1946 under the title *29 Lieder*. Most were to texts by Ferdinand Schell, but others were by his friend Bernhard Moser, three by Wilhelm Voss, one by Johann Gottfried Herder, one by the Solothurn poetess Olga Brand and one by Richard Dehmel. Most are love-songs. The first is dedicated to the singer Paula Adam-Girard (who had sung in his Mass back in 1931), but many are dedicated to Maria Schell, some to Rita and five to Maria Bangerter. It cannot have been easy for Rita to see that the songs dedicated to Maria Schell included settings of lines such as 'you are my only lover', nor that

No. 26, entitled 'Three Words' and ending 'Ich liebe dich' was dedicated to Maria Bangerter. The effusive descriptions of the last Maria in Flury's autobiography must have hurt her too. Nevertheless, consoling herself elsewhere, she seems to have accepted things as they were. Maria Bangerter later recalled having been invited to dine with the Flurys along with Maria Schell; Rita cooked goulash for them all, and it was very pleasant, Maria Bangerter recalled.

A few months after finishing the *Sketchbook from the Bucheggberg*, Flury found another young girl to adore. Her name was Rosette Schaad. She was about eighteen years old and played the violin in her spare time, taking lessons from Willy Hug, a gifted musician and visual artist who lived in Büren an der Aare. He had written a *Festspiel* for a shooting festival in Büren an der Aare in the summer of 1950, and Rosette was playing in the orchestra.[9] Flury knew Hug well, and as a favour joined the orchestra to help fill out the violin section. Rosette was a blonde, in appearance somewhat similar to Maria Schell. Flury told Rosette she looked as lovely as 'the light of the moon' and offered to teach her. She accepted – she had always been a little apprehensive of Hug, who had a bad temper, she said – and henceforth went to Flury's house for two hours every Wednesday after work. He proved a sympathetic teacher and also helped her to get to know the literary classics – Schiller, Goethe and the like. Rosette already had a boyfriend – they would marry a few years later – and Flury knew it, but in any case remained the perfect gentleman throughout. It was to him, she recalled,[10] that she owed her real education in the arts and literature. He dedicated his next violin sonata to her, also composed in 1950 – No. 8 in A major, perhaps the loveliest of his sonatas. The next year, she received the dedication of a *Berceuse*, this time worded 'to my dear Rosette for Christmas 1951'.

There were yet other 'Schwärme' of Flury's, as they seem to have been termed by those who knew him ('crush' is the closest English equivalent) and their precise number remains vague. But the proliferation of dedications bearing women's names suggests that they were numerous. One of his later crushes was Marie-Louise Geiser, who was in her late teens when she got to know Flury in about 1957. She was attending the commercial college attached to the Kantonsschule and took piano lessons with Erich Schild (and later with Charles Dobler, Flury's former pupil). She used to see Flury in the corridor in between lessons, then started visiting him in his room during breaks because he didn't mind her smoking, which was otherwise forbidden for pupils on the school premises. The teachers all noticed that Flury was enamoured of her – but whereas today that sort of thing might prompt investigations, hearings, reports and admonishments, the other teachers used to joke with Marie-Louise about it. Her English teacher even

[9] Walter Winkler, 'Das "Büreliedli" im neuen Kleid', *Grenchner Tagblatt*, 14 April 2009.

[10] Conversation with the author, February 2016, Basel.

Rita and Richard Flury playing at a wedding in Zuchwil

said 'Soon he'll be writing a symphony for you'. There was no symphony, but Flury did dedicate his *Ten Romantic Pieces for Piano* to her in 1958. Not long after, she moved to Winterthur to attend college there, but kept in touch with Flury whenever she was back in Solothurn.

All these crushes are a little perplexing. The ladies in question whom I have been able to interview[11] have been remarkably open. Without any prompting (for it would have been indecorous to pry), they confirmed that for them there was no erotic element to their relationship, nor did Flury ever openly express any such interest in them – although they could not rule out that he harboured such notions and yet left them unexpressed. As one of the ladies put it, to them he was 'an old man' and thus of no sexual interest. Flury also tended to fall for girls who by any measure were extremely attractive (in this respect, Maria Schell was only one of several), and who already inspired considerable jockeying among their male contemporaries. But all these ladies were adamant that they got much in return. One of them, who came from a poor family and who had completed primary school and little else, told me openly: 'My looks were my only talent', and she used her beauty to get the attention of the males around her (in fact, she was in fact unduly modest, for even well into her eighties she possesses a fiercely sharp mind). Flury had educated her, she said, he had introduced her to all the beauties of culture that she had never known at home, and she regarded her friendship with him as the most significant of her life (and a very successful

[11] Discretion obliges me not to state precisely who said what to me in the remainder of this chapter.

life it turned out to be, too). Although it is common to assume that the power in such relationships lies automatically with the older male, not with the school-age girl – especially in the male-dominated society of post-War Switzerland – one should nevertheless refrain from assuming that the girls in question were without agency. One of these ladies, when asked (not by me, though in my presence) 'You were one of Richard's crushes, weren't you?', replied with what can best be described as a knowing smile (hackneyed though that sounds): 'Yes, a *massive* crush of his!' she said, clearly aware of the leverage that Flury's infatuation had given her.

Today, society rightly looks askance at such relationships between teachers and pupils, regardless of whether 'anything happens' or not. But one must beware of judging when others do not, and acknowledge that in times when power and gender hierarchies are skewed (in Switzerland in the 1940s, '50s and '60s, women didn't even have the right to vote), those adversely affected will find ways and means to circumvent hindrances. None of those interviewed expressed any sense of having been disadvantaged or 'abused'. Their friendships with Flury also seem to have remained intact for many years afterwards. One of them remarked how Flury – nearly twenty years after his initial infatuation with her – had poured his heart out to her after the death by cancer of his first son, Roger, in 1964. Another said she had been a sounding board for his problems with Rita, who was something of a 'gypsy', she said (a word Flury himself used to describe his wife in a letter to Marx of 18 November 1949). Flury had complained to her about how Rita would go out and buy things on credit – such as carpets – but would tell him nothing, leaving him to find out only when the bills started to arrive.

Rita seems to have accepted the presence of these young girls as a fact of life in her marriage, though she was friendlier to some than to others – perhaps she felt some to be a threat in a way that others weren't. In one case, Richard lied to her that he was going off to his composing room to work, when in fact he was meeting one of his 'crushes' in town. But Rita found out and was furious with him. As for the carpets on credit and suchlike, Rita was neither the first nor the last spouse to use expenditure as a means of reprisal in a rocky marriage. But she also had other means at her disposal. The occasional banishment from the marital bed to which Flury refers in the letter quoted at the beginning of this chapter became permanent in the later years of his life. And Rita did not follow her husband in keeping a physical distance from the opposite sex. Her affair with Johannes von Spallart seems to have overlapped or alternated with her relationship with Cäsar Spiegel, a gifted artist who happened to be the nephew of Richard's former mentor Richard Spiegel. Cäsar had helped Richard with his research for a little book that Flury had published in 1945 about the local Solothurn poet Josef Joachim.[12] Spiegel had then become a family friend and often came to visit

[12] Richard Flury, *Josef Joachim, Leben und Werke des solothurnischen Bauerndichters*, Kommissionsverlag Vogt-Schild, Solothurn, 1945.

and eat with the extended Flury family. The affair, which lasted off and on for a decade, was common knowledge among them all, but seems to have been accepted as much as Richard's crushes were. This affair with Spiegel became far more serious, however. A member of Rita's family, a child at the time in the mid-1950s, recalls being out walking with Rita when they came across Spiegel, sitting forlornly and (in retrospect) clearly waiting for Rita. Rita left the child at a distance and went to talk to him, but the child could see that he was weeping bitterly. The end of the affair was complex and fraught, but it was Rita who decided on termination, rather than risk the end of her marriage. Spiegel nevertheless – somehow – remained over the coming years within the Flury family's circle of friends.

So what did Flury get from his crushes, apart from occasional strife at home? There was surely an erotic aspect to these infatuations, but perhaps the fact that his own daughters had grown up without him also led him to seek substitutes for his paternal feelings. It is even possible that he saw his behaviour justified by the example of Anton Bruckner, who had also fallen repeatedly in love with girls in their late teens, only to be rebuffed by all of them. Flury's friend Gustav Renker in Bern had known the Bruckner family personally, and owned one of the great composer's diaries in which such attempted entanglements are detailed. Bruckner would be an odd role model for anyone, but that does not rule him out. Perhaps Flury simply felt that he needed young muses to inspire him – though he had never yet been wont to suffer from composing blocks. Some of the music they apparently prompted is not actually very inspired at all; but some of it is. At least Flury himself was sure that these girls were an inspiration. And there is enough that is indeed inspired for the matter to be laid to rest here: as an aspect of his personality that cannot be left out of an account of his life, but whose precise import will probably never be entirely fathomable. Perhaps Flury couldn't quite fathom it either.

19
The Art of the Confectioner

Richard Flury's career after the Second World War parallels in many ways that of the society in which he lived. While central Europe began the immense business of reconstruction, Switzerland's economy boomed. The borders opened again, trade and tourism with the surrounding countries increased, and cultural exchange profited too. The immediate post-War years seemed to begin with a financial setback for Flury, because his first wife, Lily, wanted to marry again, but demanded that he pay off her debts first – for once she married, his alimony payments would cease. He agreed, cashed in assorted insurance policies, and paid off what she owed. As it happened, her second marriage proved far shorter than her first, and she separated a few months later. But this development had no impact on Flury's finances, as his debts to her were over. The children from his first marriage were now largely independent – Roger, the youngest of them, briefly stayed with Richard, Rita and Urs when doing an apprenticeship as a goldsmith in the late 1940s, and Giovanna even entered the music profession, singing in the chorus of Radio Lugano and later of the Basel Theatre. By the end of the decade, Richard's financial commitments were now solely confined to his second family, and his economic situation began to improve accordingly.

Flury's teaching and conducting duties also returned to normal. He wrote to Marx in August 1947 telling him of his 25-hour week at the Kantonsschule, comprising nineteen hours of violin lessons, an hour each of orchestra rehearsals and string-quartet practice, then four hours of music theory and history. As was happening in the rest of Switzerland, Canton Solothurn, too, began investing heavily in education after the War, the most tangible result of which was the erection of a new Kantonsschule in the 1950s (including dedicated music rooms), half a mile to the north of the old cantonal school (work had begun on the new building at the time of the outbreak of war, but had been put on hold for economic reasons in 1942).

The Solothurn Orchestra no longer had to worry about its members being called up into the army for long periods, though it did suffer from one disadvantage after 1945. The star performers who had been keen to come during the War now gradually took up engagements elsewhere. For the moment, Flury was still able to engage major names such as Yehudi Menuhin, Louis Kentner (both in 1947) and Alfred Cortot (in 1948), but once the old musical centres of Europe began to function again, an amateur orchestra in Solothurn could not compete with the professionalism (or the fees) of Salzburg, Berlin, Paris or Vienna. There was, however, an older generation of composers who were only too keen to stay in Switzerland for the moment, most notably Franz Lehár – who had been allowed out of German-occupied Europe on health grounds during the War – and Richard Strauss, who arrived in the autumn of 1945. Flury had always admired both men intensely, and now took the opportunity to make their acquaintance. He visited Lehár in his room in the Hotel Baur au Lac in Zurich (the same hotel in which Franz Liszt had stayed, nearly a hundred years before), and was delighted when the old man took the trouble to listen to the *Waldsymphonie* on the radio and praised it. Flury visited Strauss more than once, first in January 1947, when Strauss was living in the Hotel Verenahof in Baden outside Zurich; a second visit took place in the Ticino in the following April. Strauss complained about modern music, modern critics and the like, but was otherwise jovial and friendly. He gave Flury a signed copy of the new *Rosenkavalier Suite* that had just been published (Flury would no doubt have been astonished to learn that Boosey & Hawkes had paid Strauss CHF 50,000 for it).[1] Flury afterwards sent him the scores of his *Waldsymphonie* and *Fasnachts-Symphonie*, and Rita packed them in with a 'Solothurner Torte', a sweet, crumbly cake that is a speciality of the city. Strauss wrote back and admitted that he had been so used to being sent scores by aspiring composers that he generally left them unopened – but the presence of the cake had saved Flury's score from a similar fate. The cake, wrote Strauss, was a 'masterpiece of the confectioner's art', and the scores were 'very estimable'. Flury joked in his memoirs that he would have preferred Strauss' judgement of cake and scores to have been the other way round – but reading between the lines, he also respected Strauss for not dishing out platitudes of empty praise.[2]

Joseph Marx also visited Switzerland after the War. He was invited to sit on the jury of Geneva's international music competition in the autumn of 1948, and made sure to spend a few days in Solothurn with Flury on the way. Their correspondence had dwindled to near-zero during the War, but they had afterwards continued where they had left off, and when they now met again – for the first time in 27 years – Marx finally offered the familial 'Du' address to his former student (in the German-speaking world the decision to use first-name terms is a prerogative traditionally enjoyed only by the elder partner in any friendship). Marx stayed as a guest of Richard's wealthy brother-in-law Fritz Moos in Biberist, and did so again when he visited Flury once more in the autumn of 1951. This time, Moos organised a sumptuous lunch reception for Marx and assorted local luminaries that was preceded by a brief song-recital by Paula Girard-Adam accompanied by Flury. According to family anecdote, Marx repeatedly told Flury before

[1] *Cf.* my *Lies and Epiphanies*, *op. cit.*, p. 115.

[2] *Lebenserinnerungen*, *op. cit.*, pp. 241–42.

Yehudi Menuhin and Louis Kentner in Solothurn, 26 April 1947, in a sketch by Flury's friend Willy Hug

and during lunch that as a *Lied* expert he would like to take Ms Girard-Adam aside and offer her a lesson 'to help improve her phrasing'. Flury advised against it, probably because he knew his brother-in-law Fritz had long harboured extra-musical longings for Ms Girard-Adam and might take offence at Marx's interest. But Marx insisted, took her into the music room, closed the glass doors, and proceeded with a coaching session. The lunch seemed to end happily; but a day or so later, Fritz Moos rang Flury to complain that Ms Girard-Adam had been mortally offended by Marx's behaviour and that he, Richard, was to blame. Flury and Fritz had never been close, and Richard's loyalty to Marx was in any case beyond question. So he took sides against his brother-in-law, hung up on him, and relations were soured between them for over a decade. For many months afterwards, Marx's letters to Flury included the question 'Is Moos still angry?',[3] but by late December 1953 Flury could at least inform him that he and Fritz Moos were greeting each other again.[4] The next year, Flury dedicated a quartet for four horns to Fritz on his 60th birthday. But it would be a long time before relations were properly restored.

Besides his continuing commitments with the Solothurn Orchestra after the War, Flury also took on an extra conducting job from 1945 to 1949, working with the amateur orchestra in Gerlafingen, the next little town down the railway line from Biberist on the way to Thun. When its conductor, Achilles Cueny, had to withdraw for reasons of illness, he asked Flury to take over for him. Flury had hoped to reduce his commitments at the time, but the orchestra was *de facto* a successor to the old Biberist orchestra run by Flury's father and his former mentor Richard Spiegel, and so for old times' sake he relented,[5] and stayed for the next four years (he would later step in once again, conducting the orchestra from 1958 until his death in late 1967). But in 1949, Flury's circumstances changed. He was advised by a friend who was also a local politician that he should apply to be relieved of teaching duties for two or three hours a week so as to be able to have more time to compose. Flury did as he suggested, and the reduction in working hours (but at the same salary) was granted. However, Flury felt that he would have to cut back on his outside commitments if he were to devote himself properly to composing, and so he gave up both his 'temporary' post with the Gerlafingen orchestra, and his long-time permanent post with the Solothurn Orchestra too. For his final concert with the latter, he was able to engage Wilhelm Backhaus again. The concert took place on 26 March 1949 in the Solothurn Concert Hall. The Orchestra played Beethoven's First Symphony and accompanied Backhaus in the Third Piano Concerto. Backhaus then played the 'Moonlight' Sonata and Flury's *Bucheggberger*

[3] Thus Marx to Flury on 23 December 1953; similar sentiments are also to be found, for example, in his letters of 24 June and 29 August 1953.

[4] Letter of 31 December 1953 from Marx to Flury.

[5] *Lebenserinnerungen*, *op. cit.*, p. 153.

Joseph Marx and Richard Flury, autumn 1948, outside the house of Fritz Moos in Biberist

Ländler, and the Orchestra closed the programme with Beethoven's *Egmont* Overture. The critics paid tribute to Flury's thirty years of service and his achievements with the Orchestra. The *Schweizerische Musikzeitung* brought only a short notice of the event in its columns 'Reports from Switzerland and abroad', but noted that Backhaus' superb playing brought 'never-ending storms of applause' and that 'the orchestra has rarely played as well as in this concert', singling out the fine balance that Flury achieved in the orchestral accompaniment to Backhaus' playing.[6] The same report continued with a review – slightly longer – of Erich Schild's latest concert with the Solothurn Chamber Orchestra, held a little over a week later. It had featured an all-Russian programme, with Stravinsky's *Apollon musagète* and Shostakovich's Concerto for Piano, Trumpet and Strings, and the reviewer was full of enthusiasm for Schild's achievement in getting a largely amateur orchestra to such a standard of performance.

Flury's retirement from the orchestras of Solothurn and Gerlafingen did not mean he gave up performing. He still conducted his own works in the coming years when invited to do so on the radio in Zurich and elsewhere, and he continued to play the violin. In June 1950 he even joined the first violins back in the Kurorchester in Interlaken for a Mendelssohn concert.

The decision on Flury's part to concentrate more on composing makes sense, too, when one considers that his music was getting more and more performances in these post-War years. Even the conductor Hermann Scherchen had begun to take an interest in it. He had been based in Switzerland since the 1920s, conducting the Winterthur Orchestra and later the Zurich Radio Orchestra. He has gone down in the annals for his performances of Mahler and of the Second Viennese School (it was he who had given the world premiere of Alban Berg's Violin Concerto in 1936), and he also often performed the music of several Swiss late Romantics such as Othmar Schoeck. Scherchen conducted Flury's *Fasnachts-Symphonie* in Zurich in 1946, and the *Waldsymphonie* there in 1949; his recording of the former has survived and, despite its scratchiness, his interpretation brings out the Mahlerian echoes in the work. Other staunch advocates of Flury's at this time included Christoph Lertz, who had conducted the radio premiere of *Die helle Nacht* in 1935 and who now conducted the *Waldsymphonie* with the orchestra of Südwestfunk in Freiburg in Germany in 1951 and Flury's *Festspiel* musics from 1922 and 1932 on Bern Radio in that same year. Performances of his music abroad were now frequent. The Swiss soprano Ria Ginster sang assorted songs by Flury on tours through England and Germany; Otmar Suitner played the *Bucheggberger Ländler* on the radio in Innsbruck in early September 1950; a few days later his Fifth Violin Sonata was performed in East Germany at a concert of the Society for German-Soviet Friendship; Otmar Nussio frequently conducted the Overture to

[6] '-ae-', 'Solothurn', *Schweizerische Musikzeitung*, Vol. 89, No. 5 (1 May 1949), p. 209.

Flury rehearsing Wilhelm Backhaus in Beethoven's Third Piano Concerto for his last concert with the Solothurn Orchestra in March 1949

Casanova e l'Albertolli on Swiss-Italian Radio; the Piano Trio was performed in Dresden in late 1951; and the Paris-based, Hungarian violin-and-piano duo of Gabriella and Attila Lengyel performed the Sixth Violin Sonata and others in Switzerland, Holland and elsewhere over the coming years.

Nor did Flury's compositional output let up. His series of violin sonatas and string quartets continued: Rosette Schaad's Sonata No. 8 of 1950 was followed by No. 9 in C major in 1951, No. 10 in D minor in 1960 (dedicated to Gabriella and Attila Lengyel) and No. 11 in A major in 1961 (dedicated to his son Urs Joseph on his twentieth birthday). After the String Quartet No. 4 of 1940 dedicated to Kurth, Flury did not return to the genre until 1955, when he composed No. 5, with No. 6 (dedicated to his sister Erika) following in 1958 and his last, No. 7, in 1964. The post-War years also saw the composition of a string trio for violin, viola and cello (1951), a piano quintet (1948), a piano quartet (1954), a second piano trio (1961), and assorted smaller pieces of chamber music, mostly for violin and piano (more minuets, berceuses and the like). With very few exceptions, his essays in the traditional genres of sonata and quartet are, like their predecessors in his output, in the standard four-movement format with the slow movement second and the scherzo (or occasionally a waltz or a polka) third. Flury's post-War chamber music on the whole signifies a further retreat (loaded though that term is) from the more advanced harmonies of his pre-War music. The overall atmosphere tends to the idyllic, with everything cast in gentle sunshine and few clouds on the horizon; at times, as in the later violin sonatas, Flury almost seems to be harking back to Mendelssohn as his harmonic and melodic model. The results are sometimes beautiful, but often bland. The Piano Quintet of 1948 is one of his few later chamber works that both aims for something bigger and generally achieves it. It was commissioned in celebration of the 80th birthday of the painter Cuno Amiet and first performed by the Brenner Quartet and the pianist Ellen Brenner-Lüthi at the opening of an exhibition of Amiet's works in the Solothurn Art Gallery on 22 September 1948. Apart from a brief review in the *Solothurner Zeitung*, the premiere of the Quintet seems hardly to have been noticed by the critics: even this local review came under the heading 'Cuno Amiet Exhibition in Solothurn'. Flury had a high regard for it himself. Although he was unable to find a publisher for most of his chamber music, he made much effort to drum up the funding to publish his Piano Quintet, which appeared a year after its completion. The local critic praised its 'extravagant [...] lyrical invention', which sounds like the kind of phrase one might concoct for want of anything better to say. But he had a point; the slow movement in particular flows almost seamlessly in an effortless interchange between the strings, underpinned by luscious, undulating figurations in the piano (Ex. 9). Harmonically, the Quintet – like much of Flury's music from the last twenty years of his life – would have been considered conservative even seventy years before. There is hardly anything here that would have sounded modern to the mature Brahms. But it never really matters.

Ex. 9

allargando
allargando

Cuno Amiet and Flury in the painter's studio in Oschwand, 1948, with two of Amiet's Flury portraits

In a CD review on the website MusicWeb International, Rob Barnett remarks on the 'ultra-conservative' style of the Quintet and observes that the work 'is not at all challenging to the listener', but he adds: 'There is nothing amiss with that when, as here, the ideas are entrancing'.[7] Even the CD reviewer of the *Neue Zürcher Zeitung*, which long tended to look askance at contemporary music that was not progressive, admitted that the

[7] *Cf.* www.musicweb-international.com/classrev/2002/Aug02/Flury_piano_gallo.htm, accessed April 2016.

Quintet is 'rarely epigonal', achieving instead a kind of 'sensuous serenity'.[8] The Quintet can be perplexing to those of a generation brought up to regard such musical conservatism with suspicion. Other works of Flury from these years are stylistically no less conservative (such as the quartets and violin sonatas) but are far easier to pigeon-hole because their conservatism often goes hand in hand with a lack of musical invention. The Quintet, by contrast, holds one's attention.

The Piano Quartet, written six years later to a commission from Radio Bern, is not of the same quality, but is still more impressive than the later string quartets. The opening movement starts off in sternly dotted, French-overture style, but soon slips into a far more genial mood situated somewhere between Brahms and the salon. The second movement is unusual for Flury in that it is in variation form, based on the south German folksong 'Jetzt gang i ans Brünnele'. It, too, is ultra-conservative – Haydn, Schubert and Mendelssohn all seem to hover in the background – but it has an irresistible, naïve charm all the same. The last movement initially galumphs along, and if it lacks the charm of the previous two, it still manages enough little harmonic twists to take the listener by surprise.

There are surprises, too, in the two large-scale chamber-music works of Flury's last years, the Octet and the Nonet, composed in 1956–57 and 1965 respectively. They are almost identical in layout: they are suites in six movements each, variously featuring minuets, a barcarole, a valse, and so on, each movement more or less three minutes in length. There is no room for the prolixity of his 'serious' chamber works here, but the number of instruments involved still allows Flury to show off his skill in instrumentation. Sometimes – such as in the Minuetto from the Nonet – the interplay of the wind and strings, coupled with sudden key-shifts, make the music charmingly witty, and it is difficult to believe that the late violin sonatas are by the same man. The Nonet also signified a final reconciliation between Flury and his brother-in-law Fritz Moos. Flury had written him a march as a 70th-birthday present in 1964, and Moos reciprocated by having his Rotary Club commission the Nonet (paid for by Moos himself).

Flury's best string music from the immediate post-War years is arguably found in the *10 Caprices for Violin Solo* of 1952, where the restrictions of the instrumentation seem to bring out the best in him. They are brief – hardly any of them is longer than one-and-a-half minutes – and their reliance on regular four-bar phrase-lengths and sequence looks unadventurous on paper. But as in *Caprice* No. 2 (Ex. 10), the music's melodic freshness and its subtle rhythmic shifts of threes and twos make for a fascinating blend of artifice and simplicity. Flury dedicated the *Caprices* to Rita as a Christmas gift in 1952. Only a few months later, Flury would complain in a letter to Marx that being married didn't prevent one from feeling 'lonely

[8] 'stue', *Neue Zürcher Zeitung*, 21 March 1996.

Ex. 10

Prestissimo ♩. = 80
mf
7
p
13
mf
f
p
19
25
f
31
Fine
Meno mosso
p
38
f
46
p
55
f
mf
f
rall poco a poco
D.C. al fine

Flury in 1948, by Cuno Amiet

and abandoned'[9] – but these *Caprices* for Rita are still as inspired as almost anything else he wrote at the time.

Flury wrote two more symphonies after the Second World War – in fact there are really three, because besides the *Liechtenstein Symphony*, which is No. 4 in C major (1950–51) and the Symphony No. 5 in B flat major (1955–56), there is also the *Altisberg Suite* of 1953, which he had initially considered calling a 'symphony'. All four works are in the standard four movements, though the Suite puts the scherzo and the slow movement second and third respectively (Flury's five numbered symphonies all put them third and second, as had been Anton Bruckner's custom). The *Altisberg Suite* is the finest of them by far; indeed, it ranks with Flury's best works for orchestra overall. It is a depiction of the Altisberg, the hill to the south of Biberist, covered in beech forests, where Flury played as a child. Its four movements are entitled 'Pastorale', 'Forest Fête', 'Nocturne' and 'On the Burghubel' (the Burghubel being the site of what was once a fortified habitation, and which Flury as a child had imagined to be a busy, mediaeval castle). The 'Nocturne' is perhaps the finest of the four movements; the generally Brahmsian/

[9] Letter to Marx from Solothurn, 21 November 1953.

Brucknerian ambiance of Flury's late orchestral works is here replaced by more Ravelian, Impressionistic colours and orchestration.

The *Liechtenstein Symphony* also has its origins in nature depiction, but not in such concrete terms as in the *Altisberg Suite*. Flury himself gave a description of it to the press at the time of its first performance:

> When I was a boy at high school, I often spent my holidays with relatives in Maria-Grün near Feldkirch in Vorarlberg [in Austria]. That led to visits in the neighbouring Principality of Liechtenstein, for whose beautiful countryside I gained a deep affection. Doesn't this little country stand like a jewel, like a peaceful, charming museum piece in the midst of restless Europe? It is above all the impressions of the landscape and my friendly relations to the Rheinberger family in the 'Rotes Haus' that prompted me to dedicate my fourth, Liechtenstein Symphony, 'in memory of Josef Rheinberger' and to Prince Franz Josef II of Liechtenstein. The 4 movements of the work are based on the form of the classical symphony, but bear the stylistic characteristics of modern Romanticism. The music follows impressions of nature without having any programme with external images.

The premiere took place in the Zurich Radio Studio under Paul Burkhard on 27 August 1952. In spite of Flury's explanatory text, it is still not quite clear why he would write a 'Liechtenstein Symphony'. There are indeed charming spots of countryside in the Principality, but they are rather dull in comparison with the natural wonders to be found immediately across the border in the Swiss canton of Graubünden. Rheinberger (1839–1901) is Liechtenstein's only composer of note – though a fine one, whose organ, choral and chamber music has been widely recorded, and who was also important as a teacher (his students included Engelbert Humperdinck and Wilhelm Furtwängler). But there was no obvious reason for Flury to dedicate a symphony jointly to a man who had died over fifty years before and to a reigning prince he didn't actually know. Flury's text sounds as if he is currying favour with the Liechtenstein powers-that-be. But Liechtenstein didn't (and still doesn't) have a professional symphony orchestra, and so it was never going to be performed there. The Prince of Liechtenstein wrote politely on 13 June 1952 to express his thanks and 'that of the country'. But it seems nothing else was gained from the dedication.

Flury thought the *Liechtenstein Symphony* to be one of his best works at the time.[10] It is difficult to agree with him. The orchestration is excellent and there are beautiful moments as always, such as the somewhat Brucknerian opening of the first and last movements (the latter with demonstratively 'Romantic' horn calls). But as in many of his other works in the classical genres, there is too much sequence, too much meandering, and if one listens to the work and then afterwards tries to recall its main themes, it is not easy.

[10] Letter from Flury to Rita and Urs Joseph from Zurich, 7 May 1952.

Flury in 1948, by Urban Zacharias Wick

The Fifth Symphony of 1955–56, dedicated to his son Urs Joseph, suffers from similar problems. Here, the opening of the first movement is even more reminiscent of Bruckner than that of the Fourth, though again without the melodic distinction and sense of a large-scale structural grasp found with the earlier composer. The last movement of the Fifth breaks the mould. It is a variation movement – not unlike the slow movement of the Piano Quartet written at this time. Its theme is the 'Wanderlied der Prager Studenten' (the 'Wandering Song of the Students from Prague'), the text of which was by the early Romantic poet Joseph von Eichendorff, and which became popular as a student song throughout the German-speaking world (though the identity of its composer remains obscure). Flury intended it as a look back at his own youth and his friends in the Dornachia fraternity and, no doubt, as a wistful glance at the youth of his own son who was now a teenager – roughly the same age as Flury had been when joining the fraternity all those years before. This last movement, with eight variations in all, is one-and-a-half times as long as any of the other movements. It is the best thing about the symphony. It is not without its uneven passages (the sixth variation, in G minor, is a little too strident and foursquare), but there are many sumptuous passages and the coda is particularly beautiful, opening with simple, chorale-like brass accompanied by slowly descending first violins but no other strings; as the textures broaden out, it begins to sound – at least to Anglo-Saxon ears – rather like Percy Grainger. Yet this movement strikes one as something of a foreign body in the symphony overall – both because of its length and because of its episodic character. It is perhaps a pity, indeed, that Flury did not use it as a separate work. The premiere took place in the studio of Radio Bern, performed by the Bern City Orchestra under Hans Haug on 9 February 1958. The surviving recording suggests either that there was little time for rehearsal, or that the work had proved to be too expansive for the broadcasting minutes available and so had to be rushed to finish it in time. Either way, Haug was audibly unable to unify the often divergent tempi chosen by the different sections of the orchestra.

Reviews of these orchestral works were almost non-existent because they took place in radio studios, not in concert halls. But the faithful Gustav Renker made sure to review Flury's new symphony in *Der Bund* on 21 February. He ignored the scrappiness of Haug's performance and wrote a highly positive review, praising Flury for staying what he always had been: a 'Romantic' for whom 'melody and beauty of sound are paramount'.

20
Romantic at Heart

In these years Flury saw himself as a 'Romantic', a fact which can perhaps help explain inconsistencies in his post-War *œuvre*. The word 'Romantic' does not occur in the title of a Flury work until 1937, namely the *Romantic Song* for cello or violin and piano, dedicated to Rita (who was probably the reason for using the word). It recurs twice more: in 1949 in his *Sketchbook from the Bucheggberg: 50 Romantic Pieces* and in the *Ten Romantic Pieces* of 1958. Since these two works were dedicated to girls to whose charms he had succumbed, the word again has an emotional context. But it otherwise occurs so often in Flury's statements about his music that it becomes almost a mantra. It is discussed towards the end of his autobiography, published in 1950, and is the topic of the essay entitled 'My belief in musical Romanticism', first published in a supplement to the *Solothurner Zeitung* on 20 January 1953.[1] Tellingly, he sets out with a discussion not of what this Romanticism is, but of what it is not:

> With regard to music and the visual arts, we live in an age in which everything that our older contemporaries had learned in their youth to regard as holy, aesthetic and legitimate has been cast aside [....] today, we are no longer dealing with a logical development, no longer with normal progress, with the growth and unfolding of artistic means, but with a break in development, with a wanton distortion of every natural feeling, an act of arbitrary reasoning that denies and violates the natural laws that are deeply anchored in the human soul.[2]

There are aspects of this essay that are perfectly reasonable – such as the notion that progress is not in itself a qualitative aesthetic category. But Flury's insistence that a 'break' had taken place leads him to construct a dichotomy between the good and the bad, i.e., between the tonal, the harmonious, the ethical, the emotional and the natural on the one hand and atonality, dissonance, anarchy, ugliness, 'intellectualism' and the unethical and unnatural on the other. Flury conveniently forgets that he, too, had written passages of music that are essentially non-tonal (such as in his opera *Die helle Nacht*[3]). Although he had never been at the forefront

[1] *Cf.* p. 13, above.
[2] *Ibid.*, p. 1.
[3] *Cf.* p. 142, above.

of musical progress, Flury's more advanced music in the late 1920s or early '30s stills belongs recognisably to the same tradition as the music by the more 'avant-garde' composers across the border such as Berg or Schoenberg. And one of his staunchest adherents was Gottfried Kassowitz, who belonged to the wider circle of the New Viennese School at the time. So however unsympathetic Flury might have found the 'atonal' music that the Schoenbergians were writing, he was aware that they had a shared heritage, and he was formulating his opinions from within it. But by the early 1950s, most of the central European Modernists of the inter-War period were either dead or irrelevant: a new generation had emerged out of the rubble and had embarked on musical developments so swift that they left Flury and many like him aghast. Comparisons are seldom useful, but if one considers that Flury wrote his *Liechtenstein Symphony* at roughly the same time that Pierre Boulez wrote his *Structures I* for two pianos – the former a Romantic outpouring with Brahms and Bruckner as its models, the latter an exercise in integral serialism – then one gets a grasp of the vast stylistic spectrum of the post-War world and can understand why Flury was convinced that a historic break had occurred.

'The soul strives for harmony, beauty and ethical perfection', he wrote in 'My belief in musical Romanticism',[4] and his music of these post-War years clearly aims at realising this goal. His earlier progressive tendencies were left behind, and he reverted instead to the Romantic models he knew and loved so well. He said as much in a radio interview with Leo Held that he gave in Solothurn in December 1964. When asked about 'Romanticism', he said:

> My [compositional] means are newer, perhaps on the level of Brahms, Bruckner or Richard Strauss [...] but music is a romantic art, it's the language of emotion [....] in this sense I am a romantic [....] my language is wholly tonal.[5]

In these post-War years, Flury was clearly pondering his legacy as a conservative artist whose home was far from the major cosmopolitan centres of culture. Issues of local neglect and redress were prominent in the 70-page book he published on the Solothurn poet Josef Joachim (1834–1904) in 1945, and in 1950 Flury published his own autobiography[6] and sent copies of it far and wide, both to those he knew and to many he didn't, such as the poet Hermann Hesse, whom he had never met but who took the trouble to leaf through the opening pages despite his poor eyesight, and then wrote a polite thank-you note in reply.[7] That same year, Flury gave his manuscripts to the cantonal library in Solothurn, long before such donations became customary among Swiss composers.

[4] Flury, 'Mein Bekenntnis', p. 12.

[5] Radio interview with Leo Held, Solothurn, December 1966, held by the Zentralbibliothek Solothurn.

[6] *Lebenserinnerungen, op. cit.*

[7] Letter from Hesse to Flury, dated February 1951 (no day given).

The composer at work, 1950

In aesthetic terms, Flury seems to have seen himself as part of a rearguard action to uphold the true and the good. It was in this spirit that he also attempted to shift the policy of the Swiss Musicians' Association in early 1952. The Association was still holding its annual festivals comprising three or more concerts, rotating around the main Swiss towns (and a few smaller ones). Paul Sacher had succeeded Frank Martin as President after the War, and had prompted the Association to affiliate to the International Society for Contemporary Music for the first time. Flury wrote a round letter on 7 April 1952, complaining that older composers of a Romantic persuasion were being ignored by the progressive members of the annual juries, and proposing that every member of the Association be allowed to have a work performed every fifteen years, regardless of the decision of any jury; furthermore, no composer should be allowed to appear on the Festival programmes more than once every three years.[8]

He had a point, for certain names did crop up repeatedly in the 1950s, though they were hardly diehard avant-gardists, being composers whose aesthetic was more Neo-Classical, such as Franz Tischhauser (1921–2016, performed in 1952 and 1953), Rolf Looser (1920–2001, performed in 1951 and 1953) and Armin Schibler (1920–86, performed in 1951 and 1952).[9] He also found support from several colleagues including René Matthes (1897–1967), like Flury a former Hans Huber pupil. Flury and Matthes were invited to discuss his proposals with the board of the Association on 2 May 1952, and although his suggestions were rejected, Flury was invited to participate in the jury in future (he declined) and was allowed to bring his proposals before the plenary session at the Festival in Aarau.[10] They were rejected here, too.[11] In his report on the Festival, Willi Schuh wrote as follows in the *Schweizerische Musikzeitung*:

> The fact that composers still wish to be heard at the Association's festivals was shown by the proposal that was made by the conservatives at the annual general meeting in Aarau, that *all* [Schuh's emphasis] musical styles should have a place in these concerts. The subsequent broad, urbane discussion did not lead to the acceptance of the proposal, which was not a very happy one, but may result in the jury […] deciding to show the same understanding of the colleagues whose roots are in late-Romanticism, and to give them the same chances, as the representatives of 'modern' stylistic tendencies who naturally, and rightly, are in the foreground.[12]

On the face of things, there was something of a compromise. Paul Sacher wrote to Flury on 21 May to assure him that the juries would in future try to be more accommodating to different styles, and urging him again to join the jury himself.[13] But since Willi Schuh's writing was generally a model of decorum and good taste, his adjective 'urbane' is here probably a metaphor for a discussion that was fairly unpleasant. The insistent tone of Flury's lecture on 'Romanticism' the following year certainly reads as if he were reacting to something vitriolic in the recent past, and wanted to reply in kind.

It was also in 1952, the year of his abortive attempt to change the Association's policy, that Flury composed a group of piano pieces in what is

[8] Copies of the letter are in Flury's archives.

[9] Board of the Schweizerischer Tonkünstlerverein, *Tendenzen und Verwirklichungen. Festschrift des Schweizerischen Tonkünstlervereins aus Anlass seines 75-jährigen Bestehens (1900–1975)*, Atlantis Verlag, Zurich, 1975, pp. 70–77.

[10] Minutes of the board meeting are held in Flury's archives.

[11] Schweizerischer Tonkünstlerverein, *Tendenzen und Verwirklichungen*, p. 74.

[12] Willi Schuh, 'Das 53. Schweizerische Tonkünstlerfest in Aarau (17./18. Mai)', *Schweizerische Musikzeitung*, Vol. 92, Nos. 7/8 (15 July 1952), p. 303.

[13] Letter from Paul Sacher, Pratteln, 21 May 1952, in Flury's archives.

perhaps the most emphatically tonal genre of all: a set of 24 Preludes in all the keys (though the ordering of the keys seems not to follow any specific pattern). Flury did not write fugues to accompany his preludes: fugue was a form in which he seems never to have become particularly comfortable. His Preludes are almost all less than two minutes long and are essentially character pieces. Many of them are in waltz-time, No. 18 is a kind of chorale, and No. 12 is even a funeral march after a fashion. They don't really hang together as a set, but individually they sparkle, and often offer the kind of gentle harmonic twists that are familiar from Flury's earlier sets of piano pieces. There could hardly be a more determined statement of the 'eternal' values of tonality than the act of writing a set of pieces in each key of a technical standard suitable for talented young players. But they don't come across as in any way didactic, and would be ideal, say, for livening up the collections of graded piano pieces published by the music examining boards of the Anglo-Saxon world. They are far more successful than his *Liechtenstein Symphony* – and far more fun: Charles Dobler reputedly regarded them as his finest collection of pieces for solo piano.[14]

Flury's traditionalist stance is further confirmed by the composition of no fewer than three Masses with orchestra in the 1950s: a *Missa brevis* composed in February and March 1954, a *Missa in honorem Sancti Lucae* from 1958, composed for the 400th anniversary of the St. Lukas-Bruderschaft – the 'Fraternity of St Lukas' in Solothurn, to which Richard and his brother Adolf belonged – and a *Missa in honorem Sanctae Margarithae* completed in late 1959. The *Missa brevis* in particular has proven popular over the years, as it is the easiest to perform, but in fact all three works are an improvement on his Mass in D minor from 1931, partly because they largely eschew the ecclesiastical, imitative style of the earlier work, but also because they are far less ostentatious and more practical in intent, having been written specifically for liturgical use.

Flury's aesthetic opinions in these post-War years were supported by Joseph Marx, who in his letters ranted against atonality and its 'talentless' adherents.[15] Marx helped Flury in getting occasional performances in Vienna in the 1950s, such as a concert of songs and chamber works, including the Piano Quintet, in the Musikverein in January 1957. Unfortunately, Flury's 'Romantic' stance, coupled with his friendship with Marx, also began to bring him the kind of friends that make enemies superfluous. There is a letter in his archives of 4 July 1960 from Alois Melichar (1896–1976), an Austrian conductor and composer who was another former pupil of Marx. Melichar praises their former teacher and urges Flury to keep to his chosen stylistic path, reassuring him that the 'nonsense' of the atonal composers will soon come to an end. He also tells

[14] Information relayed to the author by Urs Joseph Flury.

[15] *Cf.*, for example, Marx's letter to Flury of 25 December 1956 from Graz, in which he complains about Frank Martin having converted to the 'avantgardists'.

Poster for Flury's concert in the Musikverein in Vienna

him about his forthcoming book *Schönberg und die Folgen* ('Schoenberg and his Consequences').[16] Melichar had recently taken the Swiss musicologist Hans Oesch to court over a review in which the latter had referred to Melichar's support of the Nazis. Melichar won the case, and Oesch had to pay a hefty fine. But in fact, Melichar had lied (and continued to do so for several years), for he had been deeply involved in musical activities in support of the Nazis from the early 1930s onwards, and had provided music for large-scale German propaganda films in the early 1940s (such as *Mein Leben für Irland* and *Reitet für Deutschland*, both from 1941). Melichar's vicious attacks against everything modern – Schoenberg in particular – are difficult to separate from his earlier support for the anti-Semitic regime in Nazi Germany.[17] Mercifully, Flury seems not to have maintained contact with him. In any case, Flury was no ideologue. To be sure, he made a point of confiscating any jazz records that his son Urs Joseph was given by friends, for jazz was beyond the pale. But when Leo Held asked him what he thought of atonality,[18] Flury did not feel a need to go on the attack, but stressed that it just wasn't his style. In conversation with Paul von Arb, who studied harmony and counterpoint with Flury in the early 1960s, I asked

[16] Letter from Alois Melichar to Flury, Munich, 7 July 1960, in Flury's archives.

[17] *Cf.* Fred K. Prieberg, *Handbuch deutscher Musiker 1933–1945*, [self-published], Auprès de Zombry, 2004, pp. 46–51, where he reveals the extent of Melichar's involvement with the Nazis, and of his efforts to cover it up after the War.

[18] In the 1964 interview quoted above (*cf.* p. 210).

specifically if Flury had criticised other musicians during their lessons. Von Arb replied in the negative. To be sure, Flury didn't like atonal music, he said – that was clear – and his teaching methods were traditional, using a book by Marx to teach harmony,[19] and Kurth's book on Bach's music to teach counterpoint. But Flury didn't spend his time criticising what others were doing.

If Flury was already upset at the course of Swiss music in the early 1950s, what came later must still have been a shock. The Association of Swiss Musicians held its annual Festival again in Solothurn in 1961, as it had done thirty years earlier. As so often, the Association was keen to include the locals, and so the opening concert of the Festival, on 27 May 1961 – with the Bern City Orchestra conducted by Erich Schild – began with a new work by Flury, the *Overture 1960* for orchestra. The rest of the concert, with works by Walther Geiser, Jean Perrin, Peter Mieg, Hugo Pfister and Roger Vuataz, was still largely Neo-Classical, but even in this context Flury's work must have come across as utterly anachronistic. The *Overture 1960* doesn't sound very promising at first, but after the ponderous introduction is over it turns out to be a charming, well-orchestrated piece that would delight any audience at an evening of light classics. The *Overture* exists in two versions; the second, apparently made shortly after the first, is identical to it except for a fast fugato coda over 150 bars in length that replaces the last eight bars of the previous version. Perhaps Flury felt he needed to show off his technical credentials at the coming Festival. But fugato or not, at a showcase of modern Swiss music in 1961, the *Overture 1960* will have stuck out like a sore thumb. The report by Hans Ehinger on the Festival in the *Schweizerische Musikzeitung* was appropriately condescending (though perhaps unintentionally so):

> one can expect nothing new of those born before the turn of the century. It was thoroughly acceptable that the doughty [*wacker*] Richard Flury, who has placed his energies solely at the disposal of Solothurn [...] should have been given the task of opening the symphony concert on the Saturday evening [...].[20]

Ehinger refrains from saying anything about the Overture itself. Hans Oesch was more obviously condescending in the *National-Zeitung* in Basel, writing that 'the overture by Richard Flury (Solothurn), a touching late greeting to Richard Strauss, seems well-nigh sympathetic because this honourable score harbours no ambitions whatsoever'.[21] The chamber concert the following morning – which Flury presumably also attended – was much more adventurous, including Klaus Huber's beautiful, post-Webernian

[19] Presumably Joseph Marx and Friedrich Bayer, *Harmonielehre*, Universal Edition, Vienna, 1933.

[20] Hans Ehinger, 'Das 62. Schweizerische Tonkünstlerfest in Solothurn', *Schweizerische Musikzeitung*, Vol. 101, No. 4 (July/August 1961), p. 249.

[21] Hans Oesch, 'Helvetischer Durchschnitt', *National-Zeitung*, 29 May 1961.

Urs Joseph and Rita Flury in Milan, late 1950s

chamber cantata *Auf die ruhige Nachtzeit* of 1958. If Flury hadn't yet felt too old-fashioned at the Saturday concert, the Sunday one must have made him feel utterly left behind.

21
Naughty but Nice

It would have been natural for Flury to have shied away from the theatre in the post-War years. In 1945 he had experienced his abortive *Festspiel* with Peter Lotar, an equally unsuccessful attempt to get *Die helle Nacht* performed in Bern,[1] plus the disappearance from the programme of his ballet *Die alte Truhe* after its brief run late that same year. But none of these setbacks dimmed his enthusiasm for trying to find yet another topic for the stage. He considered several possible operas in the years thereafter. The writer-painter Albert J. Welti (whose drama *Steibruch* had provided Maria Schell with her film debut) wrote to Flury on 2 April 1948 to tell him that he had 'sketched a plan for the opera', his use of the definite article suggesting that they had already discussed something concrete. But no more is known about it. Emil Schibli from nearby Lengnau wrote on 26 June 1950, also clearly after an initial discussion with Flury. He mentions Gottfried Keller's novella *Der schlimmheilige Vitalis* ('Naughty Saint Vitalis') but says 'I don't think it's suitable as a singspiel. It's the stuff of a short comic opera (and splendid stuff too!) [...] two scenes are already finished'. But nothing came of this collaboration either (perhaps Schibli's remark 'The music is your business; I don't understand anything of that' was not conducive to a fruitful working relationship). On 5 June 1952, the writer Jakob Stebler wrote, enclosing two texts (no longer extant), one of which was for a 'stewardess operetta'. Perhaps mercifully, nothing came of this suggestion, either. In Flury's archives there is also a letter from Arnold Schwengler, the editor of the cultural section of the Bernese newspaper *Der Bund*, suggesting his drama from 1935, *Rebell in der Arche*, as a possible topic. Again, it came to nothing. Flury's hankering for something dramatic was partly stilled in the 1950s by two smaller-scale works: another ballet for Solothurn, *Der magische Spiegel* ('The Magic Mirror'), composed in 1954 and given its first performance on 4 March 1955; and another *Festspiel*, *Die Insignien der Bruderschaft* ('The Insignia of the Fraternity') for soprano, alto, tenor and small orchestra to a text by Hans Enz, composed – as was Flury's *Missa in honorem Sancti Lucae* – for the 400th anniversary of the Fraternity of St Lukas. *Die Insignien der Bruderschaft* was an occasional piece, like all *Festspiele*, so it is not surprising that it has never been performed again; but the ballet music, too, suffered a similar fate. Its first run had to be

[1] Letter from Nikolaus Aeschbacher in Flury's archives, Bern, 20 March 1945.

halted after only five performances because of a suicide attempt by the main dancer, Ursula Michel, who was involved in an unhappy love-affair.[2] Numbers from the ballet were broadcast twice on Radio Lugano before the end of the 1950s, and Flury himself conducted an outdoor performance of a few numbers in Biel in 1964. It has not been heard since.

Flury returned to *Der schlimmheilige Vitalis* at some point after the death of his initial collaborator, Schibli, in 1958. The gap of over a decade between the idea and its realisation suggests an unwillingness on Flury's part to collaborate with Schibli, coupled no doubt with some feeling of obligation towards the man. Any such obligation must have died with the writer, and it was now Franz Johann Danz, a staff producer and actor at the Biel-Solothurn Theatre, who wrote the libretto for Flury. Keller's *Der schlimmheilige Vitalis* is one of his *Seven Legends* – a set of novellas that are among the glories of nineteenth-century German prose. This particular story tells of Vitalis, a monk who pretends to be dissolute in order to convert fallen women. He visits prostitutes regularly, but – unknown to the populace, who assume he is a rake – he spends his nights with them praying chastely until they agree to abandon their immoral ways and join a convent. He is finally caught out by the wiles of a local girl, Jole, who falls in love with him and manages to prompt him to reciprocal feelings. Vitalis thereupon abandons his celibacy and they live happily ever after.

Danz possessed a fluency with words and rhyme, but his text doesn't really sparkle, nor does it leave the composer too much room to let his music speak. There is a lot of dialogue in the opera, and vestiges of the old operatic-number format remain in the form of short arias and ensembles. The libretto is cast in five acts, though the last of them is somewhat superfluous, merely confirming the happy fate of Jole and Vitalis. There are four main roles, six smaller roles and yet another six even smaller roles to be taken by members of the chorus. The orchestra is modest, given the forces available in Solothurn – these were the years when the theatre was offering Tchaikovsky's *Eugene Onegin* and other grand nineteenth-century staples with one cello in the pit. Flury employs one each of flute, oboe, bassoon and trombone; two clarinets, two horns and two trumpets; and timpani, harp and strings.

Flury finished the piano score on 7 July 1962 and the full score on 7 May 1963; the first performance took place in the Solothurn Theatre on 30 October 1963. The run continued for a further eight performances, including three in Biel and one guest performance each in Burgdorf and Olten. A radio recording has survived, including brief speeches by Flury, Danz and the theatre director, Marcus Breitner (Breitner jokes that the chorus members have been promised a fee, and expresses the hope that the money will be found for it). The orchestra, conducted by Wolfgang

[2] Remark by Flury in his typescript work catalogue, no date.

Flury and the conductor Wolfgang Kretschmer in a rehearsal for Der schlimmheilige Vitalis, *1963*

Kretschmer, is a little ropey now and then – the brass occasionally sound as if they haven't waited for the post-performance party to begin drinking, though that is hardly an unknown occurrence in an opera pit. The orchestral personnel in general was variable in those years: Flury's son Urs Joseph, by now out of his teens and a fine violinist, had to jump in to play in the pit at short notice when one of the violinists dropped out. But the overall quality of performance is surprisingly high, especially among the singers. The reviews were good, though they were mostly from the surrounding region. There was a review in the *Neue Zürcher Zeitung* by Max Favre, who praised Flury's melodic gifts – and a similar comment was made by Hans Ehinger in the *Basler Nachrichten* (he who had referred condescendingly to the *Overture 1960*), who also expressed astonishment at what the composer was able to get out of such modest orchestral forces. Flury invited a number of old friends to the opening night. Maria Schell was sent an invitation but declined on account of preparations for a play she was due to perform in Paris.[3] Joseph Marx was similarly unable to come, but Gottfried Kassowitz did attend, and wrote to Flury afterwards from Vienna to affirm how much he'd enjoyed it, and that he had given Joseph Marx a full report. He praised the transparency of the orchestration and the 'dramatic tension' that was

[3] Undated letter from Maria Schell (presumably second half of 1963) in Flury's archives.

kept throughout the performance.[4] *Der schlimmheilige Vitalis* also attracted the attention of the local carnival societies, who featured a cartoon of it in one of their festive posters for Fasnacht in early 1964. The erotic delights of the opera were here compared with Hamburg's red-light district and Richard von Krafft-Ebing's late-nineteeth-century study of sexuality.

In spite of the positive reception afforded *Der schlimmheilige Vitalis* at the time, it is difficult to be so enthusiastic with hindsight. There are charming melodic passages, but the consistently syllabic setting of a lot of text means there are not as many moments of lyrical repose as one might wish – this kind of thing works for Verdi in *Falstaff*, but the comparison is unfair. Flury chooses an operetta-like style for much of the work, and the orchestra has a largely accompanying function; leafing through the vocal score reminds one not a little of Gilbert and Sullivan. There is a charming orchestral interlude in pastoral style between the Fourth and Fifth Acts, but it is a rare island in a sea of dialogue and patter. The opera lasts only an hour-and-three-quarters in the extant recording, but it seems longer. *Der schlimmheilige Vitalis* lacks the lyrical *italianità* of *Casanova e l'Albertolli*, the erotically charged harmonies of *Die helle Nacht* and the concision of *Eine florentinische Tragödie*. Flury's former pupil Alban Roetschi remarked of *Der schlimmheilige Vitalis* that it was weak because it aimed too often at cheap effects to please the public. As with the *Liechtenstein Symphony*, the overall impression of it is charming but nondescript.

Flury retired from his position at the Kantonsschule when he turned 65 in March 1962. Once he had put the exertions of his opera production behind him, he thus had more time to devote to composition. And however disadvantaged he might have felt as a Romantic surrounded by Modernists, he also enjoyed considerable local recognition in his last years. He was awarded the Solothurn Arts Prize in 1964, and in 1966 the Solothurn Theatre held a Flury matinee on 27 March on the occasion of his 70th birthday, featuring assorted songs, piano pieces, three of the *Caprices* for solo violin, the Violin Sonata No. 11 and his First Piano Trio. In the following October, the Solothurn Central Library honoured him with an exhibition in belated celebration of his birthday. It was opened on 23 October 1966 with a concert in which Flury (viola) and Rita and Urs Joseph (violins) were joined by Jost Meier on the cello to perform the Seventh String Quartet.

In this birthday year, Flury wrote his Fourth Violin Concerto for Rita as a 50th-birthday present (which she had in fact celebrated the year before) and three *Caprices* for solo violin and orchestra. These were followed by a fourth *Caprice* for the same forces the following year. But in these last years, Flury's strengths remain most evident where he is writing within specific constraints, on a smaller scale, and without any pressure to justify himself in the big genres. His *St Anne Mass* of 1964 is such an example.

[4] Letter from Kassowitz to Flury, Vienna, 12 January 1964.

Der schlimmheilige Vitalis *in a carnival poster, Solothurn, 1964: 'Men from Solothurn who, in days gone by, would go abroad to St Pauli [in Hamburg] or the Prater [in Vienna], now go to the [Solothurn] Theatre, where Flury craftily shows in his Naughty St Vitalis what they lack at home: sexual psychopathy'*

Flury had been excommunicated when marrying for the second time, but was received back into the Catholic Church in his last years (to this end, he had to swear that he had given up sexual relations with his wife several years before and was living in celibacy). Flury struck up a friendship with Gottlieb Dietiker, who was the priest in the tiny village of Gänsbrunnen, north of Solothurn on the other side of the Weissenstein mountain, and he now wrote an *a cappella* Mass for the Gänsbrunnen church choir. It is for only three voices (soprano, tenor and bass) because the village is tiny (its population is under 200) and its choir correspondingly modest. In order to liven up the three-part choral texture, Flury added a solo violin part to be played *ad libitum*. The work is thoroughly tonal, tuneful, concise, and the effect of the solo violin is striking. It is not surprising that this *Missa in honorem Sanctae Annae* has proven one of his most popular works.

Given his advancing age, these last years were marked by the deaths of several of Flury's friends. The writer Bernhard Moser died in 1959, Cuno

Flury in his study, 1963

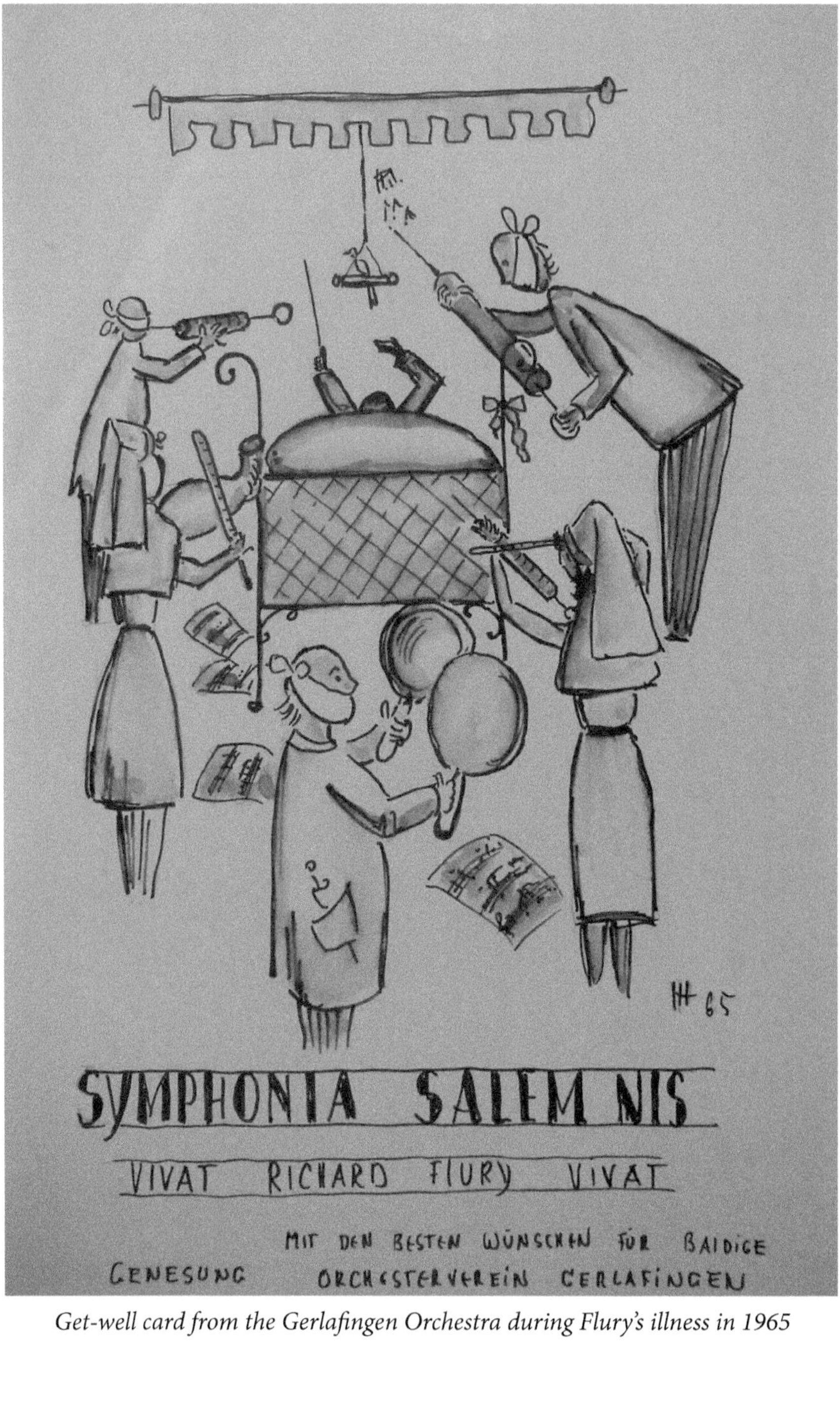

Get-well card from the Gerlafingen Orchestra during Flury's illness in 1965

Amiet in 1961 and Joseph Marx in September 1964, a few weeks after writing to Flury to praise the fragments of *Der schlimmheilige Vitalis* that he had managed to hear, and to rage one last time about the 'speculators and the swindlers' on the new music scene.[5] Gustav Renker, one of Flury's earliest supporters, died on 23 July 1967, and his old violin-teacher Maria Lochbrunner (*née* Schaad) passed away in the following October. The death that hit Flury hardest was that of his son Roger, the youngest child of his first marriage, who died of cancer at home in Cureglia in Canton Ticino on 13 March 1964. The cause was a birthmark that his parents had neglected to have removed at an early age and that had now turned cancerous. Inevitably, issues of blame arose. It was Lily who had taken Roger away from Solothurn when he was a few months old, but the bickering of both parents during Richard's visits probably diverted the attention of both away from matters as seemingly banal as dealing with a birthmark on a baby. And when Roger lived with Richard and Rita in his late teens during his apprenticeship as a goldsmith, no one had taken any action either. Roger also seems to have been the black sheep – there were family rumours about his getting involved in dubious dealings, although precisely what he is supposed to have done, and whether or not there were real grounds for suspicion, is not clear. His funeral was fraught; Lily was unable to stop herself telling Richard that he was 'no doubt glad it was this son who died, not the other one'.[6]

Flury had enjoyed robust health throughout his life (except for a bout of nettle rash in about 1960). But in early spring 1965 he had to enter hospital for a prostate operation, and a little over two years later, in early summer 1967, stomach cancer was diagnosed and surgery carried out to try and halt it. When he emerged from hospital, the first thing that Flury insisted on was going to a restaurant to eat saddle of venison.

Flury continued his conducting commitments with the Gerlafingen orchestra; his last concert with it was on 29 October 1967 in the Werkhotel in Gerlafingen. Jost Meier played Haydn's Cello Concerto in C major, the orchestra played Schubert's 'Unfinished' Symphony, and Jost Meier and Eugen Huber made up the rest of the programme with solo numbers, including six piano pieces by Flury and the premiere of his Third Cello Sonata. Life went on almost as if nothing were wrong; on the following 8 November Flury gave a lecture to a local society about his former teacher Edmund Wyss, in commemoration of the hundredth anniversary of his birth.[7] Flury also played the viola on this occasion, joining his wife, son, Werner Giger and Jost Meier to perform his Piano Quartet. Marguerite Ritter-Lochbrunner and Hans Meister sang *Lieder*. A large-scale Flury concert took place just over two weeks later, on 25 November in Solothurn.

[5] Letter from Marx to Flury from Warmbad-Villach, 17 July 1964.

[6] Flury family reminiscence.

[7] Richard Flury, 'Würdigung des Solothurner Komponisten Edmund Wyss zu dessen 100. Geburtstag', lecture given to the Töpfergesellschaft Solothurn.

Urs Joseph, Richard and Rita Flury outside their home, 1963

The last photo of Flury, with Hans Meister and Marguerite Ritter-Lochbrunner at Flury's Edmund Wyss lecture, 8 November 1967

Erich Vollenwyder conducted the Orchester des Kaufmännischen Vereins Zürich in the *Waldsymphonie* and *Fasnachts-Symphonie*, and the Oberaargauischer Lehrergesang-Verein, conducted by Alban Roetschi, sang the Te Deum. Flury's family was centre-stage on this occasion, with Giovanna, his daughter, singing the soprano solo part in the Te Deum, while Urs Joseph gave the premiere of three of the four *Caprices* for violin and orchestra under Vollenwyder's baton.

But the operation in the summer had not been a success. The cancer had returned and spread to Flury's liver, resulting in the yellow discoloration of the skin that is typical of the disease. On Saturday, 16 December, Flury played chamber music with his wife and son. By now, the cancer had spread to his bowing arm, and he remarked that if things got any worse, they would have to find another violist. On Sunday, 17 December, the family went to eat at a fish restaurant on the banks of Lake Biel. The next day, Flury felt sick and went to bed, where he stayed for the rest of the week. On Friday, the pianist Paul Baumgartner came to visit, and Flury engaged in a lively conversation that offered no suggestion that this might be their last meeting. That evening, his doctor came and gave him an injection; Flury passed away, at three o'clock in the morning on Saturday, 23 December. The end came so suddenly that his family long harboured suspicions that it might have been a result of something administered by his doctor. Not until some three decades later did the doctor's widow confirm the possibility that her husband might have given Flury something to ease his pain by hastening what was clearly an imminent, inevitable end. Before the funeral, a death mask was made by Walter Peter, one of Flury's friends since the days of the 'Künstlerstübli'.

Eugen Huber published a long obituary in the *Solothurner Zeitung* on Tuesday, 26 December, to which the paper devoted over half a page.[8] The funeral took place the next day, 27 December. Among those present were Marie-Louise Geiser, now married to a diplomat from Ecuador, whom she had joined in his home country in 1965. They were visiting Switzerland and were travelling by car across the country when the news of Flury's death came over the radio. They went straight to Solothurn and stayed to attend the funeral at the Catholic Church in Biberist, presided over by Flury's friend, Fr Albert Weingartner. Weingartner offered his own reminiscences, Peter Waldner spoke on behalf of the Kantonsschule, and Eugen Huber paid tribute to Flury the musician and composer. The music played was all by Flury; the Harmonie wind band of Biberist played the *Larghetto* from Flury's *Suite für Blasorchester* (composed for them back in 1963), Marguerite Ritter-Lochbrunner sang the song 'Adagio' from 1946, Urs Joseph Flury and Werner Bloch played the 'Ninna-Nanna' from the Suite for Two Violins of 1942, and the Gemischter Chor of Biberist under Theo Frei sang the Kyrie and the Agnus Dei from Flury's *Missa brevis*. In his final weeks, Flury had begun writing preludes and fugues for organ; Erich Vollenwyder now gave the first performance of those in F and C major.[9]

The first issue of the *Schweizerische Musikzeitung* in 1968 devoted a whole page to Flury – giving him more space in death than it had when he was alive. This obituary, by Flury's Solothurn colleague Werner Bloch, was an unusually emotional contribution to what was usually a very sober journal:

> There was something unusual and tragic about the dying of this man, who in his sphere of activity enjoyed a popularity among colleagues, friends, pupils and many sections of the population such as is granted only to few people [....] Richard Flury loved Solothurn, the city, the countryside, the whole region that was his home, but Solothurn loved and honoured 'its own' Richard Flury [....] His funeral was a unique offering of thanks that will remain unforgettable to all those who were present.[10]

[8] Eugen Huber, 'Der Komponist Richard Flury gestorben', *Solothurner Zeitung* No. 299 (26 December 1967), p. 9.

[9] *Cf.* sl., 'Abschied von Richard Flury', *Solothurner Zeitung* No. 301 (28 December 1967), p. 17.

[10] Werner Bloch, 'Richard Flury', *Schweizerische Musikzeitung* Vol. 108, No. 1 (January/February 1968), p. 40.

Walter Peter's monument to Richard Flury in Biberist, erected in 1976

Over the ensuing decades, Flury's music itself proved less unforgettable, as is so often the fate of composers in the years after their death. But his home city of Solothurn continued to perform his music, largely thanks to the efforts of his son Urs Joseph, who not long after was appointed the conductor of the Solothurn Chamber Orchestra – the same ensemble that had been the rival of his father's City Orchestra, and which had caused Richard Flury such grief when it was founded. Much of his music is available in recordings today, even if many of his biggest works – such as the operas and the Second and Third Symphonies – still await rediscovery. Nor did Biberist forget Flury. Nine years after his death, the local authorities commissioned an imposing monument from Walter Peter, and Flury's body was exhumed and reburied at the foot of it. It stands a brief walk from the Emmenbrücke where he lived as a boy.

A composer can be performed, however, only if his music is available. And in this, Flury has not been quite so lucky. Much of his music had been published in his lifetime, though with very few exceptions it had been printed by Hug in Zurich under commission, at the composer's expense. The publisher was contractually obliged to maintain stocks of his scores in its warehouse, as they were in effect the composer's property. But at some point in the 1970s the company decided to clear things out. Flury's scores – all of them – were removed and destroyed as waste-paper, without any advance notification to his heirs. Copies of his printed music survive in libraries and in private hands, and are to be found with some regularity on the usual antiquarian websites and in second-hand bookstores in Switzerland. But the bulk of it was consigned to the flames. Not even Flury, in his trepidation at the future of his *œuvre*, could have imagined that.

Conclusion

The opening chapter mentioned Richard Flury as one of several Swiss composers of the nineteenth and twentieth centuries who possessed a similar career trajectory: studies at home followed by studies at a prominent city abroad (usually in Germany, but occasionally Paris or – in Flury's case – Vienna), and then a return home to the perceived drudgery of school-teaching and/or conducting jobs with amateur choirs, orchestras or bands, all while trying, with varying degrees of success, to establish a profile as a composer. This pattern was begun with Theodor Fröhlich (1803–36) in the nineteenth century and continued through Wilhelm Baumgartner and Johann Carl Eschmann down to numerous composers in the second half of the twentieth century. Flury fits in here as well as anyone. Several of these composers did enjoy occasional success, and one or two – such as Erich Schmid – even went on to attain international reputations as performing artists. But the isolation of neutral Switzerland during the two World Wars and the economic and political vortex between them meant that composers who obtained jobs at cantonal high schools tended not to venture abroad again and generally preferred to stay at home. Some became so despairing of their composing career in the Swiss provinces that they more or less abandoned composition altogether (such as Schmid again, or Marcel Sulzberger).

The early career-path of the major German and Austrian composers from Wagner onwards was in their early stages not so different from the Swiss, but their galley years were often crowned by positions in world-class opera houses (such as Wagner in Dresden, Mahler in Vienna and New York, or Strauss in Berlin and Vienna), whereas Switzerland had nothing similar to offer to those who stayed at home; and so in superficial terms, by staying put in Solothurn, teaching at the local high school and conducting the local amateur orchestra, Flury had much in common with his Swiss contemporaries, some of whom were a lot unhappier than he was. But unhappy composers, like families, are unhappy after their own fashion. And every profession has its caste system, so that within the small-scale world of the German-Swiss music-scene, the least unhappy were those in positions of power in the Protestant cities of Basel, Bern and Zurich, where the most important conservatoires, opera houses and symphony orchestras were situated, and where the main music-critics lived and worked. Solothurn, by contrast, was tiny and Catholic, and had neither a professional orchestra, a proper opera house, a conservatoire nor a major newspaper. When Flury felt disadvantaged because of where he lived and worked, he wasn't

Flury in 1961

merely imagining it. He was also disadvantaged in never having a regular relationship with a publisher: he had to fund almost all his publications himself, or get patrons to do it for him.

As a gifted artist who by his own admission was unhappy at being a small-town boy, Flury deserves sympathy. But one should not forget that there is a simple answer for anyone faced with such a problem: get out. And yet he didn't. To be sure, he had many reasons not to do so: the political situation, the economic situation, his personal situation. But most of all, Flury lacked either the confidence or the will to take the plunge and seek personal fulfilment elsewhere in uncertain circumstances, and so he sought reasons not to take it. In the mid-1920s he was conducting regularly in Zurich and Bern and could have looked out and found enough work in one of those cities to support himself while easing into metropolitan musical life. Instead, just when his career seemed to be taking him away from Solothurn, he got his girlfriend pregnant (prophylactics were freely available in Switzerland from the early twentieth century onwards, although, of course, this kind of 'accident' still happens all the time). Even then, despite the *mores* of the day, his family – i.e., his brother Adolf – advised him against marriage and offered a way out. But Richard didn't take it. He married, and went on to get his wife pregnant three more times in rapid succession – and so when Flury wrote to Marx not long afterwards to tell him he was so desperate to live and work in Vienna that he would even take on a job as a boot-polisher,[1] he clearly wasn't, and wouldn't, and had already created all the reasons he required as to why he couldn't. There is a certain irony in that while Flury was dreaming about getting away from Solothurn and the duties of family life, it was his wife who finally did what he wanted to, but couldn't: she got out. And this act, in turn, provided another reason that Flury felt he had to stay: Solothurn offered the financial security that he wanted (or needed, or thought he needed) for his absent family.

Trying to determine where chance ends and subconscious volition begins is an impossible exercise. But it does seem that Flury, somewhere in his psyche, had decided that he should stay in Solothurn, or that Solothurn was the only feasible option open to him. Perhaps he had so internalised the idea of himself as a slow starter from the provinces that he was afraid that exposing himself to the demands of a 'big city' (be it only Zurich) might reveal his self-perceived inadequacies to others. And so he stayed, and continued to complain about being stuck in the provinces and about being condemned to work on the amateur scene. It is noteworthy that such comments occur most often in his correspondence with Marx – almost as if he complains because he feels Marx expects it of him in order to take him seriously. He wanted Marx's approval, but was perhaps afraid it might be

[1] Flury's letter to Marx of 17 May 1932.

Flury out walking near his home, 1963

withdrawn if Marx suspected him of being comfortable in Solothurn, and of staying there out of choice.

Although Flury is somewhat typical of the Swiss condition outside the Austro-German metropolises, he also fits a further pattern found among many composers of the early twentieth century: one that is stylistic, not geographical, for it crosses national boundaries. In this schema, a luscious youthful exuberance turns towards a Modernist stringency before stepping back from the brink of atonality (however defined) to resume a kind of cosy conservatism. The most famous example was in many senses the model for all the rest: Richard Strauss, who reached the forefront of the Modern with *Elektra* but moved into a proto-post-Modernism with *Der Rosenkavalier* and never ventured back. But there are many other, not dissimilar examples of composers whose forays into (near-) atonality was followed by a return to tonality. Prime cases are Béla Bartók and Paul Hindemith; in Switzerland, Flury's compatriot Othmar Schoeck was a home-grown example. But although some late conservatives – like Schoeck – lacked the white heat of passion found in their earlier, more extreme works, 'conservatism' is a relative concept and does not necessarily imply a search for comfort. It would take a brave man to argue that, say, Bartók's Concerto for Orchestra is somehow inferior to his two violin sonatas simply because it is more obviously tonal and easier on the ear than they are, or that Strauss' *Four Last Songs* are for the same reason inferior to *Elektra*.

In my opinion, Flury's finest works, with some notable exceptions, date from the mid-1920s to the mid-1930s when he was expanding his harmonic palette and experimenting with tonality as a consequence – works such as the First String Quartet, several of his shorter piano pieces and the operas *Eine florentinische Tragödie* and (more especially) *Die helle Nacht*. They are good, not because they are (in relative terms) experimental, but because these experiments took Flury out of his comfort zone and compelled him to find ways of maintaining formal coherence in a musical language that, for him, was new and unusually complex. In these early operas, he also chose to work within a genre that was far enough removed from his hitherto familiar sphere of experience to provide a dramatic challenge equal to the musical one (namely the 'genre' – if one may call it that – of sexualised music-drama set in early Renaissance Italy as established in the early twentieth century by Korngold, Schillings, Schreker and others). Not all his works from this period are as strong. Some are weak, such as the Second and Third String Quartets, in which the composer seems to be striving more than achieving. There is also an element of hit-and-miss about the works of these years, with no discernible reason why a series of weak works might be followed by a stronger piece.

Flury wrote his harmonically 'advanced' music some twenty to thirty years after similar advances had been made elsewhere. An opera such as *Die helle Nacht* might have had a better chance of success before the First World War, at the time when Zifferer wrote its text and when the German

Late Romantics and early Modernists were composing their lurid veristic-Expressionistic operas of adultery and murder. But that style was already old-fashioned by 1935. And after the Second World War, like many of his generation, Flury found that the musical progressives had by now gone so far that he could no longer comprehend them. He gave expression to his feelings of being left behind in self-justificatory writings such as his 'avowal' as a musical Romantic of 1953,[2] and in letters to the like-minded such as Marx in which he upheld a narrow ideal of what he now believed to be eternal truths, including a vaguely defined notion of 'beauty'. There were indeed composers who were excited by the new possibilities and embarked on a stylistic shift to accommodate them – such as Frank Martin, who wrote some of his best music after the Second World War. But others, like Flury, reacted instead with retrenchment.

Problems of quality can arise when a composer perceives an ideological pressure to impose a conservative aesthetic on his music that runs counter to what, in retrospect, seems to have been its hitherto natural trajectory. If a composer develops a fixed conception of what he should be (in Flury's case a 'Romantic', writing music recognisably in the tradition of Schumann, Brahms and Bruckner), then he can feel under duress to write music that reflects it. Othmar Schoeck is in this respect an extreme example. He had ventured much further than Flury into Modernism in the mid-1920s, but in the last years of his life – which were marked, admittedly, by grievous ill health and waning strength – he began to imagine Modernist enemies on all sides, and gradually and intentionally removed as many traces of the Modern from his music as he possibly could. In the process, he also succeeded in excising what actually made his music interesting in the first place, effectively erasing his own personality from it. The music of Flury's last two decades also tends to avoid harmonic complexity, as if he were consciously trying to write the kind of 'Romantic', 'beautiful' music that he talked and wrote about, while just as consciously avoiding the kind of music he felt a 'Romantic' composer should not be writing. Sometimes he still succeeded in writing fine music despite himself – the Piano Quintet is such an example. And, occasionally, some of the old grittiness returns to considerable effect – as in parts of the *Altisberg Suite*. But there is much blandness in the later years. When former pupil Alban Roetschi remarked of his opera *Der schlimmheilige Vitalis* that it aimed at cheap effects to please the public, he had a point. The music sometimes comes across as if the composer is not merely writing an opera, but self-consciously trying to write his idea of what a Romantic comic opera *should* be. If he is trying to 'please' anyone here, it is surely, first and foremost, himself.

It is ironic that Flury actually had a real gift for the popular and had no need of what Roetschi termed those 'cheap effects'. This 'popular' Flury

[2] *Cf.* p. 209, above.

can be heard in some of his best works from throughout his life, from his assorted gavottes for violin and piano to his Viennese waltzes and his opera *Casanova e l'Albertolli*. But Flury seems to have endeavoured to keep these two sides of his personality separate. Perhaps this division can explain the odd fact that a composer who was a natural melodist could later write symphonic works and sonatas that suffer from undistinguished thematic material. It is as if, when writing his sonatas and symphonies, Flury was concerned to offer the world a 'serious' face, that of a latter-day Bruckner or Brahms – the kind of composer he felt Joseph Marx expected him to be – and at the same time to conceal the more popular, 'Viennese' side of his composing nature. When circumstances required him to write music that was both serious and accessible, the results are qualitatively far better than almost anything he composed in the big, classical instrumental genres – in *Casanova e l'Albertolli*, say, or his music for Hauptmann's play *Hanneles Himmelfahrt*. As I have already suggested, Flury's ability to write on demand, his gift for melody and his undoubted dramatic gifts would have surely made him an ideal film composer. The pre-eminent Swiss film composer of the mid-twentieth century, Robert Blum, was only four years younger than Flury, but his Neo-Classical bent and technical facility, coupled with his network of connections on the Zurich scene and his natural self-confidence, all meant that he was ideally placed to ease himself into the burgeoning Swiss film industry in Zurich. Living in Solothurn meant that Flury didn't have access to the same opportunities – and the Swiss film industry was in any case too small at the time to offer a livelihood to more composers; Blum proved so successful and so quick at his work that he composed the music for most of the main Swiss films in the 1940s and '50s, turning down an offer from Hollywood only because his wife refused to emigrate. When Flury was at last approached by a local entrepreneur with an offer to write music for a film, some years after the Second World War, it did not appeal, and he turned it down.[3]

In many respects, then, Flury was typical of his land of origin and of his time. But a typical composer is hardly going to be a composer worthy of particular consideration, and a focus on his existence on the 'periphery' risks over-emphasising his absence from the centre, instead of considering how Flury's status as a 'conservative' composer in a provincial setting might have contributed to what was best about his music. Being a big fish in a pretty small pond can have its advantages too. Although Flury had to find the cash to publish many of his works, he was also helped out by well-off locals and on occasion by the cantonal and city authorities. The rector of the Kantonsschule granted him time off on a permanent basis so he could compose more, the local orchestras and choirs performed his music with regularity even after he gave up conducting in the city, and towards the

[3] Flury family anecdote.

end of his life he was awarded the Solothurn Arts Prize. Had he been active in Zurich or Basel, competing with his Swiss contemporaries in the cities where most of them lived and worked, he would probably not have enjoyed any such preferential treatment. What's more, the post-War aesthetic meant that the 'progressive' factions won an increasing proportion of local commissions and official subsidies in the bigger centres. Had he been a smaller fish in a bigger pond, Flury might have been tempted to embrace the New (after the example of Frank Martin), but he would more probably have suffered the same neglect of which his fellow Late Romantics complained. Being the main composer in a small town with a theatre was what gave Flury the chance to write his ballets and his incidental music to *Hanneles Himmelfahrt*, and these same circumstances compelled him to write them in the accessible style that came most naturally to him.

Flury never disappeared altogether from concert programmes in the years after his death, unlike his Swiss contemporaries Volkmar Andreae, Fritz Brun and others. Admittedly, performances have centred on Solothurn and have in large part been thanks to the activities of Flury's son Urs Joseph, who has been responsible for many of the recordings made of his father's music over the past thirty years. Flury still does not feature on the concert programmes of the larger Swiss orchestras, although that in itself is hardly surprising. As a perusal of the annual programmes of Zurich, Geneva and elsewhere can show, they hardly perform any Swiss music at all.[4] But enough of Flury's music has been recorded for the interested listener to get to know much of his output.

On the whole, those composers who deserve to be forgotten remain forgotten, and although the converse is less often true, those who deserve to be heard do find their way into the public arena, even if only decades after their deaths. I do not doubt that Flury's best music will attain a place in the repertoire, even if sheer logistics mean that more expensive works to perform, such as his First Piano Concerto and his *Altisberg Suite*, will not figure large in it in the foreseeable future. But it is surely time for a new generation of string players to rediscover his First Quartet, for example, or to programme his Piano Quintet. And the sheer quality of his unperformed opera *Die helle Nacht* will prompt someone to record it – if not to stage it – at some point in the not-too-distant future. In the end, all that counts is the quality of the music. And the best of it belongs not in the archives but in the concert halls and in the theatre, irrespective of the geographical confines of its composer's biography. In his lifetime, Flury's music seemed to many – not least to himself – to lag behind its time. But perhaps its time is coming only now.

[4] There are exceptions to prove the rule; Mario Venzago, currently Chief Conductor of the Bern Symphony Orchestra, has made several superb recordings of music by Othmar Schoeck.

Appendix
Catalogue of Works

This catalogue is based on several sources, primarily on the manuscripts and printed music by Flury held in his archives at the Zentralbibliothek Solothurn, and on the work catalogue kept by Flury himself as a card-index and continued after his death by his son, Urs Joseph. Where possible, information on dates, places and performers, etc., has been complemented and cross-checked by reference to contemporary reviews, concert posters and personal reminiscences of those involved. Overtures and orchestral interludes to stage works have not been listed separately, unless these were arranged for separate performance (such as the *Lustspiel Ouvertüre* for strings, which is Flury's arrangement of the overture to his *Casanova e l'Albertolli*). All dedications are given in English translation.

Abbreviations

Performing forces
pic – piccolo; fl – flute; ob – oboe; eng hn – cor anglais; cl – clarinet; bcl – bass clarinet; s-sax – soprano saxophone; a-sax – alto saxophone; bar-sax – baritone saxophone; b-sax – bass saxophone; bn – bassoon; cbn – contrabassoon; hn – horn; tpt – trumpet; trbn – trombone; btrbn – bass trombone; flugelhn – flugelhorn; a-hn – alto horn (in E flat); t-hn – tenor horn (in B flat); bar-hn – baritone horn; tb – tuba; timp – timpani; cast – castanets; cym – cymbal(s); glock – glockenspiel; tamb – tambourine; tamt – tam-tam; trgl – triangle; xyl – xylophone; hp – harp; org – organ; pf – piano; cel – celeste; vn – violin; va – viola; vc – cello; db – double bass; str – strings; S – soprano; A – alto, contralto; T – tenor; Bar – baritone; B – bass

The 'Althorn' is generally referred to in US English as the 'alto horn', in British English as the 'tenor horn'. I here retain Flury's nomenclature throughout; his 'Althorn' (here alto horn, 'a-hn') is thus the saxhorn in E flat, while his tenor horn (here 't-hn') is in B flat. Where 'hn' is used below on its own, it refers only to the French horn. Where Flury's band music requires instruments such as a piccolo in D flat or a metal clarinet, it is clearly marked as such.

Other abbreviations
FP – first performance
Instr. – instrumentation
Publ. – publication
cond. – conducted by

Operas

Eine florentinische Tragödie
Opera in one act
Libretto: Oscar Wilde's play *A Florentine Tragedy* in the German translation by Max Meyerfeld, slightly abridged by Richard Flury
1926–28 (date of completion: 14 December 1928)
Dramatis personae:
Bianca – soprano
Simone – baritone
Guido – tenor
Date and place: Florence, 1500s
Instr.: 2 fl (2+pic), 2 ob, 2 cl, 2 bn – 4 hn, 2 tpt, 3 trbn – timp, bass drum, cast, cym, glock, side-drum, tamb, tamt, trgl – hp – str
FP: 9 April 1929 in the Solothurn City Theatre. Ensemble of the Städtebundtheater Biel-Solothurn, cond. Gottfried Kassowitz

Die helle Nacht
Opera in two acts
Libretto: Paul Zifferer's play of the same name, slightly abridged by Richard Flury
1932–35
Dramatis personae:
Doctor – baritone
Solange, his wife – soprano
The Knight – tenor
Robert – tenor
Céline – soprano
Herold – bass
A fool – buffo bass
SATB chorus
Date and place: Paris, 1514, on the night after Princess Mary Tudor marries King Louis XII of France
Instr.: 2 fl (2+pic), 2 ob, 2 cl, 2 bn – 4 hn, 2 tpt, 3 trbn, tb – timp, bass drum, cast, cym, glock, side-drum, tamt, trgl, tubular bells from D flat to f, xyl – hp – str
Publ.: Hug, Zurich
FP: 17 May 1935 in Radio Bern. Bern City Orchestra, cond. Christoph Lertz (concert performance)

Casanova e l'Albertolli
Commedia lirica in two acts
Libretto by Guido Calgari (a performing translation in German was made by the composer)
Orchestrated by Eduard Favre
1937
Dramatis personae:
Principal roles:
Giocondo Albertolli, an artist from the Ticino – tenor
Lucia Morosini, a pretty girl from Lugano – soprano
Giacomo Casanova – baritone

Vittor Giuseppe von Roll, Landvogt of Lugano – baritone
Maria Anna Ludovica von Roll, his wife – contralto
Pietro Taglioretti, the innkeeper of the Albergo Svizzero – basso buffo
Doctor Agnelli, theologian and publisher – baritone
a shepherd – tenor (yodeller)
a tenor (for the 'Barcarola d'Agosto', No. 21bis)

Secondary roles:
Il Bargello, captain of the archers – tenor
La Marcofa – soprano
Conte Carlo Riva, detto in Arcadia 'Ligerio Dianteo', friend of Casanova – tenor
Il Capo dei Sindicatori (Bernese) – baritone
A mother who sings the 'Ninna-nanna' – contralto
Tomaso – silent role
priest – spoken role
herald – spoken role
il Trovatore – spoken role
una marcolfa di Sassello
I dodici Sindacatori elvetici, women of Lugano, men of Lugano, staff of the Albergo, guardie e cavalieri, artisans and artists, Italian merchants, Swiss merchants, girls of Lugano, fishermen, heralds: SATB chorus

Date and place:
Act One: 10 August 1769, the feast day of San Lorenzo, patron saint of Lugano, in the Albergo Taglioretti in Lugano
Act Two: 7 October 1769, feast day of the Madonna of the Rosary, in the Piazza Castello in Lugano
Instr.: 2 fl (2+pic), 2 ob, 2 cl, 2 bn – 2 hn, 2 tpt, 3 trbn – timp – hp – str
Publ.: Hug, Zurich, Lugano
FP: 1 October 1938, Lugano, festive hall on the Campo Marzio in Lugano, cond. Otmar Nussio
Recording (only Overture, *Introduzione pastorale* and *Marcia Svizzera*): Sinfonieorchester Biel, cond. Urs Joseph Flury. Gallo CD-1385 (2011)

Der schlimmheilige Vitalis
Opera in five acts
Text after the legend of the same name by Gottfried Keller in a free reworking for the theatre by Franz Johann Danz
Dramatis personae:
Principal roles:
Vitalis, a monk – tenor
Jole, the daughter of a rich merchant – soprano
Jucunda, a prostitute – contralto
soldier – baritone

Secondary roles:
innkeeper – bass
abbot – bass
night watchman – bass
merchant – baritone

maidservant – mezzo-soprano
second monk (emissary of the abbot) – baritone
Voices from the chorus:
craftsman – tenor
constable – baritone
citizen – tenor
another soldier – tenor
girl – soprano
woman – mezzo-soprano
the people, soldiers, citizens: SATB chorus
Date and place: A village and its environs, presumably in the late Middle Ages
Instr.: fl, ob, 2 cl, bn – 2 hn, 2 tpt, trbn – timp – hp – str
FP: 30 October 1963 in the Solothurn City Theatre. Ensemble of the Städtebundtheater Biel-Solothurn, cond. Wolfgang Kretschmer

Ballets

Kleine Ballettmusik
Not intended for stage performance. See **Orchestral Works**

Die alte Truhe
Ballet in one scene by Bet Hauschild-Sutter
20 September 1945 (date of completion)
Instr.: fl (+pic), ob, cl, bn – 2 hn, tpt, trbn – harp – timp, cast, cym, glock, side-drum, tamb, tamt, trgl – vn solo, str
FP: 15 December 1945, Solothurn City Theatre, cond. Richard Flury
Recording: Metelka Michal (solo violin), Czech Symphony Orchestra Prague, cond. Urs Joseph Flury. Gallo CD-860 (1995)

Der magische Spiegel
Ballet in three scenes after a story in the *Gesta Romanorum* in the translation by Arthur von Arx
1954
Instr.: fl, ob, 2 cl, bn – 2 hn, tpt, btrbn – timp, cym, glock, side drum, tamb, tamt – vn solo, str
FP: 4 March 1955 in the Solothurn City Theatre. Ensemble of the Städtebundtheater Biel-Solothurn, cond. Christian Vöchting

Festspiele

Festspielmusik zum 400jährigen Jubiläum der Stadtschützen Solothurn
For tenor solo, baritone solo, bass solo, children's chorus, TTBB chorus and orchestra
Sung texts by Walther von Arx; spoken text by Cäsar von Arx
1922
Instr.: pic, 2 fl, 2 ob, 2 cl, 2 bn – 4 hn, 2 tp, 3 trbn, tb – timp, bass drum, cast, cym, glock, side-drum, tamb, trgl, tubular bells – vn solo, str
Publ.: Hug, Zurich (only vocal score)
The published vocal score contains only excerpts from the *Festspiel*.

FP: 1 August 1922, Zuchwil, cond. Richard Flury

Schweizer Turner. Drei Festakte zum Eidg. Turnfest 1932 in Aarau
For soprano solo, girl soprano solo, boy soprano solo, tenor solo, boys' chorus, girls' chorus, chorus of small children, TTBB chorus, SATB chorus and orchestra
Text by Bernhard Moser
1932
Instr.: 2 fl (2+pic), 2 ob, 2 cl, 2 bn – 4 hn, 2 tpt, 3 trbn, tb – timp, bass drum, cym, glock, side drum, tamb, trgl – hp – str
Publ.: Organisations-Comité des Eidg. Turnfestes, Aarau (only piano score)
FP: 9 July 1932, festival hall in Aarau, cond. 'Music Director Dr Graf' (probably Georg Graf)

Mutterland
Festspiel for the Eidgenössisches Sängerfest 1935
Text by Karl Weber
1934
Only the vocal score exists. Submitted in competition with other composers, but did not win, and so was neither orchestrated nor performed.

Der Scholle treu. Festspiel zur Liga in Zollikofen bei Bern
For soprano, tenor and bass solo, boy soprano solo, boys' chorus, children's chorus, women's chorus (SSAA), SATB chorus and wind ensemble
1935
Text: Hans Zulliger
Instr.: pic, 2 fl, 2 ob, E flat cl, 3 cl, 2 E flat alto cl, bcl, 2 bn – B flat cornet, 3 tpt, 2 hn, 2 flugelhn, 4 a-hn, 3 t-hn, bar-hn, 3 trbn, E flat tb, B flat tb – timp, bass drum, cym, glock, side-drum – db
Orchestrated by Eduard Favre
Publ.: Krompholz, Bern (vocal score only)
FP: 31 August 1935 in the festival hall in Zollikofen, cond. Ernst Ruprecht

St. Urs und St. Viktor. Ein Solothurner Mysterienspiel
Text by Peter Lotar
1945
Dramatis personae:
St Urs – spoken role
St Viktor – spoken role
Herold – spoken role
The Devil – baritone
Angel – soprano
SATB Chorus
Instr.: fl + pic, ob, cl, bn – 2 hn, 2 tpt, trbn – timp – str
FP (concert performance): 11 May 1996 in the Solothurn Concert Hall. Sinfonieorchester Biel, Domchor St Urs Solothurn, Rosmarie Hofmann (sop), Markus Oberholzer (bar), cond. Urs Joseph Flury
Recording: Forces as at the first performance. MGB CD 6141 (1996)

Die Insignien der Bruderschaft. Festspiel für das Jubiläum der St. Lukasbruderschaft 1559–1959
For SAT chorus and small orchestra
Text by Hans Enz
6 September 1958 (date of completion)
Instr.: fl, cl, bn – hn – str
There are only two short numbers with chorus, the rest is an orchestral accompaniment to the pageant.
FP: 24 January 1959 in the Landhaussaal, Solothurn, cond. Richard Flury

Incidental Music

Incidental music to the play *Hanneles Himmelfahrt* by Gerhart Hauptmann
7 December 1941 (date of completion)
Instr.: fl, ob, cl, bn – 2 hn, tpt, trbn – timp, side drum, tubular bells – hp – str
1. Overture
2. 'Der Maurer Matten'
3. 'Musik zur Frauengestalt'
4. Intermezzo
5. 'Der Dorfschmied'
6. 'Trauermarsch'
7. 'Der gläserne Sarg'
8. 'Der Heilige'
FP: 14 December 1941 in the Solothurn City Theatre. Solothurn City Orchestra, cond. Richard Flury
Recording: Czech Symphony Orchestra Prague, cond. Urs Joseph Flury. MGB CD 6141 (1996)

Overture to the play *Adam Zeltner* by Bernhard Moser, 1947.
Apparently conceived as an independent orchestral work, not as incidental music.
See **Orchestral Works**

Orchestral Works

Konzertouvertüre No. 1 in C major
1911
Instr.: fl, cl – hn, tpt, trbn – bass drum, side-drum – pf – str
FP: 6 January 1912 in the Hotel Bahnhof in Biberist. Orchesterverein Biberist, cond. Richard Spiegel

Ouvertüre No. 2
1912
Instr.: fl, cl – hn, tpt, trbn – side drum – str

Ouvertüre No. 3
1912
Instr.: 2 fl, 2 cl – hn, 2 tpt, trbn – timp, bass drum, side-drum – pf – str

Concertwalzer No. 1
1912 (November)
Instr.: fl, cl – 2 tpt, trbn – side drum, trgl – pf – str
FP: 5 January 1913 in the hall of the restaurant St Urs in Biberist. Orchesterverein Biberist, cond. Richard Spiegel

Tarquinius-Ouvertüre
1913
Instr.: 2 fl, cl – hn, 2 tpt, trbn – timp, bass drum, cym, trgl – pf – str

Konzertwalzer No. 2
12 September 1914 (date of completion)
Instr.: 2 fl, 2 ob, 2 cl, 2 bn – 2 hn, 2 tpt, trbn – timp, bass drum, cym, side-drum – str
FP: 31 October 1915 in the hall of the restaurant St Urs in Biberist. Orchesterverein Biberist, cond. Richard Spiegel

Konzertwalzer No. 3
1915
Instr.: fl, 2 cl, sax – 2 tpt, hn, trbn – bass drum, cym, side-drum, trgl – pf – str

Ouvertüre No. 4
1919
Instr.: pic, 2 fl, 2 ob, 2 cl, 2 bn – 4 hn, 2 tpt, 3 trbn, tb – timp, bass drum, cym, side-drum – str

Ruppigoner Festmarsch
1920
Instr.: 2 fl, 2 ob, 2 cl, 2 bn – 4 hn, 2 tpt, 3 trbn – timp, bass drum, cym – str
Extant also in a version for solo piano. See **Piano Works**
FP: 2 May 1920 in the Solothurn Concert Hall. Solothurn Orchestra, cond. Richard Flury
Recording: Czech Symphony Orchestra Prague, cond. Urs Joseph Flury. Gallo CD-860 (1995)

Pastorale
1920
Instr.: 2 fl, 2 ob, 2 cl, 2 bn – 4 hn, 2 tpt, 2 trbn – timp – hp – str
FP: 5 July 1921 in the Kursaal in Interlaken. Kurorchester Interlaken, cond. Eduard Favre
Recording: Czech Symphony Orchestra Prague, cond. Urs Joseph Flury. Gallo CD-860 (1995)

Spanischer Tanz
1920
Instr.: 2 fl, 2 ob, 2 cl, 2 bn – 2 hn, 2 tpt, 2 trbn – cast, tamb, bass drum, cym, side-drum – str
FP: Late June (?) 1921 in the Stadtgarten, Solothurn. Solothurn City Orchestra, cond. Richard Flury
Recording: Czech Symphony Orchestra Prague, cond. Urs Joseph Flury. Gallo CD-860 (1995)

Menuet viennois
For string orchestra
1921
Arranged by the composer from the piece of the same title for violin and piano. Exists also in an arrangement for orchestra by Eduard Favre
Recording (in the arrangement by Favre): Czech Symphony Orchestra Prague, cond. Urs Joseph Flury. Gallo CD-860 (1995)

Schützenmarsch zum 400-jährigen Jubiläum der Stadtschützen Solothurn
1922
Instr.: pic, 2 fl, 2 ob, 2 cl, 2 bn – 4 hn, 2 tp, 3 trbn – timp, bass drum, cym, glock, side-drum, trgl – str
This march was extracted from Flury's *Festspiel* of 1922; however, it seems to have been conceived for possible separate performance right from the start. The piano version was published separately from the *Festspiel* and in a different key (B flat) from the orchestral version (which is in A major). See ***Festspiele***: *Festspielmusik zum 400jährigen Jubiläum der Stadtschützen Solothurn.*
FP: 1 August 1922 in Zuchwil, cond. Richard Flury

Symphony No. 1 in D minor
1922-3
Instr.: pic, 2 fl, 2 ob, 2 cl, 2 bn – 4 hn, 2 tpt, 3 trbn – timp, bass drum, cast, cym, side-drum, tamb, tamt, trgl, tubular bells – hp – str
1. *Allegro molto*
2. *Andante con moto*
3. Scherzo (*Allegro molto*)
4. Finale: *Allegro*
Dedication: To the Solothurn Orchestra and its president, Arthur Baumgartner
FP (first three movements): 27 June 1923 in the Kursaal in Interlaken. Kurorchester Interlaken, cond. Richard Flury; (complete): 23 March 1924 in Solothurn. Bern City Orchestra, cond. Richard Flury
Recording: Sinfonieorchester Biel, cond. Urs Joseph Flury. Gallo CD-1385 (2011)

Kleine Ballettmusik für Orchester
1925
Instr.: pic, 2 fl, 2 ob, 2 cl, 2 bn – 4 hn, 2 tpt, 3 trbn, tb – timp, bass drum, cast, cym, side-drum, tamb – hp – str
1. Arabesque
2. Melodie
3. Alla Polacca
4. Valse pastorale
5. Tambourin
6. Chilbimarsch
Dedication: To my dear friend and Italian teacher Prof. Dr Emil Misteli
No. 6 is taken from the *Festspielmusik zum 400jährigen Jubiläum der Stadtschützen Solothurn.*
FP: 30 July 1926, in the Kursaal in Interlaken. Kurorchester Interlaken, cond. Richard Flury

Fasnachts-Symphonie
For large orchestra in one movement
1928
After the ballad 'Der Zeughausviggi und der Tod' by Carl Robert Enzmann.
Instr.: pic, 2 fl, 2 ob, eng hn, 2 cl, bcl, 2 bn, cbn – 4 hn, 2 tpt, 3 trbn, tb – timp, bass drum, cast, cym, glock, large bells (on E and a), side-drum, tamb, tamt, trgl – cel – hp – str
Dedication: To Emil Brunner, malt manufacturer
Publ.: Hug, Zurich
FP: 29 August 1928 in the Kursaal in Interlaken. Kurorchester Interlaken, cond. Richard Flury
Recording: Studio-Orchester Beromünster, cond. Richard Flury (1954). Gallo CD-1397 (2013)

Wienerwalzer No. 1
1931
Instr.: 2 fl (2+pic), 2 ob, 2 cl, 2 bn – 4 hn, 2 tpt, 3 trbn – timp, bass drum, cym, glock, trgl – str
Dedication: To Eduard Favre
Publ.: Hug, Zurich (only piano score and orchestral parts)
FP: 25 August 1931 in the Kursaal in Interlaken. Kurorchester Interlaken, cond. Richard Flury

Symphony No. 2 in A minor (*Ticino Symphony*)
1936
Instr.: 2 fl (2+pic), 2 ob, 2 cl, 2 bn – 4 hn, 2 tpt, 3 trbn – timp, bass drum, cym, side-drum, trgl – hp – str
1. *Allegro* (based on the bells of Pazzolino, which were also the call sign for Swiss Italian Radio)
2. *Andante* (based on the Ticino folksong 'Vieni sulla barchetta')
3. *Allegro molto* (Scherzo) (based on the Ticino folksong 'Quattro cavai che trottano')
4. *Allegro Finale* (based on the Ticino folksong 'Addio la caserma')
FP: 1 August 1936 in Radio Lugano. Orchestra della Radio Svizzera italiana, cond. Richard Flury

Lustspiel Ouvertüre
For string orchestra
1941
Arrangement by the composer for string orchestra of the overture to his opera *Casanova e l'Albertolli*
FP: 7 March 1942 in the Solothurn Concert Hall. Solothurn City Orchestra, cond. Richard Flury

Poème nocturne
13 September 1939 (date of completion)
Instr.: 2 fl (2+pic), 2 ob, 2 cl, 2 bn – 4 hn, 2 tpt, 3 trbn, tb – timp, bass drum, cym, side-drum, tamt, tubular bells, xyl – hp – str
Dedication: To my friend Fritz Fallert

FP: 16 October 1939 in the Kasinosaal, Bern. Bern City Orchestra, cond. Richard Flury

Waldsymphonie in einem Satz
1942
Instr.: 2 fl (2+pic), 2 ob, 2 cl, 2 bn – 4 hn, 2 tpt, 3 trbn, tb – timp, bass drum, cym, glock, tamt, trgl – hp – str
Dedication: To Regierungsrat Dr Oskar Stampfli
Publ.: Hug, Zurich
FP: 6 November 1942 in the Zurich Radio Studio. Studio-Orchester Beromünster, cond. Richard Flury
Recording: Orchestra della Radio Svizzera italiana, cond. Richard Flury (1959). Gallo CD-1397 (2013)

Symphony No. 3 in B minor (*Bucheggberger Symphonie*)
July–August 1946
Instr.: 2 fl (2+pic), 2 ob, 2 cl, 2 bn – 2 hn, 2 tpt, 3 trbn, tb – timp, bass drum, cym, glock, side-drum, tamt, tubular bells, xyl – hp – str
1. *Allegro*
2. *Andante*
3. *Molto vivace* (Scherzo)
4. *Allegro Finale*
Dedication: To Maria Bangerter
FP: 22 September 1946 in the Solothurn Concert Hall. Winterthur City Orchestra, cond. Richard Flury.

Overture to the play *Adam Zeltner* by Bernhard Moser
1947
Instr.: 2 fl, 2 ob, 2 cl, 2 bn – 2 hn, 2 tpt, 3 trbn – timp – str
Dedication: To Bernhard Moser on his 50th birthday, 26 March 1947
FP: 13 October 1947 in the Zurich Radio Studio. Studioorchester Radio Beromünster, cond. Paul Burkhard

Bucheggberger Ländler
For small orchestra
Instr.: fl, ob, 2 cl, bn – 2 hn, tpt, 2 trbn – timp – hp – str
Version for small orchestra of Flury's piano work of the same name
FP: 20 October 1948 at the Lugano Radio Studio. Orchestra della Radio Svizzera italiana, cond. Richard Flury

Symphony No. 4 in C major (*Liechtensteinische*)
1950–51
Instr.: 2 fl (2+pic), 2 ob, 2 cl, 2 bn – 2 hn, 2 tpt, 3 trbn – timp, tamt – str
1. *Allegro*
2. *Andante*
3. *Scherzo*
4. Finale
Dedication: To the Prince of Liechtenstein, in memory of Josef Rheinberger
FP: 27 August 1952 in the Zurich Radio Studio. Studioorchester Radio Beromünster, cond. Paul Burkhard

Recording: Studio-Orchester Beromünster, cond. Paul Burkhard. Richard Flury-Gesellschaft RFG CD 260 412 (2008)

Wienerwalzer No. 2
1951
Instr.: 2 fl, 2 ob, 2 cl, 2 bn – 4 hn, 2 tpt, 3 trbn – timp – str
Dedication: To Grety Wirz-Luterbacher for Christmas 1951
FP: 11 March 1953 in the Solothurn Concert Hall. Orchestra of the Kantonsschule Solothurn, cond. Richard Flury

Altisberg Suite
1953
Instr.: 2 fl (2+pic), 2 ob, 2 cl, 2 bn – 2 hn, 2 tpt, 3 trbn – timp, cym, glock, side-drum, tamt, trgl – hp – str
1. Pastorale
2. Waldfest
3. Nocturne
4. Auf dem Burghubel
Dedication: To Grety Wirz-Luterbacher, in admiration
FP: 10 January 1954 in the Zurich Radio Studio. Studio-Orchester Beromünster, cond. Paul Burkhard
Recording: Studio-Orchester Beromünster, cond. Paul Burkhard. Gallo CD-1397 (2013)

Symphony No. 5
1955–56
Instr.: 2 fl (2+pic), 2 ob, 2 cl, 2 bn – 2 hn, 2 tpt, 3 trbn – timp – str
1. *Allegro moderato*
2. *Andante sostenuto*
3. *Prestissimo* (Scherzo)
4. Variationen über das 'Lied der Pragerstudenten'
Dedication: To my dear son Urs Joseph
FP: 9 February 1958 in the Bern Radio Studio. Bern City Orchestra, cond. Hans Haug

Suite for string orchestra
1959
1. Intrada (*Allegro*)
2. *Andante*
3. Valse
4. Finale (*Allegro vivace*)
Dedication: To Dr Gustav Renker on his 70th birthday
FP: 15 March 1961 in Solothurn. Solothurn Chamber Orchestra, cond. Erich Schild
Recording: Orchestra della Radio Svizzera italiana, cond. Richard Flury. Gallo CD-1423 (2014)

Kleine Suite
1964 (date of compilation)
1. Aufmarsch der Kadetten (from *Festspiel der Stadtschützen 1922*)
2. Walzer (from *Der magische Spiegel*)

3. Intermezzo (from the opera *Der schlimmheilige Vitalis*)
4. Fugato (from *Der magische Spiegel*)
5. Bolero (from *Der magische Spiegel*)

Instr.: 2 fl, 2 ob, 2 cl, 2 bn – 4 hn, 2 tpt, 3 trbn, tb – timp, side-drum – str
FP: (apparently only the first three movements) 7 July 1965 in Radio Lugano. Orchestra della Radio Svizzera italiana, cond. Otmar Nussio

Overture 1960
1960
Instr.: 2 fl, 2 ob, 2 cl, 2 bn – 2 hn, 2 tpt, 3 trbn, tb – timp, cym, glock, side-drum, tamb, tamt, trgl – hp – str
Dedication: To Otmar Nussio in admiration
This *Overture 1960* exists in two versions; the second features a long fugal coda of 157 bars to replace the final eight bars of the first version. The rest of the work is identical.
FP (second version): 27 May 1961 in the Solothurn Concert Hall. Bern City Orchestra, cond. Erich Schild

Kleine Suite
1967 (November; date of compilation)
For school orchestra (strings)

1. Choral
2. Gavotte
3. Ninna-nanna
4. Ländler

No. 1 is an arrangement of No. 10 from the *12 Kleine Stücke* for piano of 1951; Nos. 2 to 4 are arrangements of movements 4, 7 and 3 from the Suite for Two Violins of 1942.
FP: 23 March 1968 in Grenchen. Grenchen School Orchestra, cond. Wilhelm Steinbeck
Extra, optional parts for flute and oboe were later added by Urs Joseph Flury

Andante sostenuto
1967
Instr.: 2 fl, 2 ob, 2 cl, 2 bn – 2 hn – timp – str
Dedication: To Gottfried Kassowitz on his 70th birthday
FP: 4 May 1973 in the Solothurn Concert Hall. Solothurn Chamber Orchestra, cond. Urs Joseph Flury
This work was unfinished at Flury's death in 1967; the extant piano sketch was orchestrated by his son Urs Joseph.

Concertos

Concerto for Piano and Orchestra No. 1, in one movement
1927
Instr.: 2 fl, 2 ob, 2 cl, 2 bn – 4 hn, 2 tpt, 3 trbn, tb – timp – str
Originally entitled *Konzertstück* ('Concert Piece')
Dedication: To Miss Mädy Meusburger
FP: 27 November 1927 in the Solothurn Concert Hall. Dino Ghisalberti (piano), Solothurn City Orchestra, cond. Richard Flury

Recording: Margaret Singer (piano), Czech Symphony Orchestra Prague, cond. Urs Joseph Flury. Gallo CD-865 (1995)

Concerto for Violin and Orchestra No. 1
11 August 1933 (date of completion)
Instr.: 2 fl, 2 ob, 2 cl, 2 bn – 4 hn, 2 tpt, 3 trbn, tb – timp, bass drum, cym, glock – hp – str
1. *Allegro*
2. *Andante*
3. *Allegro molto*
FP: 25 August 1933 in the Kursaal in Interlaken. Luigi Valerio (violin), Kurorchester Interlaken, cond. Richard Flury
Recording: Ulrich Lehmann (violin), Czech Symphony Orchestra Prague, cond. Urs Joseph Flury. Gallo CD-865 (1995)

Concerto for Violin and Orchestra No. 2
1940
Instr.: fl, ob, cl, bn – 2 hn, tpt, trbn – timp – str
1. *Allegro*
2. *Andante*
3. *Allegro molto*
FP: (with piano accompaniment, only second and third movements) 16 November 1940 in Biberist. Rita Flury (violin); Richard Flury (piano)
Dedication: To Rita [Flury] on her birthday
Flury did not orchestrate the concerto. It was orchestrated by his son Urs Joseph after Richard's death.
FP with orchestra: 14 November 1969 in the Solothurn Concert Hall. Urs Joseph Flury (violin), Solothurn City Orchestra, cond. Corrado Baldini
Recording: Ulf Hoelscher (violin), Sinfonieorchester Biel, cond. Urs Joseph Flury. Gallo CD-1385 (2011)

Concerto for Piano and Orchestra No. 2
1943
Instr.: 2 fl, 2 ob, 2 cl, 2 bn – 2 hn, 2 tpt, 3 trbn – timp – str
1. *Andante sostenuto – Allegro molto*
2. *Andante sostenuto*
3. *Allegro vivace*
Dedication: To Paul Baumgartner, pianist and friend
FP: 5 November 1943 in the Zurich Radio Studio. Paul Baumgartner (piano), Studioorchester Radio Beromünster, cond. Richard Flury
Recording: Margaret Singer (piano), Czech Symphony Orchestra Prague, cond. Urs Joseph Flury. Gallo CD-865 (1995)

Concerto for Violin and Orchestra No. 3
1943-4
1. *Allegro moderato quasi recitativo – Allegro molto*
2. *Andante*
3. *Presto*
Instr.: 2 fl, 2 ob, 2 cl, 2 bn – 2 hn, 2 tpt, 3 trbn – timp – str

All the sources give the date of composition as 1944, but the draft of the work (with the orchestral part in piano score) is dated '15 May 1943'.
FP: 2 February 1946 in the Bern Radio Studio (but broadcast only on 18 February). Georg Kulenkampff (violin), Bern City Orchestra, cond. Kurt Rothenbühler
Recording: Georg Kulenkampff (violin), Bern City Orchestra, cond. Kurt Rothenbühler. Podium Legenda POL-1014-2

Concerto for Violin and Orchestra No. 4
1966
1. *Allegro*
2. *Andante sostenuto*
3. *Molto vivace*
Instr.: fl, ob, cl, bn – hn – str
FP: 26 January 1967 in the Solothurn Concert Hall. Urs Joseph Flury (violin), Solothurn Chamber Orchestra, cond. Erich Schild
Dedication: To Rita [Flury] on her 50th birthday
Recording: Urs Joseph Flury (violin), Orchestra della Radio Svizzera italiana, cond. Bruno Amaducci. Richard Flury-Gesellschaft RFG CD 260402 (2005)

3 Caprices for Solo Violin and Orchestra
1966
1. Caprice (*Allegro agitato*)
2. Caprice-Polka (*Bewegtes Polkatempo*)
3. Caprice (*Prestissimo*)
Instr.: fl, ob, cl, bn – 2 hn, tpt, trbn – timp – str
No. 2 is an arrangement of the Polka from Violin Sonata No. 10; No. 3 is an arrangement of the second of the *10 Caprices for Solo Violin* of 1952.
FP: (Nos. 2 and 3) 25 November 1967 in the Solothurn Concert Hall. Urs Joseph Flury (violin), Orchester des Kaufmännischen Vereins Zürich, cond. Erich Vollenwyder

Caprice 1967 for Violin and Orchestra
1967
Instr.: fl, ob, cl, bn – 2 hn, tpt, trbn – timp – str
FP: 25 November 1967 in the Solothurn Concert Hall. Urs Joseph Flury (violin), Orchester des Kaufmännischen Vereins Zürich, cond. Erich Vollenwyder

Music for Wind Band or Brass Band

Militär-Marsch für Blechmusik
5 September 1917 (date of completion)
Instr.: E flat cornet, 2 B flat cornet, 2 B flat bugle, 3 a-hn, 3 t-hn, bar-hn, 3 trbn, E flat tb, B flat tb – bass drum, cym, side-drum

Parademarsch für Blechmusik
14 September 1917
Instr.: E flat cornet, 2 B flat cornet, 2 B flat bugle, 3 a-hn, 3 t-hn, bar-hn, 3 trbn, E flat tb, B flat tb – bass drum, cym, side-drum

Marsch
[1917?l
Instr.: E flat cornet, 2 B flat cornet, 2 B flat bugle, E flat bass tpt (or a-hn), 3 a-hn, 4 t-hn [?], bar-hn, trbn, E flat tb, B flat tb
Only manuscript parts extant; Flury has at a later date added the title 'Marsch?' (*sic*) and the date '1917?'

Festmarsch zum 50jährigen Jubiläum der Musikgesellschaft 'Harmonie' in Biberist
April 1924 in Solothurn
Instr.: D flat pic, D flat fl, E flat cl, 3 cl, a-sax, t-sax, bar-sax – 2 bugle, 3 tpt, 4 a-hn, 3 t-hn, bar-hn, 3 trbn, E flat tb, B flat tb – timp, bass drum, cym, side-drum
Dedication: To Mr Hugo Schaad, music director, Biberist [unclear if this is a dedication or a postal address]

Militärmarsch für Blechmusik
1939
Instr.: E flat cornet, 3 tpt, 2 bugle, 2 flugelhn, 3 a-hn, 3 t-hn, bar-hn, 3 trbn, E flat tb, B flat tb – bass drum, cym, side-drum
Dedication: To Bat. 178

Grenzbesetzung 1939
9 September 1939 (date of completion)
Not orchestrated; in short score only
Dedication: To General Guisan

Dem Regiment Bötzberg. Marsch
1940
Instr.: D flat pic, fl, ob, E flat cl, 3 cl – E flat cornet, 2 B flat cornet, 2 bugle, 3 a-hn, 3 t-hn, bar-hn, 2 trbn, E flat tb, B flat tb – bass drum, cym, side-drum

Militärmarsch
1940
Not orchestrated; in piano score only

Urs Graf (Marsch im alten Stil)
1940
Instr.: E flat cornet, 2 B flat cornet, 2 bugle, 3 a-hn, 3 t-hn, bar-hn, 2 trbn, E flat tb, B flat tb – bass drum, cym, side-drum

Vindonissa. Marsch
1940
Instr.: E flat cornet, 2 B flat cornet, 2 bugle, 2 flugelhn, 3 a-hn, 3 t-hn, bar-hn, 3 trbn, E flat tb, B flat tb – bass drum, cym, side-drum
Dedication: To Colonel Max Schilt

Marignano (Marsch im alten Stil)
1941
Instr.: E flat cornet, 2 flugelhn, 3 tpt, 3 a-hn, 3 t-hn, bar-hn, 3 trbn, E flat tb, B flat tb – bass drum, side-drum, cym

Militärmarsch
1941
Not orchestrated, but intended for brass band; only the melody line is fully notated

Jubiläumsmarsch
May 1942
Instr. D flat pic, 2 fl, 2 ob, bn, a-sax – E flat cornet, 2 tpt, 2 flugelhn, 3 a-hn, 3 t-hn, bar-hn, 3 trbn, E flat tb, B flat tb – bass drum, cym, side-drum
Listed in Flury's work catalogue as *Marsch zum 50. Geburtstag meiner lieben Schwester Rosa.*
Only parts are extant. The sole bassoon part is marked 'Fagott I', and so it is possible that some parts are missing.

Treu dem Banner
15 October 1942 in Interlaken (date of completion)
Instr.: 'Trumpets, flugelhorns, tenor horn, baritone horn, [3] horns, [3] trombones, bass tubas'; this is the description given in the short score, which is the only extant source
Dedication: To Colonel Emil R. Zetter

Oberst Wyss-Marsch
1942
Instr.: D flat pic, 2 fl, 2 ob, E flat cl, 3 cl – E flat cornet, tpt/flugelhn, 4 a-hn, 2 t-hn, bar-hn, 3 trbn, E flat tb, B flat tb – bass drum, cym, side-drum
Dedication: To the Commandant of the AHQ in Interlaken
The opening is similar to the *Marsch des A.H.Q.*
Publ.: Musikverlag R. Boggio, Bätterkinden (Bern) [no date]

Bimor Marsch
1942
Instr.: D flat pic, 2 fl, 2 ob, E flat cl, bcl, bn, a-sax, bar-sax – E flat cornet, 2 flugelhn, 2 tpt, 3 a-hn, 3 t-hn, bar-hn, 3 trbn, E flat tb, B flat tb – bass drum, cym, side-drum
Dedication: To my friend Robert Rudolf

Marsch des A.H.Q.
11 January 1943
Instr.: 'Bugles & trumpets, I tenor horn, baritone, accompanying horns, [3] trombones, basses'; this is the description given in the short score, which is the only extant source (A.H.Q. = Armeehauptquartier, i.e. army headquarters)
Dedication: To the Commandant of the AHQ Colonel Wyss

Stans, Marsch für Blechmusik
May 1943
Instr.: E flat cornet, 2 bugle, 2 tpt, 3 a-hn, 3 t-hn, bar-hn, 3 trbn, E flat tb, B flat tb – bass drum, cym, side-drum

Oberst Moos-Marsch [No. 1]
May 1943
Identical to the march *Stans*, extant only in short score
Dedication: To my dear friend and brother-in-law Fritz Moos

Oberst Moos-Marsch [No. 2] *(Marsch im alten Stil)*
29 March 1944 (date of completion on the short score; the full score is dated 3 April 1944)
Instr.: 2 fl, 3 ob, E flat cl, 3 cl, bcl, bn, cbn, a-sax, t-sax, bar-sax – E flat cornet, 3 tpt, 2 flugelhn, 3 a-hn, 3 t-hn, bar-hn, 3 trbn, E flat tb, B flat tb – bass drum, cym, side-drum

Oberst Moos-Marsch [No. 3]
3 April 1944 (date on full score)
Instr.: D flat pic, 2 fl, ob, E flat cl, 3 cl, bcl, bn, a-sax, t-sax, bar-sax – E flat cornet, 2 bugle, 2 tpt, 4 a-hn, 3 t-hn, bar-hn, 3 trbn, E flat tb, B flat tb – bass drum, side-drum, cym
Dedication: To my dear brother-in-law on his 50th birthday

Festmarsch
August 1951
Instr.: D flat pic, 2 fl, 2 ob, E flat cl, 3 cl, 2 bn, s-sax, a-sax, t-sax, bar-sax, b-sax – 2 tpt, 2 flugelhn, 3 a-hn, 2 t-hn, bar-hn, 3 trbn, E flat tb, B flat tb – timp, bass drum, side-drum, cym
Dedication: To my friend Willy Wirz

Ouvertüre
1962
Instr.: E flat cornet, 2 flugelhn, 3 tpt, 4 a-hn, 3 t-hn, bar-hn, 3 trbn, E flat tb, B flat tb – timp, bass drum, cym, side-drum
Composed for the 75th anniversary of the Musikgesellschaft Deitingen, commissioned by the town associations ('Ortsvereine')

Werner Wohlfahrt-Marsch
1962
Instr.: D flat pic, 2 fl, 2 ob, E flat cl, A flat cl, 3 cl, B flat metal cl, bcl, 2 bn, a-sax – E flat cornet, solo tpt, 3 tpt, 2 flugelhn, 4 a-hn, 2 t-hn, bar-hn, 3 trbn, E flat tb, B flat tb – bass drum, cym, glock, side-drum – db

Suite für Blasorchester
1963
1. Vorspiel
2. *Larghetto*
3. Tarantella
Instr.: D flat pic, fl, 2 ob, E flat cl, 3 cl, bcl, bn, a-sax, t-sax, bar-sax – 2 tpt, 2 flugelhn, 2 hn, 2 a-hn, 2 t-hn, bar-hn, 3 trbn, E flat tb, B flat tb – timp, bass drum, cym, glock, side-drum
Composed for a performance of the Harmonie Biberist wind band at the Expo 1964 in Lausanne

Jubiläumsmarsch dem Schützenbataillon 5
1964
Instr.: D flat pic, fl, ob, E flat cl, cl, B flat metal cl – 3 tpt, 2 flugelhn, 2 hn, 4 a-hn, 3 t-hn, bar-hn, 3 trbn, E flat tb, B flat tb – bass drum, cym, side-drum
Dedication: To Lieutenant Colonel Eduard Pfister

Geburtstagsmarsch zum 70. Geburtstag von Oberst Fritz Moos
1 May 1964 (date of completion)
Instr.: D flat pic, fl, ob, E flat cl, a-sax – 3 tpt, 2 flugelhn, 2 hn, 3 a-hn, 2 t-hn, bar-hn, 3 trbn, E flat tb, B flat tb – bass drum, cym, side-drum
The two French horn parts are marked I and III
Dedication: To my dear brother-in-law on his 70th birthday (3.VI.1964)

Jubiläums-Ouvertüre
1965
Instr.: D flat pic, fl, ob, E flat cl, 3 cl, bn, a-sax, t-sax, bar-sax – 2 tpt, 2 flugelhn, 2 hn, 2 a-hn, 2 t-hn, bar-hn, 3 trbn, E flat tb, B flat tb – timp, bass drum, cym, glock, side-drum – db
Written in honour of the 100th anniversary of the Biberist Paper Factory and dedicated to the Eisenmann family [the long-time owners of the factory]

Der Grenchner Knabenmusik. Marsch
1967
Instr.: fl, E flat cl, 3 cl, a-sax, t-sax – 3 tpt, 2 flugelhn, 3 hn, t-hn, bar-hn, 3 trbn, E flat tb, B flat tb – bass drum, cym, side-drum

Chamber Music and Works for Solo Violin

Duet for Two Violins
1911

Trio for 3 Violins
June 1911
Alternatively for two violins and viola

Gebet
For violin and piano
30 October 1912

Freude [No. 1]
For violin and piano
February 1914

Erotikon
For violin and piano
February 1914
FP: Richard Flury (violin), Heinrich Wydler (piano), 20 March 1914 in Solothurn

Wiegenlied
For violin and piano
March 1914

Traum Tanz
For violin and piano
19 April 1914

Morgengebet
For violin and piano
20 April 1914

Freude [No. 2]
For violin and piano
19 June 1914

Albumblatt
For violin and piano
31 July 1914

Liebeslied
For violin and piano
7 August 1914

Marcato
For violin and piano
8 August 1914

Andante
For violin and piano
28 November 1914

Sonata No. 1 for Violin and Piano, in G major
April – July 1918
1. *Allegro molto*
2. *Andante*
3. Scerzo [*sic*]
4. *Allegro finale*

Sonata No. 2 for Violin and Piano, in A major
September 1918
1. *Allegro*
2. *à la Marche funèbre*
3. Shcerzo [*sic*]
Dedication: To Grety Kunz
FP: Richard Flury (violin), Adolf Flury (piano), 3 May 1919 in Biberist (only the slow movement); 21 June 1919 in Biberist (the whole sonata)

Sonata No. 3 for Violin and Piano, in E flat major
November 1918
1. *Andante*
2. Scherzo
3. *Andante mit Variationen*

String Quartet in D minor
1918-1919
1. *Allegro moderato*
2. *Adagio*
3. Scherzo (quasi 'Ländler')

[Suite movements for solo violin]
March-May 1919
Composition exercises for Ernst Kurth in Bern

Gavotte for Violin and Piano
6 December 1919
Publ.: Hug, Zurich
Dedication: To my dear violin teacher in Geneva, Prof. Paul Miche
FP: Paul Miche (violin), 11 April 1921 in Solothurn

Ständchen
For violin and piano
30 November 1920
Dedication: To Emil Wiedmer on his 31st birthday, 5 December 1920

Menuet Viennois
For violin and piano
December 1921
Publ.: Hug, Zurich
Dedication: To my violin teacher in Vienna, Sigmund Bondi
Flury calls his teacher 'Sigmund' in all the sources, but Bondi published under the name 'Samuel'.
FP: Emmy Born (violin), 4 November 1922 in Solothurn

Kleine Serenade
For violin and piano
26 September 1922

Solo Violin Sonata in G minor
10 November 1925 (date of completion)
1. *Andante – Allegro*
2. Scherzo
3. *Andante*
4. Leidenschaftlich
Recording: Urs Joseph Flury. Richard Flury-Gesellschaft RFG CD 26 0402 (2005)

Suite Pastorale
For oboe and piano
4 July 1926 (date of completion)
1. Aubade
2. Gavotte
3. Scherzo
4. Serenade
5. Tambourin
Dedication: To my dear friend George Schären
Publ. (only the Gavotte, in an arrangement by Flury for violin and piano): Senart, Paris (see below)
FP: Marcel Saillet (oboe), Solothurn, 28 October 1943
Recording: Hanspeter Thomann (oboe), Margaret Singer (piano). Richard Flury-Gesellschaft RFG CD 260 399 (2002)

String Quartet No. 1 in D minor
August 1926
1. *Allegro*
2. *Andante*
3. Scherzo
4. *Allegro vivo*
Dedication: To Pfarrer Otto von Tobel
Publ.: Hug, Zurich
FP: Hélène Isler, Hans von Arx (violins), Richard Flury (viola), Otto von Tobel (cello), Solothurn, 11 September 1926

Gavotte No. 2 for Violin and Piano
December 1926
Publ.: Senart, Paris
Dedication: To Roger Pfähler
An arrangement of the Gavotte from the *Suite Pastorale* for oboe and piano of July 1926
FP: Alphonse Brun (violin), Willi Burkhard (piano), Bern, 21 February 1927

Suite for Cello and Piano (*Suite Pastorale*)
1926?
An arrangement of the *Suite Pastorale* for Oboe and Piano
FP: Jehanne Rauch-Godot (cello), Dino Ghisalberti (piano), Concert Hall Solothurn, 13 January 1929
Recording: Svetlana Kossyreva (cello), Attila Lengyel (piano). Richard Flury-Gesellschaft RFG CD 260 410 / 260 411 (2007)

Scherzo
For violin and piano
20 December 1927
Composed for the Christmas party of the 'Künstlerstübli'

String Quartet No. 2
24 August 1929 (date of completion)
1. *Allegro*
2. *Andante sostenuto*
3. Scherzo (*presto*)
4. *Allegro finale*
Dedication: To the Schiffmann Quartet
FP: Schiffmann Quartet, Solothurn, 19 January 1930

Gavotte for Violin and Piano
1 March 1930
Dedication: For Rita [Gosteli, later Rita Flury]

Träumerei
For two violins and piano
24 February 1935
Publ.: Hug, Zurich
Dedication: To my dear mother [Rosa Flury died on 1 March 1935]

FP: Frici Goitein and [?] Schwarzenberger (violins), unknown (piano), 13 September 1935 in Schaffhausen

String Trio
For violin, viola and cello
December 1935
Only one movement extant, in parts, marked '*Allegro finale*' on the cover, '*Presto Finale*' on the first page of music. Flury's work catalogue describes it as a 'fourth movement'.
FP: Frici Goitein (violin), [?] Schwarzenberger (viola), [?] Teege (cello), 13 December 1935 in Solothurn

Gavotte for Violin and Piano
21 December 1935
Dedication: To my dear Lily [Flury] for Christmas 1935

Sonata No. 4 for Violin and Piano
9 December 1936 (date of completion)
1. *Allegro*
2. *Andante*
3. *Allegro molto*
Dedication: To Rita [Gosteli, later Flury]
FP: Werner Bloch (violin) and Paul Danuser (piano), 26 October 1938 in Solothurn

Romantisches Lied
For cello and piano
12 February 1937
Dedication: To Rita Gosteli [later Rita Flury]
Recordings: Stefan Thut (cello), Margaret Singer (piano). Richard Flury-Gesellschaft, RFG CD 260 399 (2002); Svetlana Kossyreva (cello), Attila Lengyel (piano). Richard Flury-Gesellschaft RFG CD 260 410 / 260 411 (2007)

Sonata No. 1 for Cello and Piano
27 August 1937 (date of completion)
1. *Sostenuto, Allegro molto*
2. *Quasi andante*
3. *Allegro molto*
Dedication: To Mrs [Jehanne] Rauch-Godot
FP: Lorenz Lehr (cello), Willy Girsberger (piano), Radio Bern, no date known.
Recording: Svetlana Kossyreva (cello), Attila Lengyel (piano). Richard Flury-Gesellschaft RFG CD 260 410 / 260 411 (2007)

String Quartet No. 3
28 December 1938 (date of completion)
1. *Allegro*
2. *Andante*
3. Scherzo (*Allegro molto*)
4. *Presto finale*
Dedication: To the Reisacher Quartet in Basel
FP: Reisacher Quartet, 6 May 1939 in Solothurn

Three Pieces for Violin and Piano
December 1939
1. Melodie
2. Gavotte
3. Serenade
Dedication: To my dear Rita for Christmas 1939
No. 3 is taken from the *Suite Pastorale* for Oboe and Piano
Publ.: Hug, Zurich
FP: Rita Flury (violin), 16 November 1940 in Biberist
Recording: Sibylle Tschopp (violin), Isabel Tschopp (piano). Swiss Radio International, Musica Helvetica MH CD 90.2 (1995)

Sonata No. 5 for Violin and Piano
17 December 1940 (date of completion)
1. *Allegro*
2. *Andante sostenuto*
3. *Scherzo vivace*
4. *Allegro molto*
Dedication: To Rita [Flury]
Publ.: Hug, Zurich
FP: Rita and Richard Flury, 31 January 1942 in Gerlafingen

Sonata No. 2 for Cello and Piano
May 1941
1. *Allegro*
2. *Andante*
3. *Vivace*
4. *Allegro molto*
Dedication: To my brother Adolf on his 50th birthday
FP: Walter Häfeli (cello), Dino Ghisalberti [?] (piano), 25 September 1941 in Solothurn
Recording: Svetlana Kossyreva (cello), Attila Lengyel (piano). Richard Flury-Gesellschaft RFG CD 260 410 / 260 411 (2007)

Trio for Violin, Cello and Piano No. 1
18 September 1941 (date of completion)
1. *Allegro molto*
2. *Andante*
3. Scherzo
4. *Allegro molto*
Publ.: Hug, Zurich
Dedication: To Rita on her birthday 1942
FP: Audor Dula (violin), Hans Volkmar Andreae (cello), Leopoldo Casella (piano), 7 March 1942 in Solothurn
Recording: Gabriella Lengyel (violin), Endre Lengyel (cello), Attila Lengyel (piano). Richard Flury-Gesellschaft RFG CD 260 397 (1999)

String Quartet No. 4
11 November 1940 (date of completion)
1. *Allegro*

2. *Andante*
3. *Vivace*
4. *Allegro molto*
Dedication: To my revered teacher Prof. Dr Ernst Kurth in gratitude
FP: Audor Dula, Corrado Baldini (violins), Michele Corbellini (viola), Hans Volkmar Andreae (cello), 7 March 1942 in Solothurn

Suite for Two Violins
December 1942 (composed during military service in Interlaken)
1. *Allegro* (Präludio)
2. Tambourin
3. Ländler
4. Gavotta di Urs Joseph
5. Melodie
6. Scherzo
7. Urslis Wiegenlied (also known as 'Ninna-Ninna')
8. Menuetto
9. Finale
Dedication: For Rita at Christmas 1942; Nos. 4 and 7 are individually dedicated to Rita's mother, Mrs Frigerio.
Publ.: Hug, Zurich
FP: Rita and Richard Flury, 11 April 1943 in Zuchwil
Recording: Ulrich Lehmann and Urs Joseph Flury (violins). Richard Flury-Gesellschaft RFG CD 2016 (2016)

Three Little Pieces for Two Violins
Early 1943
1. *Andante*
2. Menuett
3. *Allegro molto*
Dedication: To his dear Verena [Flury] on her 18th birthday [12 May 1943]

Duo for Violin and Cello
23 September 1943 (date of completion)
1. *Andante – Allegro molto*
2. *Andante*
3. *Molto vivace*
4. *Presto*
Dedication: To my dear former violin teacher Gustav Langenhagen, former Prussian regimental Kapellmeister
Publ.: Amadeus, Winterthur
FP: Franz Gellert (violin) and David Altyzer (cello), 2 June 1944 in Radio Basel

Sonata No. 6 for Violin and Piano
December 1943
1. *Allegro molto*
2. *Andante*
3. *Vivace* (Scherzo)
4. *Presto finale* (Rondo)
Dedication: To Rita

FP: Cesare Bertoni (violin) and Mariadele Bertoni (piano), 21 November 1944 in Radio Lugano

Dance Suite for Two Violins
16 August 1944 (date of completion)
1. *Prestissimo*
2. *Andante*
3. *Allegro molto*
4. *Vivace*
5. *Allegro molto*
6. *Allegretto*
7. *Tempo di Minuetto*
8. *Andante*
9. *Tempo di Gavotta*
10. Tarantella

Weihnachtsgavotte
For violin and piano
15 December 1944
Dedication: To Rita

Piano Quintet
For two violins, viola, cello and piano
4 February to 31 May 1948
1. *Andante, Allegro*
2. *Andante*
3. *Vivace* (Scherzo)
4. *Presto* (Finale)
Dedication: To Dr Cuno Amiet, the great Solothurn painter, on his 80th birthday
Publ.: Hug, Zurich
FP: Brenner String Quartet, Ellen Brenner-Lüthi (piano), 22 September 1948 in the Solothurn Art Museum
Recording: Margaret Singer (piano), Ulrich Lehmann, Urs Joseph Flury (violins), Erich Meyer (viola), Stefan Thut (cello). Gallo CD-866 (1996)

Sonata No. 7 for Violin and Piano
24 December 1948 (date of completion)
1. *Allegro*
2. *Andante*
3. *Scherzo*
4. Rondo finale
FP: Gabriella Lengyel (violin), Attila Lengyel (piano), 18 December 1949 in Büren an der Aare
Dedication: To Rita

Trio for Clarinet, Cello and Piano
17 July 1950 (date of completion)
Commissioned by Radio Bern on its 25th anniversary
Publ.: Amadeus, Winterthur

FP: Willi Trautenhan (clarinet), Lorenz Lehr (cello), Willy Girsberger (piano), 25 October 1950 in Radio Bern
Recording: Trio La Tâche. Soundcatcher SC 2005.5 (2005)

Three Small Duets for Two Violins
June–July 1950
1. Volksliedchen
2. Gavotte
3. Finale
Dedication: To my dear friend Rosette Schaad

Seven Small Duets for Two Violins
June–July 1950
1. Präludium
2. Melodie
3. Polka
4. Menuetto
5. Barcarole
6. Rondo
7. Kleines Lied
Dedication: For Rosette Schaad, in admiration

Berceuse
For violin and piano
13 September 1950
Dedication: To Charles and Hanny Frei

Sonata No. 8 for Violin and Piano
October 1950
1. *Allegro molto*
2. *Larghetto*
3. Scherzo
4. Rondeau
Dedication: To Rosette Schaad in Büren an der Aare
FP: Gabriella Lengyel (violin), Attila Lengyel (piano), 28 November 1950 in Büren an der Aare
Recording: Urs Joseph Flury (violin), Gérard Wyss (piano). Richard Flury-Gesellschaft RFG CD 26 0402 (2005)

Sonata No. 9 in C major for Violin and Piano
5 February to 27 April 1951
1. *Allegro molto*
2. *Andante barcarole*
3. *Molto vivace* (Scherzo)
4. *Andantino*
5. *Molto vivace* (Finale)
Dedication: To Mrs Margreth Wirz-Luterbacher
FP: Gabriella Lengyel (violin), Attila Lengyel (piano), 10 October 1951 in Radio Bern
Recording: Gabriella Lengyel (violin), Attila Lengyel (piano). Richard Flury-Gesellschaft RFG CD 260 397 (1999)

String Trio
For violin, viola and cello
28 May 1951 (date of completion)
1. *Allegro*
2. *Andante*
3. *Molto vivace* (Scherzo)
4. *Presto*
FP: Leonello Righetti (violin), Herbert Brügger (viola), Gilbert Rossi (cello), 5 June 1952 in Radio Bern
Recording: Urs Joseph Flury (violin), Françoise Pellaton (viola), Stefan Thut (cello). Richard Flury-Gesellschaft RFG CD 260 399 (2002)

Berceuse
For violin and piano
19 December 1951
Dedication: To Rosette Schaad at Christmas

Suite for Violin and Piano
16 December 1951 (date of completion)
1. *Allegro molto*
2. *Andante* (Gavotte)
3. *Andantino*
4. Valse
5. *Larghetto*
6. *Molto vivace*
Dedication: To Rita, at Christmas 1951
FP: Gabriella Lengyel (violin), Attila Lengyel (piano), 5 February 1952 in Büren an der Aare

Three Pieces for Two Violins and Piano
1951
1. *Prestissimo*
2. *Andante*
3. Gavotte
An arrangement by Flury of three movements from the *Dance Suite* for two violins of 1944

Suite for Violin and Piano
9 August 1952 (date of completion)
1. Valse
2. *Andantino*
3. Fuga
Dedication: To my dear son Urs Joseph on his birthday
FP: Urs Joseph Flury (violin) and Iren Franz (piano), 16 September 1968 in Solothurn

10 Caprices for Solo Violin
December 1952
1. *Allegro molto*
2. *Prestissimo*

3. *Andantino*
4. *Vivace*
5. *Moderato*
6. *Allegro vivace*
7. *Presto*
8. *Vivo*
9. *Allegro*
10. *Andantino*

Dedication: For Rita at Christmas
Publ.: Hug, Zurich
FP: Gabriella Lengyel (violin), 27 January 1953 in Büren an der Aare
Recording: Ruggiero Ricci. Richard Flury-Gesellschaft RFG CD 260 399 (2002)

Quartet for Four Horns
May 1954
1. *Allegro*
2. *Andante*
3. *Scherzo*
4. Finale

Dedication: To my brother-in-law Fritz Moos on his 60th birthday
FP: Horn Quartet of the Berner Stadtorchester, 29 September 1954 in Radio Bern
Recording: Hornquartett Zürich. MGB CD 6227 (2004)

Piano Quartet
For violin, viola, cello and piano
July to August 1954
1. *Allegro*
2. *Andante*
3. Variations on the folk song 'Jetzt gang i ans Brünnele'

Commissioned by Radio Bern
FP: Giorgio Silzer (violin), Karl Eugen Kremer (viola), Gilbert Rossi (cello), Eugen Huber (piano), 9 March 1955 in Radio Bern
Recording: Urs Joseph Flury (violin), Walter Kägi (viola), Jost Meier (cello), Eugen Huber (piano). Richard Flury-Gesellschaft RFG CD 260 399 (2002)

String Quartet No. 5 in C major
30 August 1955 (date of completion)
1. *Allegro molto*
2. *Andante sostenuto*
3. *Bewegtes Walzertempo*
4. *Allegro molto*

Dedication: To Mr and Mrs Gustav Eisenmann
FP: Silzer Quartet, Milan, 1955

Octet
For flute, oboe, clarinet, bassoon, violin, viola, cello and double bass
30 October 1956 to 15 January 1957
1. Entrada
2. Menuetto
3. Barcarole

4. Capriccio
5. Valse
6. Berceuse
7. Finale

Commissioned by Radio Bern
Publ.: Amadeus, Winterthur
FP: Ensemble of Radio Bern, cond. Christoph Lertz, 30 September 1957 in Radio Bern
Recording: Kammermusikvereinigung des Österreichischen Rundfunks, cond. Eugen Huber. Richard Flury-Gesellschaft RFG CD 260 404

String Quartet No. 6 in C major
April 1958

1. *Allegro*
2. *Andante*
3. *Vivace*
4. *Allegro molto*

Dedication: To my dear sister [Erika] on her 60th birthday, 11 December 1958
FP: Das neue Wiener Streichquartett, Radio Bern, 4 November 1958
Recording: Das neue Wiener Streichquartett. Gallo CD-1423 (2014)

Sonata No. 10 for Violin and Piano
30 June 1960 (date of completion)

1. *Allegro molto*
2. *Andante sostenuto*
3. Polka
4. Rondo

Dedication: To the siblings Gabriella and Attila Lengyel
FP: Gabriella Lengyel (violin), Attila Lengyel (piano) in the Werkhotel, Gerlafingen, 13 November 1960
Recording: Gabriella Lengyel (violin), Attila Lengyel (piano). Richard Flury-Gesellschaft RFG CD 260 397 (1999)

Wienerwalzer No. 3
For two violins and piano
21 June 1961 (date of completion)
Dedication: To Mrs Gertrud Bühler-Triebold on her wedding
FP: Urs Joseph and Rita Flury (violins), Richard Flury (piano), Lucerne, 24 June 1961

Menuetto
For violin and piano
17 July 1961
Dedication: To Johanna Geissbühler from Gerlafingen on her birthday, 4 August 1961

Berceuse
For violin and piano
18 July 1961
Dedication: To Heidy Heidelberger on her birthday, 8 August 1961

Sonata No. 11 for Violin and Piano
16 August 1961 (date of completion)
1. *Allegro molto*
2. *Allegretto*
3. Scherzo (*Vivace*)
4. Rondo finale (*Presto*)
Dedication: To my dear Urs Joseph on his 20th birthday, 25 August 1961
Publ.: Hug, Zurich
FP: Urs Joseph Flury (violin), Urs Jäggi (piano), 24 August 1961 in the Gewerbeschulhaus Solothurn
Recording: Urs Joseph Flury (violin), Eugen Huber (piano). Richard Flury-Gesellschaft, RFG CD 26 0402 (2005)

Trio for Violin, Cello and Piano No. 2
1961
1. *Allegro*
2. *Larghetto*
3. Variations on the Emmental song 'Niene geits so schön und lustig'
Dedication: To my dear brother Adolf on his 70th birthday
FP: Ulrich Lehmann (violin), Gilbert Rossi (cello), Eugen Huber (piano), 5 September 1962 in Radio Bern

String Quartet No. 7 in D minor
19 November 1964 (date of completion)
1. *Allegro molto*
2. *Andantino*
3. *Vivace*
4. *Allegro moderato* (Fuga)
Dedication: To Dr Franz Kienberger
FP: Reist String Quartet, Radio Bern, 12 January 1966
Recording: Urs Joseph Flury, Jean-Pierre Moeckli (violins), Walter Kägi (viola), Jost Meier (cello). Gallo CD-1423 (2014)

Nonet
For flute, clarinet, bassoon, horn, two violins, viola, cello and double bass
1965
1. Intrada
2. Minuetto
3. Intermezzo
4. *Andante*
5. *Presto* (Scherzo)
6. Fuga
Publ.: Amadeus, Winterthur
FP: Urs Joseph and Rita Flury (violins), Richard Flury (viola), Jost Meier (cello), Edgar Kremsa (double bass), Heinz Andres (flute), Bruno Pfluger (clarinet), Ernst Zurschmiede (bassoon), Fred Zurschmiede (horn), 1 May 1966 in the Solothurn City Theatre
Recording: Ensemble Radio Bern, cond. Eugen Huber. Richard Flury-Gesellschaft RFG CD 260 404

Sonata No. 3 for Cello and Piano
5 August 1966 (date of completion)
1. *Allegro*
2. *Andante*
3. *Lebhaftes Ländlertempo*, Polka
4. *Allegro agitato*
Dedication: To Jost Meier
FP: Jost Meier (cello), Eugen Huber (piano), 29 October 1967 in Gerlafingen
Recording: Svetlana Kossyreva (cello), Attila Lengyel (piano). Richard Flury-Gesellschaft RFG CD 260 410 / 260 411 (2007)

String Trio
For 2 violins and viola
July 1967
1. *Allegro*
2. *Andante*
3. Menuetto
4. Finale
Dedication: To the dear friend of my youth, Emmy Ringier
Recording: Urs Joseph Flury, Rita Flury (violins), Richard Flury (viola). Richard Flury-Gesellschaft RFG CD 2016 (2016)

Piano Works

Gruss an Biberist (Marsch)
1912
Scored for brass by K. Schell

[Five] Waltzes
December 1912

March for Piano
27 July 1913

Allegro appassionato
21 September 1914

Suite for Piano
Christmas 1918
1. Menuetto
2. *Andante*
3. Rondo
Dedication: To Grety Kunz

[Counterpoint exercises for Ernst Kurth]
24 March to 18 July 1919
Eight inventions
Two menuets
Canon
Three-part fugue
Three-part prelude

Three-part chorale canon
Two three-part inventions
Three-part chorale canon

Ruppigoner Festmarsch
1920
Also scored for orchestra by the composer
FP: Dino Ghisalberti (piano), 1920 in the Hotel Metropol in Solothurn (no further details known)

Sonata in D minor
February 1920
1. *Allegro*
2. *Lento*
3. Rondo finale
Dedication: In memory of Gertrud Getzner
Publ.: Hüni, Zurich, later Hug, Zurich
FP: Dino Ghisalberti, 1920 in the Hotel Metropol in Solothurn
Recording: Margaret Singer (piano). Richard Flury-Gesellschaft RFG CD 260 396 (1998)

Intermezzo No. 1
25 October 1921
Composition exercise for Joseph Marx in Vienna
Recording: Margaret Singer (piano). Gallo CD-1460 (2014)

Intermezzo No. 2
4 November 1921
Composition exercise for Joseph Marx in Vienna
Recording: Margaret Singer (piano). Gallo CD-1460 (2014)

Prelude in A minor
5 November 1921
Composition exercise on the white notes for Joseph Marx in Vienna
Recording: Margaret Singer (piano). Gallo CD-1460 (2014)

Prelude in F minor
28 November 1921
Composition exercise for Joseph Marx in Vienna
Recording: Margaret Singer (piano). Gallo CD-1460 (2014)

Schützenmarsch zum 400jährigen Jubiläum der Stadtschützen Solothurn
May 1922
Publ.: Hug, Zurich
This piano version was published separately from Flury's *Festspiel* to which it belongs, and in a different key (B flat major) from the orchestral version (which is in A major). See ***Festspiele***: *Festspielmusik zum 400jährigen Jubiläum der Stadtschützen Solothurn*, and **Orchestral Works:** *Schützenmarsch zum 400jährigen Jubiläum der Stadtschützen Solothurn*

4 Little Dances
1923
Dedication: Dino Ghisalberti
Publ.: Hug, Zurich
FP: Bruno Tschan Junior, 23 July 1924 in Solothurn
Recording: Margaret Singer (piano). Richard Flury-Gesellschaft RFG CD 260 396 (1998)

Fox-Trott No. 1
15 November 1929
Dedication: Dina Huber
Recording: Margaret Singer (piano). Richard Flury-Gesellschaft RFG CD 260 396 (1998)

Halottria-Foxtrott
16 November 1929
Dedication: Miss Susi Hochstrasser
Recording: Margaret Singer (piano). Richard Flury-Gesellschaft RFG CD 260 396 (1998)

Trois petites esquisses
25 February 1930 (date of No. 3)
1. Valse
2. *Moderato*
3. *Allegro*
Dedication: Composed for the Syrinx in La Chaux-de-Fonds
Publ.: In the magazine *La Syrinx* in La Chaux-de-Fonds
FP: Ms Meyer-Coen, 18 October 1930 in La Chaux-de-Fonds (no further details)

Five Preludes
1931
1. *Andante sostenuto* (Lament), 24 April 1931
2. Chant (*Andante*), 25 April 1931
3. Choral
4. Valse, 8 April 1931
5. *Andante*, 22 April 1931
FP: Anny Engelberger, 13 October 1931 in the Grenchen cinema-hall
Recording: Margaret Singer (piano). Gallo CD-1460 (2014)

Albumblätter für Klavier
1936
1. *Allegro*
2. *Allegretto*
3. *Andantino*
4. *Allegro*
5. *Andante*
6. *Tempo di valse*
Dedication: To my dear Lily on her birthday 1936 (8 December)

Four Little Piano Pieces
22 December 1944
1. *Tempo di valse*
2. Melodie
3. *Andante*
4. *Allegro*
Dedication: For Rita at Christmas

Bucheggberger Ländler
4 March 1947 (date of completion)
Dedication: Maria Bangerter in Tscheppach
Publ.: Hug, Zurich
FP: Charles Dobler, 18 March 1948 in Solothurn
Recording: Margaret Singer (piano). Richard Flury-Gesellschaft RFG CD 260 396 (1998)

Humoreske
27 May 1947
Dedication: For Martha Stuber on her birthday

Skizzenmappe aus dem Bucheggberg. 50 Romantische Klavierstücke
April – December 1949
1. 'Fangspiel'
2. 'Feierabend'
3. 'Feldweg'
4. 'Der Glockenstuhl'
5. 'Ringel-Reihn'
6. 'Polka'
7. 'Wanderung'
8. 'Gräber'
9. 'Im Gasthaus'
10. 'Walzer'
11. 'Hofstatt'
12. 'Bächlein'
13. 'Wogendes Erntefeld'
14. 'Grossmutter erzählt'
15. 'Ländler'
16. 'Der Schulmeister'
17. 'Schalkhafte Magd'
18. 'Kindermärchen'
19. 'Praeludium zur Predigt'
20. 'Schulpause'
21. 'Hirtenlied'
22. 'Flucht'
23. 'Die Magd vor dem Spiegel'
24. 'Frohe Botschaft'
25. 'Kinderspiel'
26. 'Rosenhecke'
27. 'Burgruine'

28. 'Heimfahrt'
29. 'Schöne Bauerntochter'
30. 'Gespenst im Spycher'
31. 'Hampelmann'
32. 'Die Mühle'
33. 'Der Springinsfeld'
34. 'Gemeinderat'
35. 'Klatschbase'
36. 'Schlittenfahrt'
37. 'Trauerzug'
38. 'Der Organist'
39. 'Fröhlicher Landmann'
40. 'Das Spinnrad'
41. 'Der Herr Pfarrer auf Besuch'
42. 'Für das Gästebuch des Posthüsli'
43. 'Wasserrad'
44. 'Grossvater erzählt'
45. 'Schaukelpferd'
46. 'Träumendes Kind'
47. 'Emsige Mägde'
48. 'Menuett'
49. 'Der Scherenschleifer'
50. 'Weihnachten'

Dedication: To Rita [Flury]
Publ.: Hug, Zurich
Recordings: Margaret Singer (piano). Gallo CD-1460 (2014);
Cathy Aubert-Tackett. Gallo CD-908 (1996)

Jubiläumsmarsch für die Buchdruckerei Habegger in Derendingen
1950

Fantasie
1950
Dedication: To my dear Rita, for Christmas
Recording: Margaret Singer (piano). Richard Flury-Gesellschaft RFG CD 260 396 (1998)

Festmarsch
8 August 1951
Dedication: To Willy Wirz on his birthday
Also scored for wind band

12 Little Pieces
10 November 1951 (date of completion)

1. *Allegretto*
2. *Andantino*
3. *Prestissimo*
4. *Vivace* ('Der Kuckuck')
5. *Vivace* ('Die Mühle')
6. *Allegro* ('Die Jagd')

7. *Allegro*
8. *Andante sostenuto* ('Klage')
9. *Tempo di Minuetto*
10. *Andantino* ('Chorale')
11. *Andante*
12. *Presto*

Dedication: To my dear son Urs Joseph for Christmas 1951
Publ.: Hug, Zurich
FP: Urs Joseph Flury, 4 December 1953 in Solothurn
Recording: Catherine Aubert. Gallo CD-1053 (1999)

24 Preludes
1952
Publ.: 16 Preludes in *Klavier Album*, Hug, Zurich
In all the keys
FP: Eugen Huber, 15 March 1956 in Solothurn
Recordings: Margaret Singer. Richard Flury-Gesellschaft RFG CD 260 396 (1998); Cathy Aubert-Tackett. Gallo CD 942 (1997)

Festmarsch zum 60. Geburtstag von Martha Stuber
May 1953

10 Romantic Pieces
29 January 1958 (date of completion)

1. *Allegro*
2. *Agitato*
3. *Prestissimo*
4. *Andante*
5. *Larghetto*
6. *Allegro molto*
7. *Allegretto*
8. *Andante*
9. *Walzertempo*
10. Chorale

Dedication: To Marie-Louise Geiser
FP: Eugen Huber, 13 January 1960 in Radio Bern

Bagatelle
15 July 1961
Dedication: For Vreni Probst on her birthday, 12 August

6 Miniatures
4 July 1962 (date of completion)

1. *Allegro molto*
2. *Rasches Walzertempo*
3. *Allegro*
4. *Ländlertempo*
5. *Andante*
6. *Allegretto*

Dedication: To Irene Moeschlin on her 19th birthday on 10 July 1962

3 Little Pieces
1962
1. *Tempo di valse*
2. *Andantino*
3. *Prestissimo*
Dedication: To Hanni Geissbühler on her birthday, 4 August 1962

6 Miniatures
16 August 1962 (date of completion)
1. *Allegretto*
2. *Ländlertempo*
3. *Andantino*
4. *Tempo di Minuetto*
5. *Larghetto*
6. *Allegro vivace* (Tarantella)
Dedication: To my dear friend Josef Müller on his birthday

6 Piano Pieces
3 July 1964 (date of completion)
1. Caprice (*Presto*)
2. *Adagio*
3. *Vivace*
4. *Allegretto*
5. *Allegro*
6. Fuga
Dedication: To Eugen Huber
FP: Eugen Huber, 10 January 1965 in Radio Bern
Recording: Eugen Huber. Richard Flury-Gesellschaft RFG CD 251 004 (2004)

Kleine Suite
5 October 1966 (date of completion)
1. *Allegretto*
2. *Allegro*
3. *Andante*
4. *Vivace*
Dedication: For Lotti Geissbühler on her birthday

Caprice
24 October 1966
Dedication: Bianca Sollberger on her birthday

Kleine Suite
10 February 1967 (date of completion)
1. *Allegro*
2. *Andante*
3. *Vivace*
Dedication: Beatrice Rudolf on her birthday

Organ Works

Prelude to 'O mein Heimatland' von Wilhelm Baumgartner
June 1919
FP: Miss Wittenbach in the Derendingen Reformed Church, date unknown

Prelude and Fugue in D
18 (Fugue) and 21 September 1967 (Prelude)
Recording: Bruno Eberhard. Richard Flury-Gesellschaft RFG CD 260 401 (2003)

Prelude and Fugue in F
29 September (Fugue) and 3 October 1967 (Prelude)
FP: Erich Vollenwyder, 27 December 1967 in the Biberist Catholic Church (at Richard Flury's funeral)
Recording: Bruno Eberhard. Richard Flury-Gesellschaft RFG CD 260 401 (2003)

Prelude and Fugue in C
8 September (Fugue) and 11 October (Prelude)
FP: Erich Vollenwyder, 27 December 1967 in the Biberist Catholic Church (at Richard Flury's funeral)
Recording: Bruno Eberhard. Richard Flury-Gesellschaft RFG CD 260 401 (2003)

Choral Works with Accompaniment

Die Schule
Cantata for school chorus and orchestra by J. M. Wehrli
1912
Flury wrote only the instrumental introduction and the accompaniment to the chorus part
FP: Chorus of schoolchildren, Orchesterverein Biberist, cond. Richard Spiegel, 21 July 1912 in the Catholic Church, Biberist

Tod der Schweizergarde
For TTBB chorus and piano
1 September 1917 (date of completion)
Text: Franz Achermann
FP: Katholischer Jünglingsverein, 30 December 1917 in Oberdorf

Missa solemnis
For SATB chorus and orchestra
30 January 1918 (date of completion)
Instr.: 2 fl, ob, 2 cl, bn – 2 hn, 2 tpt – timp – org – str
The organ staves in the full score are empty, though the instrument is included in the list of 'obligatory orchestral instruments' on the title page; it was perhaps intended to double the chorus parts, at least in the *a cappella* passages.
FP: Cäcilienverein and Orchesterverein Grenchen, cond. Leo Gaugler, 31 March 1918 in the Church of St Eusebius, Grenchen

Introitus
For tenor solo, SATB chorus and orchestra
1918
Instr.: fl, ob, 2 cl – 2 hn, 2 tpt, 2 trbn – timp – str
FP: Ernest Bauer (tenor), Cäcilienverein und Orchesterverein Grenchen, cond. Leo Gaugler, 31 March 1918 in the Church of St Eusebius, Grenchen

Missa solemnis
For soprano solo, SATB chorus and orchestra or organ
30 August 1919 (date of completion of the Agnus dei)
Extant only in short score, though with references to 'orchestra' and 'organ'. There is no Gloria. Each movement is in a separate score, and the numbering of Kyrie and Credo as 'I' and III' respectively suggests that a Gloria – 'II' was indeed composed, but then lost. Only the Kyrie was later orchestrated and performed as a separate work (see *Kyrie* below).

Kyrie
For SATB chorus and large orchestra
1919 – January 1920
Instr.: 2 fl, 2 ob, 2 cl, 2 bn – 4 hn, 2 tpt, 3 trbn, tb – timp – str
This was apparently the only movement of the *Missa solemnis* of 1919 (see above) that was fully scored.
FP: Frauenchor and Männerchor Schaffhausen, Männerchor Harmonie Schaffhausen, Gemischter Chor Steig, Zurich Tonhalle Orchestra, cond. Oskar Disler, 22 June 1924 in Schaffhausen

Wandermorgen
For SSA chorus and piano
13 February 1925 (date of completion)
Text: Walter Dietiker
Dedication: To the President of the Gemischter Chor Harmonie in Bern, Joseph Henzi
FP: Gemischter Chor Harmonie, cond. Richard Flury, 15 February 1925 in Bern

Mass in D minor
For SATB soli, SATB chorus and orchestra
1931
Instr.: 2 fl, 2 ob, 2 cl, 2 bn – 4 hn, 2 tpt, 3 trbn, tb – timp – hp – str
Dedication: To [the memory of] my father and Richard Spiegel
Publ.: Hug, Zurich (only the vocal score)
FP: Paula Adam-Girard (soprano), Ilona Durigo (contralto), Ernest Bauer (tenor), Felix Loeffel (bass), Cäcilienverein Solothurn, Bern City Orchestra, cond. Erich Schild, 3 May 1931 in the Concert Hall, Solothurn.

Hei cho
For two-part women's voices and piano
October 1943
Text: Josef Reinhart

Chöre der Bauern und Bäuerinnen
Little cantata for men's chorus, women's chorus, mixed chorus and piano
2 August 1944 (date of completion)
Text: Emil Schibli
FP: Frauenchor and Männerchor Lengnau, 4 November 1944 in Lengnau

2 Lieder für 3st[immigen] Frauenchor
For SSA chorus and small orchestra
1967
1. 'Abend am See' (Heinrich Federer)
2. 'Jagdlied' (Hans Zulliger)
Instr.: (No. 1): str; (No. 2): 2 tpt, B flat t-hn – str
The composer's title on the manuscript is 'for 3-part women's chorus and string orchestra', but the second song also has parts for two trumpets and tenor horn. 'Abend am See' was originally composed for SSA chorus *a cappella* in 1961, the 'Jagdlied' was arranged by Flury from his *Festspiel Der Scholle treu* of 1935.
FP: Chorus and orchestra of pupils of the secondary school in Grenchen, cond. Ernst Märki, 23 March 1968 in Grenchen

Te Deum
For SATB soli, SATB chorus and orchestra
6 June 1939 (date of completion)
Instr.: 2 fl (2+pic), 2 ob, 2 cl, 2 bn – 4 hn, 2 tpt, 3 trbn, tb – timp – org *ad lib.* – str
Dedication: To the Cäcilienverein and its conductor Erich Schild
Publ.: Hug, Zurich (only the vocal score)
FP: Elisabeth Hertig (soprano), Maria Helbling (contralto), Ernest Bauer (tenor), Werner Heim (bass), Cäcilienverein Solothurn, Zurich Radio Orchestra, cond. Erich Schild, 2 June 1939 in the monastery church, Einsiedeln

Missa brevis
For SATB chorus and orchestra or organ
February – March 1954
FP: Bellach Catholic Church Choir, cond. Richard Flury, 24 April 1955 in Bellach

Zur Weihe des Hauses. Kantate zur Einweihung des neuen Kantonsschulgebäudes in Solothurn
For SATB chorus and orchestra
12 March 1956 (date of completion)
Text: Fritz Grob
Instr.: fl, ob, cl, bn – hn, tpt, trbn – timp – str
FP: Mixed chorus and orchestra of the Kantonsschule Solothurn, with adult orchestral musicians drawn *ad hoc* from Bern and Solothurn, cond. Erich Schild, 2 June 1956 in the main hall of the new Kantonsschule, Solothurn

Die alten Schweizer
Cantata for TTBB chorus and wind band
18 September 1956 (date of completion)
Text: Heinrich Leuthold
Orchestrated by Kurt Burri

Instr.: D-flat pic, 2 fl, 2 ob, E flat cl, 3 cl, 2 bn, a-sax, t-sax, bar-sax – 3 tpt, 2 flugelhn, 4 a-hn, 3 t-hn, bar-hn, 3 trbn, E-flat tb, B-flat tb – timp, bass drum, side-drum
FP: Männerchor Zuchwil, Männerchor Biberist, Harmonie Biberist, cond. Werner Borer, 7 July 1957 in Biberist

Der Schleier der Mutter
Cantata for soprano or tenor solo, SATB chorus and orchestra
27 September 1957 (date of completion)
Texts by Robert Roetschi (choruses), Emil Wiedmer, Hermann Hesse, Isabelle Kaiser, Annette Droste-Hülshoff, Otto Zinniker, Theodor Storm, Clemens Brentano (solo movements)

1. 'Garten der Mutter' (Wiedmer)
2. 'Erde! Wir sind dein' (Roetschi)
3. 'Nach Jahren wieder daheim' (Wiedmer)
4. 'Hast du nie an Selbstmord gedacht' (Hesse)
5. 'An der Kirchhofmauer' (Roetschi)
6. 'Stufen' (Kaiser)
7. 'Frühjahrskühle Schauer' (Roetschi)
8. 'An meine Mutter' (Droste-Hülshoff)
9. 'Mutter' (Zinniker)
10. 'Wie entschlummert ruht sie' (Roetschi)
11. 'Juli' (Storm)
12. 'Abends' (Storm)
13. 'Wiegenlied' (Brentano)
14. 'Wunderbar ist alles dem Frischgenesenen' (Roetschi)

Instr.: fl, ob, cl, bn – hn – str
FP: Zsuzsa Alföldi (soprano), Oberthurgauer Kammerchor, Collegium Musicum St. Gallen, cond. Mario Schwarz, 6 July 1996 in St. Gallen
Recording: Forces as at the first performance above. K-Tonstudio, K 23.018 (1996)

Missa in honorem Sancti Lucae
For SATB chorus and orchestra or organ
1958
Instr.: fl, ob, cl, bn – 2 hn, tpt, 2 trbn – timp – str
Publ.: Cron, Lucerne
Composed for the 400th anniversary of the St. Lukas Bruderschaft in Solothurn
FP: Domchor St Urs, *ad hoc* orchestra, cond. Hermann Schaller, 24 January 1959 in the Jesuit Church, Solothurn

Missa in honorem Sanctae Margarithae
For SATB chorus and string orchestra or organ
20 November 1959 (date of completion)
Dedication: To the St. Margrithenbruderschaft in Solothurn and Obmann Forstmeister Edmund Burki
FP: Domchor St Urs, *ad hoc* orchestra, cond. Hermann Schaller, 17 July 1960 in the Heiliggeistkirche, Solothurn

Die Emme
Cantata for TTBB chorus and piano
20 April 1960 (date of completion)
Text: Hermann Misteli
1. 'Der Schachen'
2. 'Emmen-Launen'
3. 'Hochwasser'
4. 'Waldfest'
5. 'Frühe Liebe'
6. 'Die Reiterin'
Flury intended to score the accompaniment for small orchestra, but did not do so.
FP: Männerchor Biberist, Eugen Huber (piano), cond. Theo Frei, 10 April 1970 in Radio Bern

St Anna-Messe
For SAB chorus with solo violin (and organ *ad lib.*)
1964
Composed for the church choir of Gänsbrunnen
FP: Urs Joseph Flury (violin), Gänsbrunnen church choir, 26 July 1964 in Gänsbrunnen
Recording: Urs Joseph Flury (violin), Gemischter Chor der Kantonsschule Solothurn, Christkatholischer Kirchenchor zu Franziskanern Solothurn, cond. Beate Obrecht. Richard Flury-Gesellschaft RFG CD 260 414 (2010)

Choral Works *a cappella*

Gesang der Toten
For SATB chorus
1913
Text: August Graf von Platen

Frühlingsmorgen
For SATB chorus
December 1913
Text: Friedrich Fiala

Four Chorales
For SATB chorus
1918
1. 'Nun hab ich was mein Herz begehrt'
2. 'O Traurigkeit, o Herzelied'
3. 'O Heiland reiss die Himmel auf'
4. 'Oh Zährenstrom, o Tränenmeer'

Abstieg
For women's chorus
June 1925
Dedication: To Joseph Henzi, the Secretary of the Bernischer Kantonal-Gesangverein
Publ.: Hug, Zurich

FP: Frauenchor Steffisburg, no date or place

Nacht
For SATB chorus
1925
Text: Bernhard Moser
Publ.: Hug, Zurich
FP: Gemischter Chor Harmonie, cond. Richard Flury, 15 February 1925 in Bern

Wahlspruch
For TTBB chorus
1943 (?)
Text: Adolf Flury
Dedication: To the Männerchor Biberist on their 75th anniversary
Publ.: [Biberist?] [1943?], self-published
Music adapted by the composer from his Festspiel *Schweizer Turner* of 1932

Canto dei Pescatori
For SATB chorus
1946
Text: Guido Calgari
Music adapted by the composer from his *Casanova e l'Albertolli* of 1937

Ave Maria
For SSAA chorus
1946
Text: Guido Calgari
Music adapted by the composer from his *Casanova e l'Albertolli* of 1937

Stosst an
For TTBB chorus
January 1939
Text: W. Marti-Allemann
Publ.: Hug, Zurich

Schöner Wald
For TTBB chorus
30 April 1942
Text: Emil Zetter
Publ.: self-published by Richard Flury (no date)
FP: Männerchor Derendingen, 27 June 1943 in Heinrichswil

Jägerlied
For TTBB chorus
1943
Text: Emil R. Zetter
Publ.: Hug, Zurich
FP: Männerchor Biberist, cond. Werner Borer, 20 May 1944 in the St Urs Restaurant, Biberist

Der Ruppigonia Solothurn zum 50-jährigen Bestehen
For SATB chorus or TTBB chorus
1945
Text: Willy Miller
FP: *Ad hoc* student chorus, cond. Heinz Sigrist, 25 June 1945 in the old Kantonsschule, Solothurn

Hingabe
For TTBB chorus
28 August 1947
Text: Alfred Huggenberger

Mein Herz ist stark und frei
For SATB chorus
May 1949
Text: Rudolf Baumbach
Dedication: To Martha and Alexander Stuber in Lüterswil

Märchen und Träume
For SATB chorus
May 1949
Text: Otto Feier
Dedication: To Martha and Alexander Stuber in Lüterswil

Sühne
For SATB chorus
May 1949
Text: Carl Robert Enzmann
Dedication: To Martha and Alexander Stuber in Lüterswil

In der Nacht
For TTBB chorus
July 1952
Text: Nikolaus Lenau
Dedication: To Willy Wirz in friendship
Publ.: Hug, Zurich

Mondnacht
For TTBB chorus
22 July 1952
Text: Rudolf Baumbach
Dedication: To W. Wirz
FP: Männerchor Biberist, cond. Theo Frei, 11 April 1970 in the Catholic Church, Biberist

Frühling
For TTBB chorus
25 July 1952
Text: Rudolf Baumbach
Dedication: To W. Wirz
Publ.: Hug, Zurich

Wanderlied
For TTBB chorus
July 1952
Text: Rudolf Baumbach
Dedication: To W. Wirz
Publ.: Hug, Zurich
FP: All participating choruses at the Sängertag Wasseramt, cond. Werner Borer, Lohn [no date]

An den Frühling
For TTBB chorus
1957
Text: Nikolaus Lenau
FP: Männerchor Biberist, cond. Theo Frei, 11 April 1970 in the Catholic Church, Biberist

Uesers Liedli
For TTBB chorus
1957
Text: Paul Burkolter
Publ.: Hug, Zurich
The music is identical to that of *An den Frühling* above.

Die lustigen Musikanten
For SATB chorus
1957
Text: Clemens Brentano
Dedication: To the Gemischter Chor Biberist and Theo Frei
Publ.: Hug, Zurich
FP: Gemischter Chor Biberist, cond. Theo Frei, 2 May 1958 in Radio Bern

Erntetag
For TTBB chorus
20–22 August 1957
Text: Hermann Misteli
Publ.: Hug, Zurich
FP: Männerchor Bellach, cond. Armin Allemann, 16 March 1958 [? date uncertain] in Bellach

Nie gestilltes Sehnen
For TTBB chorus
1960
Text: Heinrich Leuthold

Abend am See
For SATB or SSA chorus
May 1961
Text: Heinrich Federer
Publ.: Hug, Zurich
Also arranged by Flury for SSA and small orchestra. See **Choral Works with Accompaniment**

Auf ein Grab
For SAT chorus
May 1961
Text: Heinrich Federer

Gottes Ding
For SATB or SSA chorus
May 1961
Text: Otto Feier

Heimweh
For SATB or SSA chorus
May 1961
Text: Bernhard Moser
Dedication: To Mrs Martha Stuber
Publ.: Pelikan, Zurich

Mängs Blüemli
For SSA chorus
May 1961
Text: Bernhard Moser

An einen Dichter
For SSA chorus
May 1961
Text: Nikolaus Lenau

Wenn's ame nachtet
For SSA chorus
May 1961
Text: Bernhard Moser
Dedication: To Adrienne Heizmann
Publ.: Pelikan, Zurich
FP: Gemischter Chor Recherswil, cond. Traugott Jäggi, 24 June 1962 in Lohn

Reiterlied
For TTBB chorus
May 1961
Text: Nikolaus Lenau
Dedication: To the Berner Singstudenten
Publ.: Hug, Zurich
FP: Männerchor Recherswil, cond. Traugott Jäggi, 23 June 1962 in Lohn

Liebesfeier
For SSA chorus
May 1961
Text: Nikolaus Lenau

Am ersten Morgen
For SSA chorus
May 1961
Text: Matthias Claudius

's Glück uf Aerde
For TTBB chorus
9 January 1967
Text: Otto Wolf
FP: Männerchor Selzach, cond. Josef Wolf, 11 May 1968 [in Selzach?]

Der Rekrut
For TTBB chorus
12 January 1967
Text: Otto Wolf
FP: Männerchor Selzach, cond. Josef Wolf, 11 May 1968 [in Selzach?]

Es Schärli Chinder
For TTBB chorus
14 January 1967
Text: Otto Wolf
FP: Männerchor Selzach, cond. Josef Wolf, 11 May 1968 [in Selzach?]

Songs for Voice and Ensemble or Orchestra

3 Volkslieder für Alt und Kammerorchester
1924
Texts by Hermann Löns and Heinrich Reinhardt
Instr.: pic, fl, ob, cl – 2 hn, tpt, trbn – timp, cast, glock, tamb, trgl – hp – str
1. 'Der Tausch' (Löns)
2. 'Weil ja morgen Sonntag ist' (Reinhardt)
3. 'Der eine allein' (Löns)
All three songs were composed in 1923 for voice and piano. No. 1 was also arranged for voice and ensemble in the *Nachtlieder* (see below).
The composer notes in his manuscript that Nos. 1 and 2 may be sung either by contralto or soprano

4 Lieder für eine Sopranstimme und Kammerorchester
6 August 1924 (date of completion)
Texts by Theodor Bohnenblust, Ludwig Finkh, Paul Hardmeyer
Instr.: pic, fl, ob, cl, bn – 2 hn, tpt, trbn – timp, glock – hp – str
1. 'Ein Kuss' (Finkh)
2. 'Im weissen Schnee' (Hardmeyer)
3. 'Wanderer' (Hardmeyer)
4. 'Feierabend' (Bohnenblust)
Publ.: Hug, Zurich (No. 1); Müller & Schade, Bern (Nos. 2–4)
Nos. 2 and 3 exist also in versions by the composer for contralto and chamber orchestra
FP: Amalie Roth (contralto), Orchestra of the Berner Männerchor, cond. Ernst Hohlfeld, 18 May 1924 in Bern (it is unclear whether only Nos. 2 and 3 were sung, or all four)

Sapphos Tod
For soprano and large orchestra
12 July 1928 (date of completion)
Text: Franz Grillparzer (closing monologue from his tragedy *Sappho*)
Instr.: 2 fl (2+pic), 2 ob, 2 cl, 2 bn – 4 hn, 2 tpt, 3 trbn, tb – timp, bass drum, cym, trgl – cel – hp – str
Dedication: Berthe de Vigier
FP: Berthe de Vigier (soprano), Bern City Orchestra, cond. Richard Flury, 13 January 1929 in Solothurn

Nachtlieder
28 July 1936 (date of completion of final version?)
Texts by Viktor Aufricht, Otto Julius Bierbaum, Hermann Löns, Alfons Petzold, Peter Sturmbusch
Instr.: cl, hn – vn, va, vc, db (more than one instrument per string part is intended)
1. 'Alles schweigt' (Sturmbusch)
2. 'Ein Lied' (Aufricht)
3. 'Weisst du' (Sturmbusch)
4. 'Bang ist die Nacht' (Sturmbusch)
5. 'Vom Wege' (Sturmbusch)
6. 'Herzloses Mädchen' (Sturmbusch)
7. 'Flieder' (Bierbaum)
8. 'Du' (Sturmbusch)
9. 'Traum' (Petzold)
10. 'Der Tausch' (Löns)
Dedication: Walter Schürmann, pharmacist in Lucerne (Nos. 1–8, 10), My sister Erika (No. 9).
No. 6, 'Herzloses Mädchen', is a different setting of this poem from the song Flury composed on 30 September 1921 for voice and piano (see below).
Publ.: Hug, Zurich (only for voice and piano)
FP: Lucia Delsarta (soprano), Erwin Tüller (tenor), cond. Christoph Lertz, 16 February 1934 in Radio Bern (*sic*; but see date of composition)

6 Lieder für Sopran und Streichquartett
1959
Texts by Viktor Aufricht, Heinrich Leuthold, Eduard Mörike, Otto Zinniker
1. 'Augenzauber' (Leuthold), 5 August 1951
2. 'Ob Du wohl weisst, was Liebe ist' (Zinniker), 14 June 1952
3. 'Das Kind' (Aufricht), 31 July 1951
4. 'Heisses Herz, o lern' ertragen' (Leuthold), 8 August 1951
5. 'Trinklied' (Leuthold), 15 August 1951
6. 'Nimmersatte Liebe' (Mörike), 3 August 1951
Arrangements for soprano and string quartet of six songs from the *17 Lieder* of 1951–52

11 Lieder für Sopran und Orchester
1966
Texts by Viktor Aufricht, Clemens Brentano, Annette Droste-Hülshoff, Ludwig Finkh, Isabelle Kaiser, Heinrich Leuthold, Eduard Mörike, Bernhard Moser, Hermann Ferdinand Schell, Otto Zinniker
Instr.: fl, ob, cl, bn – 2 hn, tpt, trbn – timp, glock – hp – str
1. 'Einer Frau' (Finkh)
2. 'Adagio' (Moser)
3. 'An meine Mutter' (Droste-Hülshoff)
4. 'Stufen' (Kaiser)
5. 'Wiegenlied' (Brentano)
6. 'Dir will ich gehören' (Schell)
7. 'Augenzauber' (Leuthold)
8. 'Herbstzeitlose' (Zinniker)
9. 'Ob Du wohl weisst, was Liebe ist' (Zinniker)
10. 'Heisses Herz, o lern' ertragen' (Leuthold)
11. 'Trinklied' (Leuthold)
Arrangements for soprano and chamber orchestra of assorted songs composed between 1946 and 1965

Songs for Voice and Piano

Sehnsucht
2 August 1915
Text: Rudolf Baumbach
First version

Der verrückte Geiger
August 1915
Text: Rudolf Baumbach
Dedication: Fridy Lüthi

Sehnsucht
September 1915
Text: Rudolf Baumbach
Dedication: Fridy Lüthi
Second version

Triftiger Grund
September 1915
Text: Rudolf Baumbach
Dedication: Fridy Lüthi

Die drei Zecher
10 October 1915
Text: Rudolf Baumbach
Dedication: To his dear Fridy [Lüthi]

Wenn ich in deine Augen seh
5 January 1916
Text: Heinrich Heine
First version
Dedication: To his dear Fridy [Lüthi], in remembrance

Du bist die Ruh
25 January 1916
Text: Friedrich Rückert
Dedication: Fridy Lüthi

Sehnsucht
25 January 1916
Text: Johann Wolfgang von Goethe
Dedication: To my dear Fridy [Lüthi]

An Helmine von Chezy
22 June 1917
Text: Adalbert von Chamisso
Dedication: To my friend Paula von Arx

Tote Liebe
2 July 1917
Text: Hans Böhm
Dedication: To my friend Paula von Arx

6 kleine Lieder
1917–18
Texts by Heinrich Heine, Julius Arent
1. 'Im wunderschönen Monat Mai' (Heine), 18 May 1918
2. 'Aus meinen Tränen spriessen' (Heine), 10 April 1918
3. 'Dein Angesicht so lieb und mild' (Heine), 14 June 1918
4. 'Lehn deine Wang' (Heine), March 1918
5. 'Sei mir gegrüsst' (Heine), 27 January 1918
6. 'Melancholie' (Arent), July? 1917
Dedication (published edition): 'Den Eltern gewidmet' ('To [my] parents'). The individual songs were originally dedicated to: Grety Siegrist in Thun (Nos. 1 and 2) and Grety Kunz (Nos. 5 and 6) – although in Flury's work catalogue he has crossed out the dedication of No. 6 to Grety Kunz and added the name of Paula von Arx.
Publ.: Verlag Union, Solothurn
Nos. 1–4 and 6 were published in revised versions as '5 Lieder' by Hug in Zurich in 1949 (see below)
Recording (Nos. 1, 2, 6): Juliette Bise (soprano), Eugen Huber (piano). Richard Flury-Gesellschaft RFG CD 260 413 (2009)

Die blauen Frühlingsaugen
18 April 1918
Text: Heinrich Heine

Die Lotusblume
May 1918
Text: Heinrich Heine
Unfinished

Wenn ich in deine Augen seh
19 June 1918
Text: Heinrich Heine
Second version

Der Liebende
8 March 1919 in the Café Schwarz, Bieltor, Solothurn
Text: Emil Wiedmer
Dedication: To my brother Adolf

Der Einsame singt
14 March 1919
Text: Emil Wiedmer
Dedication: To my brother Adolf

Der Dichter
8 April 1919
Text: Emil Wiedmer
Dedication: To Frau Dr. Susanne Michel in Wiedlisbach, the mother of [my] dear friend Eduard Michel

Der Irre
11 April 1919
Text: Emil Wiedmer

Ausgestorben war mein Haus
April 1919
Text: Emil Wiedmer
Unfinished

Die Mitternacht
July 1919
Text: Heinrich Heine
Dedication: To my brother Adolf

Spätherbst
25 December 1919
Text: Emil Wiedmer

6 Liedli von Josef Reinhart
1920
1. ''s Hergottsbründli', May 1920
2. ''s Mätteli', May 1920
3. 'Drü Nägeli im Garte', May 1920
4. 'Ha nemol es Liedli gwüsst', 1920
5. 'Nemol', 4 August 1920
6. 'Tröpfli im Gras', May 1920

Publ.: Hug, Zurich
Dedication: Heinrich Pilz
FP (Nos. 1, 3, 5): Hélène Stoss (soprano), Lily Mermino (piano), 14 May 1921 at the Schweizerisches Tonkünstlerfest in Lugano

Heimetvogel
2 June 1920
Text: Josef Reinhart

Herzloses Mädchen
30 September 1921
Text: Peter Sturmbusch
Dedication: Mädy Meusburger
Publ.: Hug, Zurich
A different setting of this poem from the song in the *Nachtlieder*

8 Liebeslieder
1920–22
Texts: Ludwig Finkh, Isabelle Kaiser, Karl Stamm, Peter Sturmbusch, Emil Wiedmer
1. 'Ich hab dich lieb' (Sturmbusch), 1921
2. 'Du' (Kaiser), 1921
3. 'Der Liebende: Winde wehn' (Wiedmer), 1920
4. 'Noch seh ich dich' (Finkh), June 1922
5. 'Der Liebende: Ein hohes Schwestertum' (Wiedmer), 1922
6. 'Aber' (Finkh), 1922
7. 'Ein Kuss' (Finkh), 1922
8. 'Inez' (Stamm), May 1921
Dedication: To Mädy Meusburger
Publ.: Hug, Zurich
FP (No. 3): Hélène Stoss (soprano), Lily Mermino (piano), 14 May 1921 at the Schweizerisches Tonkünstlerfest in Lugano

Weil ja morgen Sonntag ist
15 February 1923
Text: Heinrich Reinhardt

Der eine allein
1923
Text: Hermann Löns

4 Lieder
1923
Texts: Paul Hardmeyer, Theodor Bohnenblust
1. 'Im weissen Schnee' (Hardmeyer), February 1923
2. 'Wanderer' (Hardmeyer), 20 February 1923
3. 'Feierabend' (Bohnenblust), February 1923
4. 'Marusa' (Bohnenblust), 21 February 1923
Dedication: To Lily Sollberger [later Flury's first wife]
Publ.: Müller-Gyr, Bern

Flury arranged Nos. 1, 2 and 4 for soprano and chamber orchestra in 1924 (Nos. 1 and 2 also for contralto and chamber orchestra). See **Songs for Voice and Ensemble or Orchestra**: *4 Lieder für eine Sopranstimme und Kammerorchester*

Frühe
12 February 1925
Text: Bernhard Moser

Woher-wohin
24 February 1925
Text: Bernhard Moser

Fünf Rosenlieder
April 1929
Texts: Ludwig Finkh
1. 'Du legst mir allerwege'
2. 'Nur manchmal, wenn in Schauern treibt'
3. 'Vierblätter fand ich zwei im Klee'
4. 'Nachts'
5. 'Ich hab einmal ein Lied vernommen'
Dedication: Dori Geissler, teacher in Magglingen near Biel

Arie des Schäfers
23 April 1931
Text: Otto Julius Bierbaum

Agla
31 January 1933
Text: Peter Sturmbusch

Unschuld
7 February 1933
Text: Peter Sturmbusch

Nachtlieder
1923, 1933
Texts by Viktor Aufricht, Otto Julius Bierbaum, Hermann Löns, Alfons Petzold, Peter Sturmbusch,
1. 'Alles schweigt' (Sturmbusch), 13 March 1933
2. 'Ein Lied' (Aufricht), 22 February 1933
3. 'Weisst du' (Sturmbusch), 10 February 1933
4. 'Bang ist die Nacht' (Sturmbusch), 13 February 1933
5. 'Vom Wege' (Sturmbusch), 23 February 1933
6. 'Herzloses Mädchen' (Sturmbusch), 10 March 1933
7. 'Flieder' (Bierbaum), 12 April 1933
8. 'Du' (Sturmbusch), 2 February 1933
9. 'Traum' (Petzold), 1933
10. 'Der Tausch' (Löns), 20 February 1923
Dedication: To Walter Schürmann, pharmacist in Lucerne (Nos. 1–8, 10); To my sister Erika (No. 9).
Publ.: Hug, Zurich

No. 6, 'Herzloses Mädchen', is a different setting of this poem from the song Flury composed on 30 September 1921 (see above).
Recording (No. 10): Juliette Bise (soprano), Eugen Huber (piano). Richard Flury-Gesellschaft RFG CD 260 413 (2009)

Warum
17 February 1933
Text: Peter Sturmbusch

Mein
21 February 1933
Text: Peter Sturmbusch

Mein Mädchen
8 March 1933
Text: Peter Sturmbusch

Gruss der Natur an ein Mädchen
14 March 1933
Text: Viktor Aufricht

Missklang
24 March 1933
Text: Viktor Aufricht

Mein Herz
8 December 1933
Text: Nikolaus Lenau
Dedication: For Lily on her birthday [Flury's first wife]

Bitte
20 October 1935
Text: Nikolaus Lenau
Dedication: To my dear wife

Schliesse mir die Augen zu
21 October 1935
Text: Theodor Storm
Dedication: To my dear wife on her birthday 8 December 1935

Ich liebe Dich
For bass and piano
3 September 1940
Text: Gustav Renker
Dedication: To my dear Rita
A different setting of Renker's poem from that of 16 October 1942

Ich liebe Dich
For soprano and piano
16 October 1942
Text: Gustav Renker
Dedication: To my dear Rita
A different setting of Renker's poem from that of 3 September 1940

Ein lustig Lied
30 August 1942
Text: Emil R. Zetter

Ave Maria
6 October 1942
Text: Gustav Renker
Dedication: To my dear Rita

Jägerlied
1943
Text: Emil R. Zetter
Also exists in a version for TTBB chorus *a cappella*. See **Choral Works *a cappella***

Der Weg zum Sieg
9 October 1943
Text: Emil R. Zetter
First version

Der Weg zum Sieg
25 October 1943
Text: Emil R. Zetter
Second version

29 Lieder
1946
Texts by Olga Brand, Richard Dehmel, Johann Gottfried Herder, Bernhard Moser, Hermann Ferdinand Schell, Wilhelm Voss

1. 'Entgleite mir nicht in die Welt' (Schell), 5 February 1946
2. 'Immer muss ich einsam sein' (Schell), 30 January 1946
3. 'Will mich gerne niederlassen' (Schell), 9 February 1946
4. 'Wandern mit Dir' (Schell), 26 January 1946
5. 'O wär' ich bei Dir' (Schell), 2 February 1946
6. 'Trennt uns der Tod' (Schell), 23 January 1946
7. 'So gern neigt' ich mein Haupt zu Dir' (Schell), 31 January 1946
8. 'Der Zweig' (Schell), 13 February 1946
9. 'Dir will ich gehören' (Schell), 26 January 1946
10. 'Was ich erlebt' (Schell), 9 February 1946
11. 'Dir' (Schell), 12 February 1946
12. 'Hätt ich dir's doch gegeben' (Schell), 11 February 1946
13. 'Er liebt mich' (Schell), 23 January 1946
14. 'Lieber, sei gut' (Schell), 4 February 1946
15. 'Wenn Du die andre liebst' (Schell), 5 February 1946
16. 'Hoffnungslos lieben' (Schell), 29 January 1946
17. 'Wenn ich einst gestorben bin' (Schell), 25 January 1946
18. 'An den Mond' (Moser), 17 December 1946
19. 'Bitte' (Moser), 26 December 1946
20. 'Wenn vor Tagesanbruch' (Moser), 16 December 1946
21. 'Adagio' (Moser), 18 December 1946
22. 'Für mich' (Moser), 21 December 1946

23. 'Aufblick' (Dehmel), 10 December 1946
24. 'Stimme im Dunkeln' (Dehmel), 22 November 1946
25. 'Abendstille' (Voss), 23 November 1946
26. 'Drei Worte' (Voss), 4 December 1946
27. 'Deine Tulpen' (Voss), 2 December 1946
28. 'Sternentreue' (Brand), 23 December 1946
29. 'Ein Traum' (Herder), 13 December 1946

Dedications: Gritli [i.e., Maria] Schell (Nos. 1–17); Rita [Flury] (Nos. 19, 20, 22–25); Maria Bangerter (Nos. 18, 21, 26, 27); Dina Sigrist-Huber (No. 28); Martha and Alexander Stuber (No. 29)
Flury orchestrated No. 9 in his *11 Lieder für Sopran und Orchester* in 1966. See **Songs for Voice and Ensemble or Orchestra**.
Publ.: Hug, Zurich
Recording (Nos. 9, 21, 28): Juliette Bise (soprano), Eugen Huber (piano). Richard Flury-Gesellschaft RFG CD 260 413 (2009)
Recording (Nos. 2, 4, 9, 13, 21): Rosmarie Hofmann (soprano), Margaret Singer (piano). Gallo CD-866 (1996)

Ich lieb' ihn o Himmel
29 January 1946
Text: Hermann Ferdinand Schell
Dedication: For Gritli [i.e., Maria] Schell

Ich sage nichts, kein Sterbenswörtchen
8 February 1946
Text: Hermann Ferdinand Schell
Dedication: For Gritli Schell

Und wenn Du mich liebst
8 February 1946
Text: Hermann Ferdinand Schell
Dedication: For Gritli Schell

Ruf
24 December 1946
Text: Wilhelm Voss
Dedication: To the poet and his wife

Evas Klage
23 September 1949
Text: Richard Dehmel
Dedication: To Ria Ginster

5 Lieder
1949
Texts by Heinrich Heine, Julius Arent
1. 'Melancholie' (Arent)
2. 'Im wunderschönen Monat Mai' (Heine)
3. 'Aus meinen Tränen spriessen' (Heine)
4. 'Dein Angesicht so lieb und mild' (Heine)
5. 'Lehn deine Wang' (Heine)

Revised versions of 5 songs from the *6 kleine Lieder* of 1917–18
Publ.: Hug, Zurich

17 Lieder
1951–52
Texts by Viktor Aufricht, Nikolaus Lenau, Heinrich Leuthold, Eduard Mörike, Otto Zinniker

1. 'Augenzauber' (Leuthold), 5 August 1951
2. 'Libelle' (Zinniker), 30 November 1952
3. 'Herbstzeitlose' (Zinniker), 24 June 1952
4. 'Ob Du wohl weisst, was Liebe ist' (Zinniker), 14 June 1952
5. 'Jeder Tag' (Zinniker), 31 October 1952
6. 'Wie ein Birkenzweig im Wind' (Zinniker), 4 June 1952
7. 'Bekenntnis' (Zinniker), 5 June 1952
8. 'Sommerwolke' (Zinniker), 26 November 1952
9. 'Der schwere Abend' (Lenau), 21 August 1952
10. 'Schlaflied' (Zinniker), 9 June 1952
11. 'Abendwerden' (Zinniker), 1952
12. 'Vereinsamt steh ich da' (Zinniker), 3 June 1952
13. 'Heisses Herz, o lern' ertragen' (Leuthold), 8 August 1951
14. 'Trinklied' (Leuthold), 15 August 1951
15. 'Das Kind' (Aufricht), 31 July 1951
16. 'Gruss der Natur an ein Mädchen' (Aufricht), 28 March 1951
17. 'Nimmersatte Liebe' (Mörike), 3 August 1951

Dedications: Grety Wirz-Luterbacher (Nos. 1–14, 16, 17); Urban Wirz (No. 15)
Publ.: Hug, Zurich
Recording (Nos. 1, 4, 13, 16, 17): Rosmarie Hofmann (soprano), Margaret Singer (piano). Gallo CD-866 (1996); (Nos. 1–4, 8, 10, 13, 16, 17): Juliette Bise (soprano), Eugen Huber (piano). Richard Flury-Gesellschaft RFG CD 260 413 (2009)
Flury orchestrated Nos. 1, 3, 4, 13, 14 in his *11 Lieder für Sopran und Orchester* in 1966. See **Songs for Voice and Ensemble or Orchestra**. He also arranged Nos. 1, 4, 13–15 and 17 for soprano and string quartet as *6 Lieder für Sopran und Streichquartett* in 1959. See **Songs for Voice and Ensemble or Orchestra**.

Sommer
31 July 1951
Text: Viktor Aufricht
Dedication: For Grety Wirz-Luterbacher

Liederfrühling
22 August 1951
Text: Heinrich Leuthold
Dedication: For Grety Wirz-Luterbacher

Spiele, o Herr
29 May 1952
Text: Otto Zinniker
Dedication: To Grety Wirz

Noch steht ein Sternbild am Gezelt
30 May 1952
Text: Otto Zinniker
Dedication: For Grety Wirz

Ich gehe gern
9 June 1952
Text: Otto Zinniker
Dedication: For Grety Wirz

Einst lief mir alles wie im Spiel
19 June 1952
Text: Otto Zinniker
Dedication: For Grety Wirz

Hoher Sommer
24 October 1952
Text: Otto Zinniker
Dedication: For Grety Wirz

Gott
4 November 1952
Text: Otto Zinniker
Dedication: For Grety Wirz

Abends
2 July 1957
Text: Theodor Storm
FP: Juliette Bise (soprano), Eugen Huber (piano), 13 January 1960 in Radio Bern
Version for voice and piano of a song from the cantata *Der Schleier der Mutter*. See **Choral Works with Accompaniment**

Garten der Mutter
25 July 1957
Text: Emil Wiedmer
FP: Juliette Bise (soprano), Eugen Huber (piano), 13 January 1960 in Radio Bern
Version for voice and piano of a song from the cantata *Der Schleier der Mutter*. See **Choral Works with Accompaniment**

Nach Jahren wieder daheim
26 July 1957
Text: Emil Wiedmer
Version for voice and piano of a song from the cantata *Der Schleier der Mutter*. See **Choral Works with Accompaniment**

An meine Mutter
26 July 1957
Text: Annette Droste-Hülshoff
FP: Juliette Bise (soprano), Eugen Huber (piano), 13 January 1960 in Radio Bern
Version for voice and piano of a song from the cantata *Der Schleier der Mutter*. See **Choral Works with Accompaniment**

Recording: Juliette Bise (soprano), Eugen Huber (piano). Richard Flury-Gesellschaft RFG CD 260 413 (2009)

Hast Du nie an Selbstmord gedacht
27 July 1957
Text: Hermann Hesse
Version for voice and piano of a song from the cantata *Der Schleier der Mutter*. See **Choral Works with Accompaniment**

Mutter
27 July 1957
Text: Otto Zinniker
Version for voice and piano of a song from the cantata *Der Schleier der Mutter*. See **Choral Works with Accompaniment**

Stufen
27 July 1957
Text: Isabelle Kaiser
FP: Juliette Bise (soprano), Eugen Huber (piano), 13 January 1960 in Radio Bern
Version for voice and piano of a song from the cantata *Der Schleier der Mutter*. See **Choral Works with Accompaniment**
Recording: Juliette Bise (soprano), Eugen Huber (piano). Richard Flury-Gesellschaft RFG CD 260 413 (2009)

Juli
28 July 1957
Text: Theodor Storm
FP: Juliette Bise (soprano), Eugen Huber (piano), 13 January 1960 in Radio Bern
Version for voice and piano of a song from the cantata *Der Schleier der Mutter*. See **Choral Works with Accompaniment**
Recording: Juliette Bise (soprano), Eugen Huber (piano). Richard Flury-Gesellschaft RFG CD 260 413 (2009)

Wiegenlied
27 August 1957
Text: Clemens Brentano
FP: Juliette Bise (soprano), Eugen Huber (piano), 13 January 1960 in Radio Bern
Version for voice and piano of a song from the cantata *Der Schleier der Mutter*. See **Choral Works with Accompaniment**
Recording: Juliette Bise (soprano), Eugen Huber (piano). Richard Flury-Gesellschaft RFG CD 260 413 (2009)

Gebet
7 November 1957
Text: Hansruedi Forster
Dedication: Fridy Gmür-Lüthy on her 60th birthday
FP: Juliette Bise (soprano), Eugen Huber (piano), 13 January 1960 in Radio Bern
Recording: Juliette Bise (soprano), Eugen Huber (piano). Richard Flury-Gesellschaft RFG CD 260 413 (2009)

Du
7 November 1957
Text: Hansruedi Forster
Dedication: Fridy Gmür-Lüthy on her 60th birthday
FP: Juliette Bise (soprano), Eugen Huber (piano), 13 January 1960 in Radio Bern
Recording: Juliette Bise (soprano), Eugen Huber (piano). Richard Flury-Gesellschaft RFG CD 260 413 (2009)

Dem Winde mein Lied
7 November 1957
Text: Hansruedi Forster
Dedication: Fridy Gmür-Lüthy on her 60th birthday
FP: Juliette Bise (soprano), Eugen Huber (piano), 13 January 1960 in Radio Bern
Recording: Juliette Bise (soprano), Eugen Huber (piano). Richard Flury-Gesellschaft RFG CD 260 413 (2009)

Bitte
7 November 1957
Text: Hansruedi Forster
Dedication: Fridy Gmür-Lüthy on her 60th birthday
FP: Juliette Bise (soprano), Eugen Huber (piano), 13 January 1960 in Radio Bern
Recording: Juliette Bise (soprano), Eugen Huber (piano). Richard Flury-Gesellschaft RFG CD 260 413 (2009)

Vergangenes
7 November 1957
Text: Hansruedi Forster
Dedication: Fridy Gmür-Lüthy on her 60th birthday
FP: Juliette Bise (soprano), Eugen Huber (piano), 13 January 1960 in Radio Bern
Recording: Juliette Bise (soprano), Eugen Huber (piano). Richard Flury-Gesellschaft RFG CD 260 413 (2009)

Junger Ritter
7 December 1957
Text: Hansruedi Forster
Dedication: Fridy Gmür-Lüthy on her 60th birthday, 14 March 1958
FP: Juliette Bise (soprano), Eugen Huber (piano), 13 January 1960 in Radio Bern
Recording: Juliette Bise (soprano), Eugen Huber (piano). Richard Flury-Gesellschaft RFG CD 260 413 (2009)

Heckenröslein
23 September 1961
Text: Carl Robert Enzmann
Dedication: To my dear Giovanna [Flury, the composer's daughter]
FP: Juliette Bise (soprano), Eugen Huber (piano), 29 November 1962 in Radio Bern
Recording: Juliette Bise (soprano), Eugen Huber (piano). Richard Flury-Gesellschaft RFG CD 260 413 (2009)

An ein Kind
25 September 1961
Text: Carl Robert Enzmann
Dedication: To my dear daughter Giovanna
FP: Juliette Bise (soprano), Eugen Huber (piano), 29 November 1962 in Radio Bern
Recording: Juliette Bise (soprano), Eugen Huber (piano). Richard Flury-Gesellschaft RFG CD 260 413 (2009)

Einsamkeit
28 September 1961
Text: Carl Robert Enzmann
Dedication: To my dear Giovanna [Flury, the composer's daughter]
FP: Juliette Bise (soprano), Eugen Huber (piano), 29 November 1962 in Radio Bern
Recording: Juliette Bise (soprano), Eugen Huber (piano). Richard Flury-Gesellschaft RFG CD 260 413 (2009)

Gebet
30 September 1961
Text: Carl Robert Enzmann
Dedication: To my dear daughter Giovanna
FP: Juliette Bise (soprano), Eugen Huber (piano), 29 November 1962 in Radio Bern

Allerseelen
6 October 1961
Text: Carl Robert Enzmann
Dedication: To my dear daughter Giovanna
FP: Juliette Bise (soprano), Eugen Huber (piano), 29 November 1962 in Radio Bern
Recording: Juliette Bise (soprano), Eugen Huber (piano). Richard Flury-Gesellschaft RFG CD 260 413 (2009)

Das Brünnlein
26 October 1961
Text: Carl Robert Enzmann
Dedication: To my dear daughter Giovanna
FP: Juliette Bise (soprano), Eugen Huber (piano), 29 November 1962 in Radio Bern
Recording: Juliette Bise (soprano), Eugen Huber (piano). Richard Flury-Gesellschaft RFG CD 260 413 (2009)

Humor
1962
Text: Carl Robert Enzmann
Dedication: To Fiammetta Grieshaber-Schabelitz
FP: Marguerite Ritter-Lochbrunner (soprano), Eugen Huber (piano), 11 April 1970 in Biberist Catholic Church

Sei klug
1962
Text: Carl Robert Enzmann
Dedication: To Fiammetta Grieshaber-Schabelitz
FP: Marguerite Ritter-Lochbrunner (soprano), Eugen Huber (piano), 11 April 1970 in Biberist Catholic Church

Fremdes Kind
1962
Text: Carl Robert Enzmann
Dedication: To Fiammetta Grieshaber-Schabelitz

Knospen
1962
Text: Carl Robert Enzmann
Dedication: To Fiammetta Grieshaber-Schabelitz

Melodie
1962
Text: Carl Robert Enzmann
Dedication: To Fiammetta Grieshaber-Schabelitz
FP: Margarethe Ritter-Lochbrunner (soprano), Eugen Huber (piano), 11 April 1970 in Biberist Catholic Church

Nocturno
1962
Text: Carl Robert Enzmann
Dedication: To Fiammetta Grieshaber-Schabelitz

Nachts
22 March 1965
Text: Ludwig Finkh
Dedication: Hedwig Vonlanthen-Walz

Rosenlied
23 March 1965
Text: Ludwig Finkh
Dedication: Hedwig Vonlanthen-Walz

Falterlied
24 March 1965
Text: Ludwig Finkh
Dedication: Hedwig Vonlanthen-Walz

Schwermut
30 March 1965
Text: Ludwig Finkh
Dedication: Hedwig Vonlanthen-Walz

Einer Frau
18 April 1965
Text: Ludwig Finkh
Dedication: Hedwig Vonlanthen-Walz

Letzte Bitte
20 April 1965
Text: Ludwig Finkh
Dedication: Hedwig Vonlanthen-Walz

Und einmal wars...
November 1966
Text: Ludwig Finkh

Du legst mir allerwege
November 1966
Text: Ludwig Finkh

Du, siebenmal hab ich dich lieb
November 1966
Text: Ludwig Finkh

Nur deine Hand
November 1966
Text: Ludwig Finkh

Ich bin ein Falter
November 1966
Text: Ludwig Finkh

Ich wartete die ganze Nacht
November 1966
Text: Ludwig Finkh

Arrangements

Edmund Wyss:
Festmarsch zur Dornacher Schlachtfeier in Solothurn 1499–1899
Arranged for orchestra by Richard Flury
7 June 1919 (date of completion)
Instr. pic, 2 fl, 2 ob, 2 cl, 2 bn – 4 hn, 3 tpt, 2 trbn, tb – timp, bass drum, cym, side-drum, tubular bells – str

Solothurner Lied, 's isch immer so gsi!
Text: Carl Robert Enzmann
With piano accompaniment by Richard Flury
The melody for this song – the quasi-official 'city song' of Solothurn – is reputedly a folk-tune of Irish origin

Writings

Flury's more substantial writings are listed here, in chronological order. His occasional small articles for local newspapers and unpublished lectures are not included.

'Meine musikalischen Bekenntnisse', lecture given to the 'Töpfergesellschaft' in Solothurn on 12 February 1944. Self-published, 1944

Josef Joachim. Leben und Werke des solothurnischen Bauerndichters, Kommissionsverlag Vogt-Schild AG, Solothurn, 1945. Illustrated with drawings by Willy Hug

Lebenserinnerungen, Habegger AG, Derendingen, 1950

'Mein Bekenntnis zur musikalischen Romantik. Vortrag gehalten in der Jugendgemeinde für Musik in Solothurn 20. Januar 1953', special supplement to the *Solothurner Zeitung*, no date

Bibliography

'-ae-', 'Solothurn', *Schweizerische Musikzeitung*, Vol. 89, No. 5, 1 May 1949, p. 209

ANON., 'Paul Zifferer und der Kosmopolitanismus', *Ostdeutsche Rundschau*, 20 November 1917

———, *50 Jahre Städtebundtheater Biel - Solothurn 1927–1977*, no publisher indicated, Biel, 1977

———, *SKO. 50 Jahre Solothurner Kammerorchester 1936-1986*, no publisher indicated, [Solothurn], 1986.

———, *100 Jahre Bill de Vigier*, exhibition brochure [W. A. de Vigier Stiftung], [Solothurn], 2012

BECHERT, PAUL, 'Vienna', *The Musical Times*, Vol. 66, No. 984 (1 February 1925), p. 172

BLANK, STEFAN, and HOCHSTRASSER, MARKUS, *Die Kunstdenkmäler des Kantons Solothurn*, Vol. II, *Die Stadt Solothurn II. Profanbauten*, Gesellschaft für Schweizerischer Kunstgeschichte GSK, Bern, 2008

BLOCH, WERNER, 'Richard Flury', *Schweizerische Musikzeitung*, Vol. 108, No. 1 (January/February 1968), pp. 39–40.

BLUBACHER, THOMAS, '"Sorge in Freude und Leid in Vergessen wandeln!" Das Städtebundtheater Biel-Solothurn unter der Direktion von Leo Delsen 1927–1954', in Simone Gojan and Elke Krafka (eds.), *Theater Biel Solothurn - Théâtre Bienne Soleure. Geschichte und Geschichten des kleinsten Stadttheaters der Schweiz*, Chronos, Zurich, 2004, pp. 13–46

———, 'Egon Karter und Charlotte Sender' in *ibid.*, pp. 69–72

———, 'Leo Delsen und Elisabeth Delsen' in *ibid.*, pp. 62–66

BRAND, JULIANE, *et al.* (eds.), *Briefwechsel Arnold Schönberg - Alban Berg*, Vol. II, Schott, Mainz, 2007

BROTBECK, ROMAN, 'Prekäre Ambivalenzen. Arthur Honeggers Anpassungen nach 1941' in Andreas Eichhorn (ed.), *Kurt Weill und Frankreich*, Waxmann, Münster & New York, 2014, pp. 9–23

COBBE, HUGH, 'Vaughan Williams, Germany and the German tradition: a view from the letters', in Alain Frogley, *Vaughan Williams Studies*, Cambridge UP, Cambridge, 1996, pp. 81–98

DEGEN, BERNHARD, 'Arbeitslosigkeit' in *Historisches Lexikon der Schweiz*, www.hls-dhs-dss.ch/textes/d/D13924.php

EHINGER, HANS, 'Das 62. Schweizerische Tonkünstlerfest in Solothurn', *Schweizerische Musikzeitung*, Vol. 101, No. 4 (July/August 1961), pp. 248–50

———, 'Geschichtlicher Überblick' in *Musik-Akademie der Stadt Basel, Gedenkschrift zum fünfzigjährigen Bestehen der Abteilung Konservatorium 1905–1955*, Verlag der Musik-Akademie, Basel, 1955, pp. 5–46

Fischer, Kurt von, *Erich Schmid*, Hug, Zurich, 1992

Frey, Peter, and Arber, Justin (eds.), *1833–1983. 150 Jahre Kantonsschule Solothurn*, Kantonsschule Solothurn, Solothurn, 1983

Gartmann, Thomas, 'Der Schweizerische Tonkünstlerverein 1933 bis 1945. Ein Berufsverband, der sich nicht mit politischen Fragen befasst (?)', in Chris Walton and Antonio Baldassarre (eds.), *Musik im Exil. Die Schweiz und das Ausland 1918–1945*, Peter Lang, Bern, 2005, pp. 39–58

Haefeli, Anton, *Die internationale Gesellschaft für neue Musik (IGNM). Ihre Geschichte von 1922 bis zur Gegenwart*, Atlantis, Zurich, 1982

Hall, Patricia, 'The Progress of a Method: Berg's Tone Rows for "Lulu"', *The Musical Quarterly*, Vol. 71, No. 4 (1985), pp. 500–19

———, *A View of Berg's 'Lulu' through the Autograph Sources*, University of California Press, Berkeley, 1996

Hensher, Philip, 'Rake's still making perfect progress', *The Independent*, 13 August 2010

Hoster, Alex, 'Pionierin der Bewegungsschule hat ihren 100. Geburtstag gefeiert', *Der Landbote*, 29 October 2014

Huber, Eugen, 'Der Komponist Richard Flury gestorben', *Solothurner Zeitung* No. 299 (26 December 1967), p. 9

Kully, Rolf Max, 'Hanns Wagner und das Solothurner "Festspiel" vom Jahre 1581', *Jahrbuch für solothurnische Geschichte*, Vol. 55, 1982

Kurth, Ernst, *Grundlagen des Linearen Kontrapunkts: Einführung in Stil und Technik von Bach's melodischer Polyphonie*, Max Drechsel, Bern, 1917

Lotar, Peter, manuscript diary, 20 May 1943; held by the Swiss National Library in Bern, shelfmark: SLA-Lotar, C-3-a.1

Martin, Frank, and Piguet, Jean-Claude, *Entretiens sur la musique*, Editions de la Baconnière, Neuchâtel, 1967

Marx, Joseph, and Bayer, Friedrich, *Harmonielehre*, Universal Edition, Vienna, 1933

Mösch, Johann, 'Der Einfluss des Humanisten Glarean auf Solothurn', *Jahrbuch für solothurnische Geschichte*, Vol. 11, 1938

Moser, Bernhard, 'Meine "Schweizer Turner"', *Zürcher Illustrierte*, 1932, No. 29, p. 917

Musikschule und Konservatorium Basel, *Jahresbericht über den 62. Kurs 1928/29*, Basel, 1929

Oesch, Hans, 'Helvetischer Durchschnitt', *National-Zeitung*, 29 May 1961

PALMER, PETER, 'Frank Martin *et al.*', *Tempo*, Vol. 67, No. 266 (October 2013), pp. 116–17

PRIEBERG, FRED K., *Handbuch deutscher Musiker 1933–1945*, self-published, Auprès des Zombry, 2004

RINDLISBACHER, HANS (ed.), *Nachlass Delsen, Leo (1884/88–1954)*, Zentralbibliothek, Solothurn, 2003

SCHMID, NORA, and HINDEN, LEA, *Inventar Nachlass Ernst Kurth: Anhang II, Volltextbriefe zum Inventar Nachlass Ernst Kurth,* Institut für Musikwissenschaft, Bern, 2007

SCHUH, WILLI, 'Das 53. Schweizerische Tonkünstlerfest in Aarau (17./18. Mai)', *Schweizerische Musikzeitung*, Vol. 92, Nos. 7/8 (15 July 1952), pp. 303–5

SCHWEIZERISCHER TONKÜNSTLERVEREIN (ed.), *Der Schweizerische Tonkünstlerverein im zweiten Vierteljahrhundert seines Bestehens. Festschrift zur Feier des 50jährigen Jubiläums 1900–1950*, Atlantis, Zurich, 1950

———, *Tendenzen und Verwirklichungen. Festschrift des Schweizerischen Tonkünstlervereins aus Anlass seines 75-jährigen Bestehens (1900–1975)*, Atlantis, Zurich, 1975

SEVERI, RITA, '"Astonishing in my Italian": Oscar Wilde's First Italian Editions 1890–1952' in Stefano Evangelista (ed.), *The Reception of Oscar Wilde in Europe*, Continuum, London and New York, 2010, pp. 108–23

'sl.', 'Abschied von Richard Flury', *Solothurner Zeitung* No. 301 (28 December 1967), p. 17

STENGL, THEO, and GERIGK, HERBERT, (eds.), *Lexikon der Juden in der Musik*, Bernhard Hahnefeld, Berlin, 1940

WALTON, CHRIS, 'Composing Oscar: Settings of Wilde for the German Stage' in Stefano Evangelista, (ed.), *The Reception of Oscar Wilde in Europe*, pp. 217–28

———, (ed.), *Marcel H. S. Sulzberger (1876–1941)*, Amadeus, Winterthur, 2010

———, *Lies and Epiphanies: Composers and Their Inspiration from Wagner to Berg*, University of Rochester Press, Rochester, 2014

———, *Othmar Schoeck. Life and Works*, University of Rochester Press, Rochester, 2009

WINKLER, WALTER, 'Das "Büreliedli" im neuen Kleid', *Grenchner Tagblatt*, 14 April 2009

YATES, W. E., review of Hilde Burger (ed.), *Hugo von Hofmannsthal: Paul Zifferer: Briefwechsel*, *The Modern Language Review* Vol. 79, No. 4 (October 1984), pp. 987–88

Index of Flury's Works

General Index

CD Content

The music on the CD with this book offers a broad, chronological overview of Flury's *œuvre*, covering most of the genres he cultivated. They range from works for the theatre (opera, ballet and incidental music) to symphony, solo songs and short piano pieces (the last of these including both 'abstract' genres, such as the prelude and intermezzo, and programmatic character pieces). Flury's substantial output of chamber music is also well represented here, with assorted movements from works as varied as his First String Quartet of 1926, his *10 Caprices for Solo Violin* of 1952 and his late Nonet of 1965. This selection also makes clear Flury's broad stylistic range, from the near-atonality found in certain passages of his Bergian First Quartet to the effervescent, popular style of the overture to his Italian comic opera *Casanova e l'Albertolli*. Some of the recordings here are taken from old Swiss radio tapes and have been remastered. The sound quality is in such cases imperfect, but these examples are of documentary importance as they are the only extant recordings of the works in question. The excerpts from *Hanneles Himmelfahrt* and the Horn Quartet are reproduced by kind permission of the label MGB. We are grateful to the other rights-holders, in particular Gallo and Urs Joseph Flury, for permission to publish the other recordings heard here.

1. 'Im wunderschönen Monat Mai' (Heinrich Heine), for voice and piano, 1918, rec. c 1949. Rosmarie Hofmann, soprano, accompanied by Margaret Singer, piano. Source: Gallo CD-866
2. Prelude for piano No. 1, 1921. Margaret Singer, piano. Source: Gallo CD-1460.
3. *Intermezzo* for piano No. 1, 1921. Margaret Singer, piano. Source: Gallo CD-1460
4. Symphony No. 1, 3rd movement, 1922–23. Sinfonieorchester Biel, conducted by Urs Joseph Flury. Source: Gallo CD-1385
5. String Quartet No. 1, 2nd movement, 1926. Brenner Quartet. Source: Swiss radio (1955)
6. *Eine florentinische Tragödie*, opera, final scene, 1926–28. Simone: Siegfried Tappolet; Bianca: Annie Weber; Stadtorchester Bern, conducted by Christoph Lertz. Source: Swiss radio (1944)
7. Preludes for piano No. 4, Valse, 1931. Margaret Singer, piano. Source: Gallo CD-1460
8. *Casanova e l'Albertolli*, Overture, 1937. Sinfonieorchester Biel, conducted by Urs Joseph Flury. Source: Gallo CD-1385
9. *Hanneles Himmelfahrt*, 'Musik zur Frauengestalt', 1941. Czech Symphony Orchestra, Prague, conducted by Urs Joseph Flury. Source: MGB CD-6141
10. *Hanneles Himmelfahrt*, 'Der gläserne Sarg', 1941. Czech Symphony Orchestra, Prague, conducted by Urs Joseph Flury. Source: MGB CD-6141

11 Violin Concerto No. 3, 3rd movement, 1943–44. Georg Kulenkampff (violin), Stadtorchester Bern, conducted by Kurt Rothenbühler. Source: Podium Legenda POL-1014-2

12 *Die alte Truhe*, ballet, dance of the Gypsy woman (csardas), 1945. Czech Symphony Orchestra Prague, conducted by Urs Joseph Flury. Source: Gallo CD-860

13 'Immer muss ich einsam sein' (Hermann Ferdinand Schell), for voice and piano, 1946. Rosmarie Hofmann, soprano, accompanied by Margaret Singer, piano. Source: Gallo CD-866

14 'Adagio' (Bernhard Moser), for voice and piano, 1946. Rosmarie Hofmann, soprano, accompanied by Margaret Singer, piano. Source: Gallo CD-866

15 Piano Quintet, second movement: *Andante*, 1948. Margaret Singer, piano; Ulrich Lehmann, violin; Urs Joseph Flury, violin; Erich Meyer, viola; Stefan Thut, cello. Source: Gallo CD-866

16 *Skizzenmappe aus dem Bucheggberg* No. 4, 'The Belfry', 1949. Margaret Singer, piano. Source: Gallo CD-1460

17 *Skizzenmappe aus dem Bucheggberg* No. 30, 'Ghost in the Granary', 1949. Margaret Singer, piano. Source: Gallo CD-1460

18 *Skizzenmappe aus dem Bucheggberg* No. 43, 'Water Wheel', 1949. Margaret Singer, piano. Source: Gallo CD-1460

19 'Augenzauber' (Heinrich Leuthold), for voice and piano, 1951. Rosmarie Hofmann, soprano, accompanied by Margaret Singer, piano. Source: Gallo CD-866

20 *10 Caprices for violin solo*, No. 1, 1952. Ruggiero Ricci, violin. Source: Richard Flury-Gesellschaft RFG CD-260 399

21 *10 Caprices for violin solo*, No. 2, 1952. Ruggiero Ricci, violin. Source: Richard Flury-Gesellschaft RFG CD-260 399

22 *Altisberg Suite*, third movement, 'Nocturne', 1953. Studio-Orchester Beromünster, conducted by Paul Burkhard. Source: Gallo CD-1397

23 *Missa brevis*, Sanctus, 1954. Kammerchor Buchsgau, Serenata Solothurn, conducted by Bruno Späti. Source: private recording

24 *Missa brevis*, Benedictus, 1954. Kammerchor Buchsgau, Serenata Solothurn, conducted by Bruno Späti. Source: private recording

25 Horn Quartet, fourth movement, Finale, 1954. HornQuartett Zürich. Source: MGB CD-6227

26 String Quartet No. 7, third movement, *Vivace*, 1964. Urs Joseph Flury, Jean-Pierre Moeckli (violins), Walter Kägi (viola), Jost Meier (cello). Source: Gallo CD-1423

27 Nonet, second movement, *Minuetto*, 1965. Instrumentalists of Radio Bern, conducted by Eugen Huber. Source: Richard Flury-Gesellschaft RFG CD-260 404